Power in Uncertain Times

Power in Uncertain Times

STRATEGY IN THE FOG OF PEACE

Emily O. Goldman

STANFORD SECURITY STUDIES
An Imprint of Stanford University Press
Stanford, California

Stanford University Press
Stanford, California

© 2011 by the Board of Trustees of the Leland Stanford Junior University.
All rights reserved.

No part of this book may be reproduced or transmitted in any form or by any means, electronic or mechanical, including photocopying and recording, or in any information storage or retrieval system without the prior written permission of Stanford University Press.

Special discounts for bulk quantities of Stanford Security Studies are available to corporations, professional associations, and other organizations. For details and discount information, contact the special sales department of Stanford University Press.
Tel: (650) 736-1782, Fax: (650) 736-1784

Printed in the United States of America on acid-free, archival-quality paper

Library of Congress Cataloging-in-Publication Data

Goldman, Emily O.
  Power in uncertain times : strategy in the fog of peace / Emily O. Goldman.
    p. cm.
  Includes bibliographical references and index.
  ISBN 978-0-8047-5726-3 (cloth : alk. paper) —
  ISBN 978-0-8047-7433-8 (pbk. : alk. paper)
  1. Military policy—History. 2. National security—History. 3. Strategy—History. 4. United States—Military policy. 5. National security—United States—History. I. Title.
  UA11.G66 2011
  355'.033573—dc22
                                    2010011330

Typeset by Thompson Type in 10/14 Minion.

I dedicate this book to Alex, Catherine, and JR.

CONTENTS

	List of Figures and Tables	ix
	Preface	xi
1	The Fog of Peace	1
2	Strategic Choice in Uncertain Times	12
3	Post–Crimean War Period, 1856–1910	36
4	Inter–World War Period, 1918–1939	78
5	United States, 1990–2010	125
6	Consequences of Strategic Choices	162
	Notes	179
	Bibliography	209
	Index	241

LIST OF FIGURES AND TABLES

Figures

2.1	Sources of uncertainty	14
2.2	Uncertainty curve	23

Tables

2.1	Unknowns in uncertain times	16
2.2	Shaping strategies	21
2.3	Hypotheses on relative power	25
2.4	Hypotheses on complexity	26
2.5	Hypotheses on nonstructural causes	29
2.6	Case selection	31
2.7	Pure strategies	33
3.1	Russian military spending, 1856–1876	43–44
3.2	Size of the army and navy in Russia, 1856–1914	46–47
3.3	Great Britain's naval expenditures, 1889–1914	61
3.4	Distribution of British defense expenditures by department, 1904–1914	71
4.1	Great Britain's defense spending, 1910–1939	85–86
4.2	Great Britain's naval manpower, 1912–1938	87–88

4.3	Great Britain's army manpower, 1911–1937	89–90
4.4	Great Britain's Royal Air Force numbers, 1920–1939	91
4.5	Great Britain's military manpower totals, 1912–1939	92
4.6	Strength of the Indian army, 1910–1921	93
4.7	U.S. defense spending, 1910–1939	104–105
4.8	U.S. military numbers data, 1900–1939	106–107
5.1	U.S. national defense, federal spending, and gross domestic product, fiscal year 1980 through fiscal year 2007	136
5.2	U.S. active duty military personnel, 1985–2009	137
5.3	U.S. Department of Defense outlays by subfunction, fiscal year 1980 through fiscal year 2007	138–139

PREFACE

THE GREATEST DIFFICULTY of military statecraft is that decisions must deal with future uncertain contingencies. What opponents may have to be faced, with what allies, and under what circumstances? What sorts of conflicts are most likely to arise? Planning for the future is by nature beset with uncertainty, whether one is making long-term projections, monitoring emerging problems, or warning of imminent danger. Defense planners have performed most poorly when making long-term projections. Yet long-range strategic planning is the problem confronting U.S. leaders today, and the stakes are high.

The current period is more uncertain than the Cold War past, but it also presents a window of opportunity for the United States to shape the future. Some strategies take advantage of windows of opportunity to create more favorable futures; others do not. The challenge for the United States, and for all states, is not just to manage uncertainty but to prevail in spite of it.

This book examines strategic choices in uncertain times and analyzes how different strategies position states to compete in the present and future, manage risk, and prevail despite uncertainty. The empirical chapters investigate how past and current political and military leaders have responded to uncertain strategic and technological environments and assess the consequences of those strategies for their state's power and influence. Underestimating uncertainty and not thinking strategically about the future leave states ill prepared to meet future competitors. They may also miss the opportunities that uncertainty provides. Hegemons typically invest in sustaining capabilities and processes that support their power. Rising challengers leverage disruptive capabiities and processes that precipitate the decline of the leader.

Aware of this more than any other past hegemon, the post–Cold War United States tried to avoid this trap and sustain the nation's hegemonic position by out-innovating any potential challengers, be they states or nonstate actors, and by shaping the global security environment. U.S. leaders have struggled to proactively shape the security environment over the medium and long-term, rather than just defensively react to events. The question is whether that path has a chance of forestalling hegemonic decline, enhancing U.S. security, and creating a more favorable international environment for the future.

It is but a slight exaggeration to say that I have been writing this book for almost twenty years. I have many people to thank. The first person is Mackubin Owens, who planted the idea for this book in my mind when I was a visiting professor at the U.S. Naval War College in 1991–1992. The first Gulf War had ended. National security practitioners were debating how to characterize the new era. Military educational institutions were reworking their curricula to make it more relevant to the post–Cold War period. One day Mac referred to the "fog of peace" when describing the uncertainty and lack of strategic anchor characterizing the current period. This was an idea I knew I had to explore. There was no theory of strategy for times when threats were uncertain.

I benefited from the advice and support of Larry Berman, Chris Demchak, Colin Elman, Theo Farrell, Chaim Kaufman, Miko Nincic, and Andy Ross. A particular debt of gratitude goes to Nick Lambert, who patiently discussed my thesis and the evidence over many sessions. I was immensely fortunate to have several superb research assistants: Leo Blanken, Olga Bogatyrenko, Phillip Khan, and John Turpin.

Over the years I received generous financial support from the University of California's Institute on Global Conflict and Cooperation, the Smith Richardson Foundation, and the Woodrow Wilson International Center for Scholars. The editors at Stanford University Press have been both enthusiastic and patient while I completed the manuscript.

I am convinced that the subject of this book is as relevant today as it was twenty years ago. I am equally convinced that while I and a few others may have started a more considered conversation about the "fog of peace," that conversation will not—and should not—end. I hope I spur others to study this subject, develop and test theory about it, and inform policy as well as academic debates about strategic choice in uncertain times.

Three individuals have been personal inspirations to me. My son Alex Forrest inspired me with the daily commitment and intellectual focus he demonstrated as he prepared for his Bar Mitzvah. My daughter Catherine Forrest—the only girl on her tackle football team, one of two girls on her ice hockey team, and now both a wrestler and boxer—continually inspires me with her determination, strength of character, and spirit. JR Vines has believed in me more than anyone and taught me to believe in myself.

Power in Uncertain Times

1 THE FOG OF PEACE

THE UNITED STATES faces a bewildering array of strategic challenges today. The wars in Iraq and Afghanistan have dominated headlines in recent years, but the problems posed by North Korea, nuclear Iran, rising China, resurgent Russia, and spreading violent extremism vie for attention and resources. The perceptual reference points and decision frameworks that guided national security decision making since the mid-twentieth century are no longer meaningful in today's world. The strategic environment has been characterized in national security documents and debates over the past decade as uncertain and chaotic. A more accurate descriptor is "complex." There is no dominant threat, no single strategic challenger, no clear enemy. Relative to the Cold War context that forged and honed our strategic constructs, we now confront a *greater number* of threats, *greater diversity* in the types of security actors that can threaten our interests, and a *more interdependent* world in which rapidly emerging technologies quickly diffuse and are exploited by others in unanticipated ways.[1]

Geopolitical developments had already overturned Cold War givens before the terrorist attacks of September 11, 2001. Ethnic and religious extremists threatened peace. Nonstate actors, newly empowered by globalization and the information revolution, threatened to disrupt the information systems and critical infrastructure that undergird modern society. Proliferation of nuclear, biological, and chemical weapons technologies and expertise were diffusing the capability to cause massive damage and eroding prevailing international norms constraining the spread of weapons of mass destruction. Technological advances associated with an information technology revolution were beginning to transform military competition and warfare. Strategic planners always confront uncertainty as they prepare for conflict "(1) that will occur at some indeterminate point in the future, (2) against an opponent who may not yet be identified, (3) in political conditions which one cannot accurately predict, and (4) in an arena of brutality and violence which one cannot replicate."[2] Complexity exacerbates these normal difficulties because resources must be allocated, personnel must be trained, and plans must be forged in the absence of a strategic rival.

This book examines how leaders respond in a complex and uncertain world. The overwhelming power of the United States is in many ways unprecedented; but the challenges America faces are not so different from those faced by others when long-standing rivals collapsed, alignment patterns shifted, and new types of threats emerged. Some opted to react to present challenges at the expense of preparing for future unforeseen contingencies; others reversed these priorities. Some tried to shape the structure of the international system; others reactively adapted. Some crafted strategies to be robust across a range of contingencies; others adopted focused strategies. During times of rapid technological change, some acted to capture the opportunities of first-mover advantages; others postponed major investments in new and emerging technologies. These same choices confront the United States today.

QUESTIONS ADDRESSED, WHY THEY ARISE

How do states respond when they face no strategic rival and have no overarching threat? What strategies do they pursue, and what explains their strategic choices? What are the risks and consequences of different strategies for power, influence, and preparedness for war?

These questions lie at the heart of this book. They arise because they have not received adequate attention by scholars. The focus of inquiry has been on critical turning points in world history leading up to the outbreak of war or after wars end. There is a robust literature on the causes of war and sources of instability when threats are high or escalating.[3] Realist scholarship and balance-of-power theory explain why states balance, buck-pass, or bandwagon when threats are rising. The literature on deterrence, crisis management, escalation, alliance formation, and postwar institutional arrangements is also broad and deep.

In between the run-ups to major wars are longer periods when the threat is not clear or well understood. Threat uncertainty is not uncommon. It follows after the disappearance of a traditional or familiar threat. This usually occurs after a major war, but rivals may implode, as the Soviet Union did, or become partners through peaceful reconciliation. Absent a clear enemy, a state may face a number of potential threats over the horizon, no threats even at a distance, or novel, diffuse, unfamiliar threats in the near term and long term. In each case, no "burning house" exists to focus on.[4]

The field has focused disproportionately on a narrow slice of world history—periods of high threat—giving short shrift to the rest of the time, when states operate in the fog of peace. The extant literature tells us far less about the strategies adopted under these conditions and the consequences that follow.[5] Yet the problems facing strategic planners when the threat is low differ from those they confront when the threat is high. The logic of strategic choice also differs. In uncertain times, the problem is not how to respond to a specific threat. The challenges are to identify and understand a range of threats, anticipate the types of wars that may arise in the future, balance responses to present challenges with preparations for future contingencies, and ensure the state is well positioned to compete effectively when new unanticipated challenges arise.

States always plan under uncertainty. The issue here is planning in uncertain times. The timeliness of this study stems from the uncertain conditions that characterize the present security environment of the United States, that have done so for nearly two decades, and that most likely will continue to do so in the future. The United States is no longer burdened by the threat of massive nuclear exchange and possesses overwhelming conventional military superiority. It faces no peer; nor is a potential rival chasing closely behind. The European Union is an economic rival but not a military one.[6] Economic and military transformations underway in China could propel it to superpower status in the next half-century. India is also poised to emerge as a global superpower. But neither Asian state is nipping closely at the heels of the United States. History shows that strategic choices made in uncertain times have important consequences for future power and position. Surviving and thriving in the international system depend on choices made before threats coalesce, during the "fog of peace."

This study also engages the debate on unipolarity. The dominant paradigm in international relations, realism, assumes that rising contenders innovate and invest more wisely than overburdened leaders, causing a shift in the balance of power and hastening the leader's decline. Most security studies scholars, even those who argue that the United States can sustain unipolarity for some unspecified period of time, believe that hegemonic decline is *eventually* inevitable. Balance-of-power theory and hegemonic stability theory both assume that U.S. military power and preponderance will erode with shifts in relative power or that the pace of erosion will be accelerated by self-defeating behavior. On the other hand, those who think unipolarity is sustainable believe the United States should show restraint in promoting its values, act multilaterally, strengthen international institutions, and provide public goods that reassure others of America's benign intent. The United States should leverage its soft power, judiciously use military force, and bolster domestic support for internationalism, all in the service of a defensive grand strategy that gradually accommodates inevitable decline.

A consistent pattern in business is the failure of leading companies to stay at the top of their industries when technologies or markets change. In a similar fashion, leading states likewise cling to the technologies and practices that are historically valued and that underwrite their current strength. Shifts in the balance of power often come from rising challengers that launch innovations that leverage the challengers' strengths and exploit the leaders' weaknesses. But research on corporate responses to uncertainty in the marketplace shows that there are options firms have in uncertain times that are not available when competition is intense. In other words, periods of pause in great power strategic rivalry present windows of opportunity that states can exploit to shape the dynamics of competition and perpetuate their power. The logic of "shaping" has not been examined systematically. With the uncertainty from more threats, greater diversity in security actors, and a rapidly evolving technological environment that can be exploited by different actors in unanticipated ways, a proactive strategy of shaping the future has advantages over waiting for others to impose their futures. A hiatus in great power rivalry provides a rare opportunity to capitalize on competitive advantages and cement a lead. On the cautionary side, shaping is not viewed as a benign strategy. It can encourage challengers to rise and exacerbate prospects for peace.

This book puts U.S. efforts to shape its strategic environment into historical perspective. By so doing, it identifies the pitfalls of planning in peacetime. It also clarifies the conditions under which different strategies preserve, augment, or undermine state power. These choices are equally important for rising powers, like China and India, and significantly weakened states, like Russia. All have to allocate resources and make strategic choices in an uncertain world.

In this book I introduce three types of strategic responses states may make: "shaping," "adapting," and "reforming and reconstituting." I argue that environmental factors (power distribution) and complexity provide the best predictors of when states will undertake one of these strategic responses. I demonstrate how choices made during periods of strategic pause have a significant effect on what states can do once threats emerge.

ARGUMENTS ADVANCED, ANSWERS OFFERED

The focus of this book is on military strategy and grand strategy. Military strategy encompasses decisions about doctrine, force structure, and mission requirements to support grand strategy. Grand strategy brings together the economic, diplomatic, and military lines of effort to manage present challenges and prepare for future contingencies. Structural and environmental conditions and concerns about relative international standing shape strategic choices, even when a state has no strategic competitor or clear threat—in other words, during the fog of peace.

Realism is the starting point for this analysis because the theory provides the most convincing explanation for how states react to their strategic environment. It is the approach best suited to understanding the constraints and opportunities facing leaders as they strive to preserve and extend their state's power. Its starting premise is that states live in an anarchic world with no sovereign to enforce rules of behavior, and so states must look to themselves to survive. War is always a possibility, and the key to survival in war is military power. States try to increase their power when they can without excessive cost or risk, and they try especially hard to preserve the power they have. Power is relative, so states are vigilant about the attempts of others to increase their capacities. Not all states behave according to the tenets of realism, but those that do not decline in power and suffer accordingly.

Realists acknowledge that states have choices about the strategies they pursue to preserve and increase their relative power. But they have focused on conditions of rising and high threat and said less on how concerns about relative international standing influence strategic choice in uncertain times. Employing an exploratory research strategy,[7] this study builds on theories of corporate responses to uncertainty in the marketplace on the premise that the strategies modern business firms adopt can help us to understand state choices. States and firms both can be viewed as unitary rational actors in an uncertain environment. They face common problems when confronted with uncertainty, and this plays an important role in the decision-making calculus of entrepreneurs and political leaders. Research shows that the risks of uncertainty can be reduced for firms that increase their size, much as states strive to augment their power to hedge against unanticipated futures. Shaping consumer preferences, expectations, and behavior through advertising is another way for firms to deal with uncertainty, much as states use strategic communication and soft power to influence attitudes and behavior of critical audiences.[8] Both states and firms innovate to remain competitive, and their position affects the propensity to innovate. The state–firm analogy is not the only way to characterize strategic choice in uncertain times, but it highlights a number of important dimensions of the problem that are overlooked by traditional approaches to the study of international politics.[9]

By drawing on managerial theory, I do not claim that a modern state is in every respect analogous to the "ideal" of a modern business firm driven by the overriding goal of profit maximization. But both exist within competitive environments; both seek to survive, to remain competitive, and to maximize relative power, whether understood as influence or market share. In the real world, as opposed to the hypothetical world of perfect competition, the similarities increase further. Both are organizations with relatively independent action in a system, defined group boundaries, control of their internal structure and resource allocation, varying levels of domain consensus, and a good deal of organizational complexity across various competencies. Nor do the profit motive or stockholders present stark differences. Corporations do not manage up and down for profit; if they did, all losing corporations would disappear. Stockholders are usually, at best, distant from the operation of the firm, voting with as much knowledge as citizens have when they vote.[10]

From the management literature, we can derive three main strategies available to states to maintain and improve their relative standing in an uncertain world: shaping, adapting, or reforming and reconstituting. Shaping is a proactive strategy of altering the external strategic environment to channel world events down favorable paths so that serious new challengers do not emerge. Adapting is a reactive strategy that takes the current system structure as given and strives to preserve the state's position in the system and gradually improve it over time. Reforming and reconstituting make up a long-term strategy of deep and fundamental internal reform undertaken to leapfrog to a more privileged position and compete more effectively in the future. Each strategy has distinct pitfalls and risks.

The strategy a state pursues is a product of its relative power. The weakest states, those in the trough of the power curve, have little choice but to reform and reconstitute to strategically rebuild in response to defeat in war or gradual relative decline. Rising powers have an incentive to shape to overturn the current order. Declining powers have one of two options if they want to arrest their decline. They can adapt in the hopes that a fast follower strategy will forestall decline, or they can opt for a more radical strategy of reforming and reconstituting, as did the Soviet Union under perestroika.

Conventional wisdom suggests that preeminent powers, particularly hegemons, should act as conservative status quo states and adapt to maintain and preserve the prevailing order they dominate.[11] Yet preeminent states, like market leaders, also have an incentive to exploit the opportunity that their preponderant power presents to organize international politics to suit their interests, consolidate and improve their dominant power advantage, and perpetuate their lead. Shaping is an important yet understudied response to uncertainty. This may be why it was so surprising to most international relations theorists that the United States has acted like a revolutionary power by trying to shape the world with its "transformational" program of democracy promotion, regime change, and military transformation.[12] Shaping is risky because it seeks to overturn the very system the hegemon sits atop. Yet the absence of a strategic competitor presents unique opportunities for the market leader.[13] What is paradoxical from the perspective of traditional international relations theory becomes less puzzling from a management theory perspective.

Structural realism is a theory about how constraints and incentives of the geopolitical environment affect state behavior. Relative power is the logical place to start to understand strategic choices. For example, great powers, by virtue of having more power, more expansive interests that have to be promoted, and more commitments that have to be protected should face different strategic dilemmas than do lesser powers that exert power only locally or regionally. The great power must plan against a larger number of threats and probably a more diverse set of threats. However, the opportunities and constraints that derive from relative power position can be modified or reinforced in relatively predictable ways by unit-specific environmental conditions. For example, geography and proximity to potential adversaries can alter the opportunities and constraints of states that are otherwise comparable in terms of relative power. The strategic options available to insular, defensively advantaged states should diverge from those available to continental, defensively disadvantaged states.

States that face a greater number of threats, a more diverse set of consequential security actors, and a more highly interdependent or networked environment, one in which rapid change is likely to spill over and spread, confront a more "complex" external environment. The greater the complexity of one's environment, the more things one will be uncertain about. One of the biggest challenges of living in uncertain times is to balance the ability to respond to both present problems and future unforeseen contingencies. This challenge is particularly great for the most powerful states in the system because they are likely to have broader interests, more commitments, and greater ambitions. What this means for the United States today is that, despite a commitment to shape the international system and transform its military to perpetuate its power, operational demands associated with a complex strategic environment demand responsiveness to a wide variety of near-term contingencies, and these demands run counter to the shaping priority of long-term transformation.

History shows that preparedness for war is affected by lengthy periods of peace. Some states and their militaries have been prepared for future wars, and others have not. The question is why. Exploring how leaders have responded when they were uncertain about their strategic and technological environments shows the risks and trade-offs of various strategies and the consequences of contemporary policy choices.

PLAN OF THE BOOK

The argument made in this book—that states adopt particular strategies in uncertain times, that relative power should be the starting point for understanding these strategic responses, that the complexity of the state's external environment can modify strategic choice in predictable ways—is demonstrated and evaluated through a set of historical and contemporary case studies of how leaders have managed uncertainty over time. The book compares strategy formation and threat assessment today with two earlier periods, between the end of the Crimean War and the onset of World War I and between the two world wars. The case studies show that relative power and complexity explain strategic choice better than do nonstructural and nonenvironmental factors such as domestic politics, organizational imperatives, and cognitive psychology. The case studies also show the conditions under which different strategies preserve, augment, or undermine state power.

Chapter 2 describes the sources and nature of uncertainty and the logic of case selection. It discusses the specific problems facing planners and operators in uncertain times and develops the book's theoretical argument about strategic choice. It proposes a set of competing hypotheses that are evaluated in subsequent chapters.

Chapter 3 examines Russian and British policy between the Crimean War and World War I. This was a period of tremendous strategic and technological upheaval and one that has received relatively little attention compared to the pre- and post–World War II eras. In addition to the complexity introduced by rapid military change, Russian leaders faced many potential adversaries in the form of coalitions of wealthier industrialized states that risked unraveling the empire. As a defeated and recovering power, Russia opted to reform and reconstitute, setting in motion a process of reassessment that produced far-reaching military and social reforms. As a preponderant power, Britain pursued a shaping strategy that exploited its information advantages to sustain its naval supremacy. Between 1904 and 1910, the Royal Navy embarked on a strategy to achieve information dominance by establishing a chain of wireless stations around the world. The resulting information-communications network proved to be a huge strategic advantage for the British.

Chapter 4 examines British and U.S. policies between the two world wars. The inter–world war years are another example of strategic pause coupled with technological upheaval. Improvements in internal combustion engines, aircraft design, radio, and radar altered the nature of conflict dramatically. As a declining hegemon, the British faced no imminent threats but potential long-term strategic problems with all the great powers. Budget problems, competing visions of the future threat environment, a false belief in the country's ability to reconstitute with sufficient warning, and challenges across the empire resulted in a strategic posture of adapting. The United States faced no serious threats, was unhampered by imperial commitments, and was burdened with few peacetime demands on strategic resources. As a rising challenger, the United States systematically planned for a range of contingencies over the longer term and made significant efforts to shape its future strategic environment.

Chapter 5 focuses on the United States today. America's strategic response to uncertainty was one of adapting in the 1990s and shaping in the first decade of the twenty-first century. Adapting was logical for a leading power to preserve a scaled-down version of a Cold War force structure that had served the United States well. Organizational inertia reinforced adapting. By the late 1990s, shaping became closely tied to calls for military transformation. The attacks of September 11 brought home the novelty and complexity of the new security environment, and the Bush administration launched a strategy of "muscular" shaping. Military dominance, preemption, and regime change were its hallmarks. As the conflicts in Afghanistan and Iraq have dragged on, the United States has strived to simultaneously minimize near-term risk while also transforming its military, economy, and diplomacy for the long term.

Chapter 6 concludes by examining the consequences of strategic choices made over time, assessing their influence on states' power and position, and weighing the advantages and disadvantages of different strategies for the United States today.

IMPLICATIONS FOR U.S. POLICY

Hegemonic decline is inevitable. The issue is how long and by what means a preponderant power can sustain its lead and ward off competitors. Many scholars assume that U.S. preponderance is already eroding and that the pace of erosion has been accelerated by self-defeating behavior and overreliance on the military instrument of power.

The historical record is on the skeptic's side because most hegemons, like most leading firms in the marketplace, improve performance in the sustaining capabilities valued historically by the major players. Hegemons attend less to the disruptive innovations that have a competence-destroying impact on established capabilities. Leaders may even shun disruptive innovations out of fear of stimulating others to follow, accelerating decline and shifting the balance of power in a competitor's direction.[14]

Disruptive technologies by definition represent a credible threat to the competitive strength of the market leader. They are disruptive precisely because they do not augment the leader's existing strength but rather compromise traditional sources of power, growth, and profitability. They create new forms of competition and thereby new competitors.[15] So, for example, new communication and computing technologies, as well as the Internet, have facilitated the emergence, coordination, and operations of networked terrorist groups in the Greater Middle East.[16] The growth of national satellite architectures and the commercialization of space threaten to erode the United States' near monopoly in space. Coupled with missile and weapons of mass destruction (WMD) technology, even middle and small powers may be able to target forward bases and deter U.S. operations abroad. Advanced mines and human-portable antiaircraft missiles; terrorism and cyber-warfare attacks on critical infrastructure; and protracted and extremely lethal conflicts are all tailor made to exploit U.S. vulnerabilities and empower traditionally weaker actors. Combat in urban environments and other complex terrain further undermines America's competitive advantage in technology, and in fighting concentrated and in the open. "Together, the effect of these trends will be to exploit enduring U.S. military weaknesses by creating a competitive environment requiring manpower-intensive operations over a protracted period with the prospect of incurring substantial casualties."[17] Few adversaries appear willing to challenge America in areas of its traditional military dominance.

How does one stave off the decline of U.S. power in an unpredictable environment? By analyzing strategy in uncertain times, this book strives to clarify the consequences of different strategic choices for preserving the Pax Americana and sustaining, augmenting, or undermining the power that supports it.

2 STRATEGIC CHOICE IN UNCERTAIN TIMES

STRATEGIC CHOICES made in peacetime have significant effects on what states can do once threats coalesce.[1] Planning against the wrong enemy or type of enemy or preparing for the wrong type of war has produced military defeats and realignments of power in the past, usurping some states and catapulting others to positions of preeminence. This book advances three arguments. First, planning absent a clear and overarching threat raises policy dilemmas that are distinct from those that planners face during periods of high threat. Second, the management literature is instructive for international relations theorizing on peacetime planning and can easily be adapted to describe the strategies states pursue in response to an uncertain strategic environment. Third, to explain which strategy a particular state adopts in uncertain times, we should look first to the state's relative power and next to the complexity of its strategic environment. Contra much of the literature, strategic choice in uncertain times does reflect structural and environmental factors as well as states' concern with their relative international standing.

The purpose of this chapter is to flesh out each of these arguments. The first section defines uncertainty and discusses the problems of planning in uncertain times. The second section describes the strategies states adopt in response to uncertainty. The third section explains how relative power and complexity shape strategic choice. Hypotheses on the impact of structural and environmental conditions are juxtaposed with hypotheses from the organizational, institutional, domestic politics, and cognitive psychology literatures. The final section addresses methodological issues: the logic of case selection and the indicators used in the case studies to code strategic postures.

UNCERTAINTY, COMPLEXITY, AND PLANNING DILEMMAS

The classic definition of uncertainty distinguishes "uncertainty" from "risk." Risk means future events occur with measurable probability. Risk can be quantified, either on a priori grounds (a flipped coin will come up heads 50 percent of the time) or on the basis of empirical observation (14 percent of all automobile deaths involve young drivers). Uncertainty is present when the likelihood of future events is indefinite or incalculable.[2] Events cannot be measured and analyzed on a priori grounds or through empirical observation because they are too irregular or unique.[3] Risk requires controlled scenarios where the alternatives are clear. The real world is a dynamic system in which strategic planners regularly face situations that are unique and unprecedented.[4] Uncertainty is a given, whether one is making long-term projections, predicting outcomes in given contingencies, monitoring emerging problems, or warning of imminent danger. Defense planners typically have performed poorly when making long-term projections.[5]

Uncertainty is central to international relations theory, where it is typically treated as a property of the international system. Kenneth Waltz defines the international system by its gross distribution of power and argues that bipolar systems are more certain and stable than multipolar systems. A single conflict dyad means less risk of miscalculation and greater clarity about alliance formation. "Who is a danger to whom is never in doubt."[6] Stephen Van Evera also views uncertainty as a property of the international system, but he defines the system by its structure of military capabilities.[7] Uncertainty results from low distinguishability—the inability to distinguish offensive from defensive weapons, strategies, and force postures. When information about capabilities cannot be used to deduce the true nature of intentions because offensive and defensive weapons and postures are not distinguishable, status quo powers cannot signal their benign intentions by investing in defense, and uncertainty rises.

While the sources of uncertainty lie in the structure of the international system, the objects of uncertainty, or what one is uncertain about, are others' intentions. Some theorists believe that future intentions are never fully knowable, so one must assume the worst.[8] Others believe uncertainty about intentions can be reduced through reliable information about state type—whether a state is status quo and security seeking or greedy and revisionist[9]—and by monitoring capabilities, weapons acquisitions, and costly signals.[10]

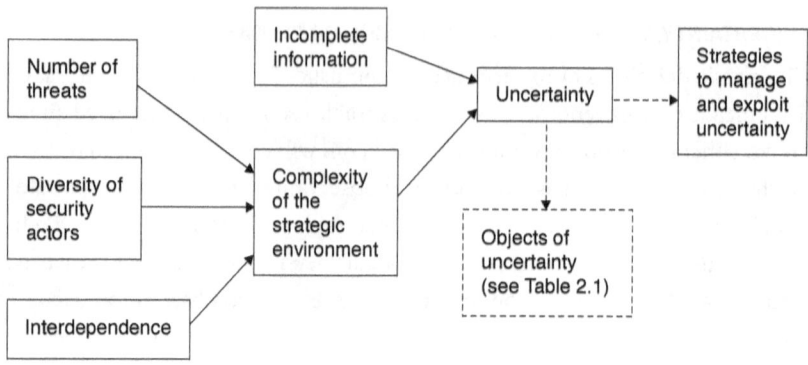

Figure 2.1. Sources of uncertainty.

Structural theories provide one approach to understanding the sources and objects of uncertainty. In this study, uncertainty is conceived as a property of humans, not their environment. Systems and structure are not uncertain; agents are. The framework diagrammed in Figure 2.1 treats uncertainty as a property of agents. Incomplete information and the complexity of the agent's strategic environment are the primary sources of uncertainty.[11]

The agent's environment is not the same as the system. Similar to Stephen Walt's balance of threat theory, complexity is a property of the external environment, and some of the dimensions of it are specific to states rather than systemwide. Complexity rises when numbers, diversity, and interdependence increase.[12] A state's external environment is more complex to the extent it faces a greater number of threats, a more diverse set of consequential security actors, and a more interdependent and networked environment in which change rapidly spreads.

A clearly defined or overarching threat simplifies strategic calculations. If a state faces a number of potential threats, it must judge the goals and capabilities of a greater number of actors, as well as the time when those potential threats are likely to become actual threats.

Diversity of consequential security actors also increases complexity.[13] The state may face qualitatively different types of threats, some of which it never confronted before, some of which come from actors that are much less obvious threats yet have the capacity to inflict harm in meaningful ways, and some of which, like terrorist groups, have different incentive structures from states. The diversification of threat types enhances the difficulty of assessing relative power. This has become more challenging with an emerging private market for military services that can rapidly transform a rival's capabilities, producing increasingly unpredictable power balances.[14] Diversity also makes it difficult to decide what type(s) of conflict(s) to prepare for (for example, major conventional war, complex irregular warfare, and so on), if only because one is more likely to face adversaries with capabilities that are dissimilar to one's own.

Finally, the more interdependent and networked the environment, the more widely and rapidly will changes diffuse, thereby complicating strategic calculations. The cases examined in this book all coincide with periods of rapid technological change, or "revolutions in military affairs" (RMAs).[15] RMAs mark fundamental discontinuities with the status quo[16] and introduce periods of considerable turmoil in the complexion of the battlefield as states respond and adapt. It is difficult to anticipate whether a new way of war will overturn existing paradigms. When an RMA occurs in a highly networked system, technologies and their applications diffuse more rapidly, to a greater number of actors, with a greater diversity in outcomes, producing more uncertainty about relative capabilities and about how new technologies will be leveraged. Planners face many unknowns: the direction of change in military technology, the impact of new methods on war making, how technology can be leveraged and by whom, and the speed of its diffusion.[17] Interdependence has increased over time and so has complexity.

Complexity does not always correlate positively with danger. The Cold War world was a very dangerous one because of the potential consequences of a U.S.–Soviet conflagration. But the structure of bipolarity minimized complexity by reducing the number and diversity of threats. There was a working consensus on the identity of the dominant adversary and reasonable agreement on Soviet intentions. The "who" and the "where" were known, and the challenge was to optimize forces for a given scenario. Now, the challenge is to understand the problem, the "who," the "where," and the "why."

Decision makers always face uncertainty; but, during periods of strategic pause, they confront a greater number and variety of unknowns. Realists claim that the most critical objects of uncertainty are the intentions and capabilities of adversaries. Agents can also be uncertain about the intentions and capabilities of friends and even be unsure of the capabilities and level of commitment their own nations can muster. Table 2.1 summarizes the unknowns that confront planners in uncertain times, and the discussion that follows demonstrates the many ways that planning in uncertain times differs from periods of high threat.

Table 2.1. Unknowns in uncertain times.

	Intentions	Capabilities
Adversaries	Identity of potential threats	Adversary's capabilities
Allies	Identity of potential allies	Level of interoperability with, and distribution of roles and missions among, allies and coalition partners
	Desirability of firm or loose diplomatic arrangements	
		Whether to trade with and transfer technology to, or contain, current partners who may become future adversaries
Self	National purpose	Balance of resources between defense and nondefense
	Reasons for engagement abroad	Balance of resources between near term and long term
	Themes to mobilize domestic support	Scope and speed of transformation

Uncertainty about the identity of potential threats is central to international relations theory.[18] It should not be reduced to uncertainty over state type—status quo versus revisionist. Threat uncertainty follows the disappearance of the prior, traditional, or familiar threat pattern. This can occur in the wake of major wars; or a rival may implode, as did the Soviet Union; or peaceful reconciliation can transform an enemy into a partner. Instead of a clearly defined enemy, several potential threats may loom over the horizon (the situation of post-Crimea Russia); there may be no threats even at a distance (the situation facing America in the 1920s); or novel, diffuse, and unfamiliar threats in the near term and distant future may populate the strategic environment (as they do for America today). RMAs have important implications for threat uncertainty. They can reduce or increase effective geographic distance, expanding or shrinking the number of actors that can pose a serious threat. Political threats may be negligible, but changes in technology, such as air power, nuclear weapons, and computers increase vulnerability by reducing the space between states.

The fundamental importance of threat uncertainty is captured by Jennifer Mitzen, who distinguishes physical security from ontological security.[19] States may be physically insecure due to offense dominance or acute rivalry but socially secure because they know who the enemy is and the type of game they are playing. This is why people talk nostalgically about the Cold War. Despite the prospect of mutual annihilation, both sides knew who the enemy was. The decline or disappearance of a major rival may increase physical security, but it reduces ontological security. Relative quiescence in great power rivalry paradoxically increases uncertainty.

Uncertainty over the identity of future adversaries creates ambiguity about whether one should prepare for an adversary with similar or dissimilar capabilities. Peer competitors possess roughly similar capabilities, and symmetry facilitates planning. Competitors that cannot match superior capabilities adopt asymmetric responses to offset superior strengths, and disruptive technologies—low-cost innovations that undermine the competitive advantage of leaders.[20] Uncertainty about adversary capabilities rises when the criteria for assessing the relative distribution of power are unclear, which is common during periods of rapid technological change.

When threats recede and the security dilemma is dampened, alliances loosen, reducing the level of cooperation in the system. Alliance uncertainty captures the ambiguity about the identity of potential allies and whether one's security is served best by permanent alliances, looser coalitions, or collective security. Collective security makes sense when threats are ambiguous because no specific adversary is identified; but this is the least flexible diplomatic option. Unilateralism maximizes flexibility to prepare for unforeseen contingencies but is very costly because it depends least on others.[21]

Uncertainty about the capabilities of allies raises challenges for managing and coordinating assets with potential partners: which partners to rely on, how extensively to rely on them, what their contributions will be, how much integration is desirable, how to ensure interface standards across multiple partners. The problem of interface standards is aggravated under conditions of military transformation when states are adapting their military forces to new technologies at different rates.

One's posture toward allies also raises questions about trade and transfer. If offensive realists are correct that future intentions can never be known, then transferring sensitive technologies even to friends is problematic. Friends today may become adversaries tomorrow, able to use advanced capabilities against the country that provided them. Opting to contain rather than engage in the area of trade and transfer does not preclude cooperation entirely. The questions are the extent and nature of economic engagement and the transfer of technologies to states that may become adversaries or that may in turn transfer or sell those technologies to others.

While realists assume uncertainty about the intentions and capabilities of others, they fail to acknowledge that states may be uncertain about their own intentions and capabilities. When external imperatives are weak, uncertainty over the nation's purpose and reasons for engagement abroad rises, and strategic postures are more vigorously contested internally. Elites face uncertainty about societal support, what Michael Howard calls the "forgotten dimension of strategy,"[22] because it is difficult to mobilize the public in the pursuit of security absent a clear threat.[23] The loss of a threat requires creation of a new theme, or national purpose orientation, around which domestic society can be mobilized.

Absent a clear and present danger, uncertainty about one's own capabilities also rises. How should leaders manage the domestic economy to preserve the ability to prevail in future conflicts? Without a clear threat, it becomes difficult to convince wary politicians and publics of the importance of peacetime defense spending. When threats subside, financial risks are perceived to overwhelm military risks, and strategic insurance appears to depend disproportionately on economic strength at the expense of military strength.

Uncertainty over the allocation of defense resources concerns more than guns versus butter trade-offs. It involves trade-offs between the near term and long term and the scope and speed of transformation that should be pursued. The trade-off between near-term spending and long-term investment will be influenced by the extent to which rapid advances in technology create "slack" that permits actors to create decisive advantage through improvements in technology and doctrine.[24] Under these circumstances, states should shift resources into research and development (R&D) to leverage rapidly changing technologies. Uncertainty calls into question the time horizon that states use to calculate their interests, forcing a choice between minimizing short-term risk and maximizing long-run opportunities. Current spending to retain the capability and readiness to meet unanticipated threats in the short run competes with long-term economic growth and recapitalization to meet unanticipated threats in the more distant future. If potential near-term threats appear serious or if current expenditure will have little negative impact for the long run, it makes sense to maintain capable forces in being. However, if potential long-run threats loom greater than short-run threats, or if the costs of failing to invest are high, it becomes more sensible to trim forces in being and channel resources into research and development for the future. The challenge can also be how to split the difference, or transform "under fire."

Uncertainty about the intentions and capabilities of others enhances the difficulty of deciding what type of conflict to prepare for. Mission uncertainty grows with the diversification of threat types because competing threats often imply conflicting mission priorities. The trade-offs become more acute during periods of financial stringency. Periods of military revolution further exacerbate uncertainty over mission priorities because they introduce fundamental discontinuities in the status quo.

States can respond to uncertainty by trying to reduce its sources or by pursuing strategies that exploit the opportunities it offers up. Improving intelligence about the broader security environment and battlefield and enhancing one's ability to collect, process, synthesize, and share vital information to a greater extent than an adversary can reduce uncertainty. This is the essence of information superiority, a capability at the centerpiece of post–Cold War U.S. defense transformation efforts.[25] States can never attain perfect information because of the limits of intelligence, the impossibility of predicting complex events with precision, and the inevitable "fog" that is a defining characteristic of war. Reducing complexity is another strategy to mitigate uncertainty. Curtailing the diffusion of sensitive technologies decreases the number of consequential security actors with the capability to inflict harm. Tethering potential adversaries to the state in peacetime reduces those aligned against the state and hence the planning scenarios one must prepare for.[26] Increasing power allows the state to prevail against a larger number of threats and across a broader range of diverse scenarios, particularly when one invests in capabilities to increase information dominance.[27] The next section presents three overarching strategies for operating in uncertain times.

STRATEGIES TO MANAGE AND EXPLOIT UNCERTAINTY

Management scholars who have examined how firms operate in an uncertain marketplace identify three strategic postures designed to leverage opportunities and stay competitive: shaping, adapting, and reserving the right to play.[28] These are analogous to strategies available to states that face a large number of unknowns about their strategic environment: shape,[29] adapt, and reform and reconstitute.[30]

Shaping is proactive and geared toward the long term. It takes advantage of periods of strategic pause to invest in order to prevent more dangerous futures. Shaping leverages opportunities to generate big payoffs instead of trying to reduce risk across a range of scenarios. The goal is to alter the shaper's domain—the nature of competition or competitors—to prevent the emergence of serious new threats. Shaping offers the highest reward but is the riskiest strategy.

Shaping is not a well-developed concept. It embraces a wide range of options. The expectations and behaviors of others can be shaped through the power of ideas or superior capabilities. Shaping can mean providing a vision that coordinates the strategies of other players, which is not costly. It may simply involve leveraging the credibility of leadership (for example, if the leader thinks this is the right way to go, it must be right) to drive the system toward a long-term favorable outcome. In the private sector, this is akin to creating a new industry standard.

Some shaping strategies are very costly, such as regime change, which aims to change potential competitors. Preventive war is another ambitious shaping strategy designed to deter the emergence of new threats by focusing on nations not yet locked into confrontation over vital interests. Although U.S. shaping strategies since the end of the Cold War have relied predominantly on the military tool, most have been less ambitious and less controversial than regime change or preventive war: expanding military assistance programs, multinational exercises, military-to-military contacts, and military presence. These shaping strategies are analogous to replicating an existing system (for example, of civil–military relations) in a new market.

While regime change is a coercive form of shaping, engagement is a collaborative way to prevent rising powers from becoming adversaries by giving the challenger a stake in the international order. This was the cornerstone of the post–World War II Marshall Plan and American efforts to integrate Germany into the postwar liberal international order. It is the desired course of those who believe China can be enticed to follow Germany's path, even if it means transforming its polity and limiting its strategic ambitions. The goal here is to influence the conduct of a specific competitor, rather than to reshape the strategic landscape or the nature of competition.

Technological innovation is a shaping strategy that involves making large capital investments to maintain leadership in the system or, if one is a rising power, to shake up the current system hierarchy. Enhancing military capabilities through innovation can place the state in a position of dominance where few can balance against it.

Table 2.2 provides examples of shaping. The strategy can target a particular actor or, more ambitiously, strive to alter the strategic landscape. Shaping can employ military and nonmilitary tools and be pursued coercively or noncoercively.

Adapting is a common response to uncertainty and conceptually familiar to international relations theorists.[31] A state or organization analyzes its

Table 2.2 Shaping strategies.

Tool	Mode	Examples
Military	Coercive	Regime change; preventive war
	Noncoercive	Technological innovation; transformation; military assistance, education and exercises
Nonmilitary	Coercive	Containment on trade and transfer
	Noncoercive	Strategic communication; engagement and integration into system

environment and commits to actions that conform to that environment. The mind-set is one of accepting the world as it is. Adapting is a reactive strategy that takes the current system structure, its evolution, and one's position in it as given. It is closest to a hedging strategy. Adapting does not challenge the status quo but tries to preserve the system and one's position in it. Adapters are rarely innovators but instead follow the shaper's lead, responding quickly to new developments and incorporating innovations into existing systems. The logic behind adapting is to incrementally modify existing postures, commitments, and capabilities as new strategic conditions arise.

A strategy of reform and reconstitute is geared to the long term. Leaders undertake deep internal reform to remedy fundamental structural deficiencies and guarantee a more competitive position in the future. To maximize power and capabilities in the long term, reformers minimize cost and sacrifice capability and flexibility in the short to medium term. Management specialists call this strategy "reserving the right to play." It is a strategy for weaker players who are not content with their position. Reforming and reconstituting requires investing in core capacity, organizational capabilities, relevant expertise, and learning. It is more than internal balancing. It resembles what Victoria Tin-bor Hui calls "self-strengthening reforms," which build up the administrative capacity and mobilize untapped resources to increase military and economic strength.[32]

Each strategy has pitfalls. Shapers are more likely to overprepare for particular futures and underprepare for others. Shaping may result in large payoffs in some scenarios but can produce large losses in others (for example, sacrificing boots on the ground for high-tech standoff weapons).[33] Former Defense Secretary Donald Rumsfeld's preference for a "high-tech low numbers on the ground" strategy for Iraq may have led to a swift victory but poorly prepared the U.S. military to conduct stabilization, reconstruction, and counterinsurgency operations. Strategies that bet on a particular outcome have greater risks than diversified strategies, so while shapers may succeed in technologically shaping the future with some adversaries, they risk falling victim to the asymmetric strategies of other adversaries. Shaping through technological innovation may also prompt others to respond, thereby undermining the shaper's technological lead. Gearing one's military, economic, and diplomatic policies to the future can undermine near-term capabilities and responsiveness. Shapers are also likely to face greater diplomatic backlashes because shaping is an offensive grand strategy that seeks to alter the status quo.[34]

Adapters are more likely to cling to preexisting assumptions about the environment, and this reinforces organizational tendencies toward incremental change and defense of the status quo. They may have hedged for a range of futures but invested insufficient resources and planning to succeed at any of them. Adapters are less likely to innovate and risk falling behind when technology is rapidly changing.

A strategy of reform and reconstitute risks leaving the state unprepared for near-term contingencies. If resources are shifted too much toward shoring up the economy at the expense of defense investment, the state may be left unprepared to meet unanticipated contingencies in the medium to long term.

SOURCES OF STRATEGY

Relative power is a useful starting point for understanding strategic responses to uncertainty.[35] I deduce hypothesized relationships between relative power and strategy. The behavior of rising powers is straightforward. Rising powers want to subvert the current order and so adopt shaping strategies. The innovations that have revolutionized warfare have typically been introduced by military underdogs bent on attaining hegemonic status. Revolutionary France created the *levée en masse*, and the treaty-restricted German military of the interwar years developed a successful operational doctrine employing highly mobile tank formations and aircraft to break the trench deadlock and quickly defeat entire armies.[36]

Preeminent powers typically adapt to preserve the status quo, but leaders have also shaped to sustain their lead. Few powers at the height of their game have, like the United States today, so willingly adopted let alone taken the lead in military transformation. For leading states, shaping through transformation risks overturning the system they dominate. Leaders may shape for a short time to prolong the apex of their power but have traditionally preferred incremental adjustments to preserve the system.

Declining powers either adapt in the hopes that a fast follower strategy will arrest their decline or pursue far-reaching changes by reforming and reconstituting. Adapting is a strategy for those seeking to hold on to their current position in the system and avert decline rather than transform the system. Once a state has reached deep decline, it has no option but to reform and reconstitute. The Soviet Union was a declining state forced to reform and reconstitute through perestroika to arrest decline.

States in the trough of the power curve reform and reconstitute to strategically rebuild because of defeat in war or gradual relative decline. Reform and reconstitute is a long-term strategy for addressing deep structural problems that must be overcome to reassert power and influence in the long run.

The relationship between state power and strategy is captured in Figure 2.2.

To evaluate the hypothesis that strategic choices reflect relative power, we need to measure power independently of actors' perceptions, and evidence must show that relative power helps predict the strategic choices leaders make. Scholars differ on how problematic perceptions of relative power are and the conditions under which it is more or less problematic.[37] To argue that relative power is causal, one must claim to measure it objectively *and* show how it creates incentives toward certain policy choices over others. A structural argument would receive additional confirmation if it could be shown that objective measures of relative power matched what actors believed to be their relative power at the time and that they acted for reasons associated with their relative power position. If the theory's predictions did not match policy outcomes, other causal forces could be at work or actors' perceptions of relative power might diverge from analysts' objective assessments.

Relative power is the proposed starting point for understanding strategic choice in uncertain times. Economic power—more specifically mobilization potential—is used to assess relative power.[38] Economic power does not translate directly into military power, but the material basis of military strength

Figure 2.2. Uncertainty curve.

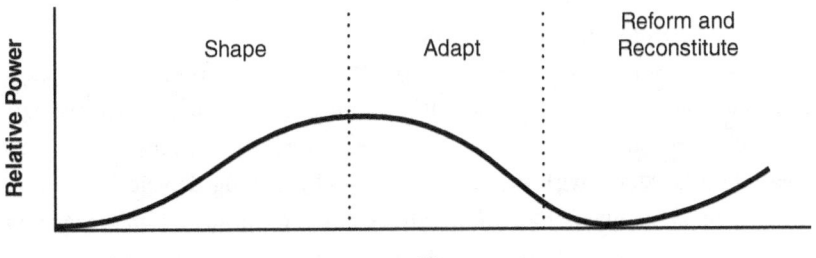

has traditionally been a starting point for assessments of military potential, and economic capacity has been treated as a necessary condition for the ability to inflict significant harm since the advent of the industrial age.[39] In 1987, Paul Kennedy observed the strong correlation between the productive and revenue-raising capacities of states and their military strength.[40] Those relationships have not been invalidated in the information age.[41]

Complexity, however, can modify the preferences of states otherwise similarly located in the distribution of power. Geographic position and distance to potential adversaries can increase the number of threats to the state or create a buffer of distance.[42] Defensive realists argue that a state can privilege long-term economic growth at the expense of near-term military preparations if the state has weak neighbors or defensible borders. Modern technology has certainly dampened the impact of geography by shrinking space and accelerating time, but states must still master their geography. The United States, for example, faces power projection problems that require a more expeditionary force structure than the one developed for the Cold War.[43]

Insular powers have traditionally not faced intense border pressure. Greater distance from powerful and potentially hostile neighbors has allowed them to adopt flexible diplomatic strategies and focus on long-term economic growth at the expense of near-term defense spending and military preparedness. With more abundant security, they have less incentive to cooperate with other states and are also more prone to neglect military innovation.

These options are foreclosed to states that face intense border pressure and possess little territorial depth. It is more difficult for defensively disadvantaged states to defend their national territory, so they devote more attention to improving their military posture and cooperating with other states. They also have greater incentive to innovate to solve strategic problems. In sum, states with few potential adversaries in close proximity should exhibit flexible diplomatic postures and long-horizon investment strategies and neglect innovation. States with adversaries in close proximity should exhibit firm diplomatic postures and near-term readiness and pursue innovation.

Existing commitments also modify preferences by affecting the diversity of threats facing the state or the diversity of markets—that is, geostrategic situations—in which the state must operate. More power means more expansive interests. States with global interests and far-flung dependencies have broader security interests and more diverse strategic priorities and face more threats and more diverse threats. The problem is most acute for hegemons.

Robert Jervis notes that "disturbances that would be dismissed in a multipolar or bipolar world loom much larger for the hegemon because it is present in all corners of the globe and everything seems interconnected."[44] Global powers need to prepare for a broad spectrum of conflict, while states with few global interests have the luxury to innovate to prevail in a local market or military environment. In these ways, the strategic preferences derived from relative power position can be modified by unit-specific environmental conditions.

Finally, complexity rises in a "rich" environment[45] where rapid advances in technology permit actors to reap significant gains by experimenting with new applications that can create decisive advantages.[46] During periods of rapid technological change, states have an incentive to shape and innovate. When the pace of technological change is stable, states have an incentive to adapt and slowly modernize to preserve their international position.

Tables 2.3 and 2.4 summarize hypotheses about the impact of relative power and complexity on strategic choice.

Other literatures attribute causality to nonstructural and nonenvironmental factors based on the proposition that, when systemic pressures are not acute, as Jeffrey Taliaferro argues, there is "an explicit role for leaders' preexisting belief systems, images of adversaries, and cognitive biases in the process of intelligence gathering, net assessment, military planning, and foreign policy decision making."[47] Domestic politics should also play a bigger role in strategic choice. As threats recede, pressure to shift resources from defense to social and economic programs rises in response to demands for a "peace dividend." Miroslav Nincic, Roger Rose, and Gerard Gorski argue that "the clearer the cues provided by the international environment, the slighter the domestic dissension concerning their interpretation." By contrast, the more uncertain one is about the external

Table 2.3. Hypotheses on relative power.

Effect of relative power on strategy

P1—Rising powers shape to overturn the status quo.

P2—Declining powers adapt to arrest their decline.

P3—Declining powers reform and reconstitute to arrest their decline.

P4—Leaders adapt to preserve the system they dominate.

P5—Leaders shape to perpetuate their position, even if this undermines the system they dominate.

P6—States in the trough of the power curve reform and reconstitute to strategically rebuild and reassert their power.

Table 2.4. Hypotheses on complexity.

Effect of border pressure on strategy (proximity of threats)

B1—Defensively advantaged states because they face fewer threats by virtue of distance from adversaries, privilege long-term investment, and neglect near-term readiness, which is consistent with shaping.

B2—Defensively disadvantaged states, because they face more threats by virtue of intense border pressure, privilege near-term readiness over long-term investment, which is consistent with adapting.

B3—Defensively advantaged states neglect innovation, which is consistent with adapting.

B4—Defensively disadvantaged states innovate to solve strategic problems, which is consistent with shaping.

Effect of global extension on strategy (number and diversity of threats)

E1—States with global interests and commitments face a larger number and wider variety of threats and adapt in response to a diverse range of missions and markets.

    E1a—States with global interests and commitments will face pressures to adapt to a larger array of near-term contingencies.

E2—States with only regional or local interests and commitments face fewer threats and shape to prevail in a specific contingency.

Effect of rapid technological change on strategy (interdependence)

I1—When technological change is rapid, states shape to reap gains from slack in the system and create decisive advantages.

I2—When technological change is stable, states adapt and slowly modernize to preserve their international position.

---

threat, the "more domestic social and political calculations dominate the thinking of policymakers,"[48] particularly in democracies where responsiveness to public pressure is likely to be greater.

Strong domestic politics arguments make more ambitious claims—that means and ends may be fashioned to serve domestic imperatives rather than strategic necessity. Foreign policy is domestic policy because the impact of international forces varies internally, advantaging some constituencies at the expense of others.[49] There are many arguments about the linkage between domestic factors and grand strategy, including the causal impact of regime type, coalitions, elite interests, and domestic instability. Few theories link domestic factors to choice of strategy. One exception is Carl Conetta's claim that RMA early adopters tend to be revolutionary or dictatorial regimes with revisionist strategic agendas. They are more risk acceptant and embrace bolder strategic agendas than democratic states or status quo powers:

> Because radical military transformation manifestly involves substantial uncertainty and risk, democratic states and *status quo* powers are seldom "first

out of the gate" in undertaking them—although desperate circumstances may sometimes compel them to act early and decisively.[50]

Other scholars focus on the domestic balance of power and argue that the preferences of the most powerful coalition explain foreign policy. What is critical is the nature of domestic cleavages—be they economic[51] or class.[52] Free traders or internationalists are hypothesized to prefer low defense spending and low-cost defense arrangements like international organizations, collective security, and arms control and to want to engage potential challengers. Economic nationalists should support higher defense spending and more coercive policies and prefer to punish potential challengers. Both internationalists and statist/nationalists in theory could opt to shape, adapt, or reform and reconstitute. Preferences for the choice of strategy cannot be deduced from such a coalitional analysis. However, the type of coalition that dominates could influence the implementation of the strategy, or the particular "options" selected, in the terminology of management theory. Internationalists should prefer cooperative or institutional shaping strategies over coercive or muscular shaping.

Other literatures predict little variance in strategic choice in uncertain times. All states and militaries display certain tendencies: focusing on technological threats, clinging to existing policies and resisting change, adopting planning shortcuts, and copying one another. These tendencies stem from the dynamics of organizational behavior, cognitive psychology, and the normative and social pressures operating in the international system.

Jan Breemer argues that rapid technological transformation induces strategic insecurity wholly independent of the level of amity and enmity among states. When technological change is rapid, threats are assessed in terms of capabilities, as opposed to intentions, for "fear that an international competitor might use a fleeting technological advantage to spring a surprise attack."[53] Breemer hypothesizes, "As the war-making intentions of potential opponents become more ambiguous, technological 'threats' will tend to become the focus of military planning."[54]

Organization theory makes predictions about the ways that organizations respond when faced with uncertainty due to the loss of their main enemies. All organizations want to minimize uncertainty[55] and maintain continuity in their operations. Members of organizations cope with uncertainty and complexity by forming, and then becoming attached to, simplified belief systems that are hard to change and resistant to discrepant evidence.[56] The result is resistance to change and reliance on standard operating procedures. If the organization does change, it is incrementally and in ways that preserve missions, budget, and autonomy.[57]

Cognitive explanations focus on what we know based on past experience and how we extract and create cues from limited information to deal with uncertainty. People rely on decision-making short cuts, or heuristics, because of their limited capacity to process information and cope with uncertainty. The availability heuristic assesses the likelihood of future events by the ease with which instances are constructed and retrieved,[58] and it often results in biased judgments because availability is affected by factors other than frequency. Easily retrievable or more familiar instances, recent occurrences, and highly salient experiences are judged to occur more frequently. The availability heuristic points to the vital role experience plays in perceptions of risk and assessments of probability under uncertainty. Familiar, recent, and highly salient experiences receive higher priority, and direct experience enhances the level of perceived risk associated with similar situations. This may account for the tendency to prepare for the last war. National security strategies are shaped by recent events, particularly when those events are *perceived* to resemble past events that are highly salient to leaders because of personal experience and/or the costs of those past events.

Sociology's new institutionalism focuses on the way that institutional pressures stimulate the spread of forms and practices across societies and professions. Of relevance here is the claim by Paul DiMaggio and Walter Powell that "when organizational technologies are poorly understood, when goals are ambiguous, or when the environment creates symbolic uncertainty, organizations may model themselves on other organizations."[59] Modeling is an easy way to adopt a successful practice without investing resources in a search for alternative options. The mimicry predicted by organizational sociologists could also result from the competitive pressures of the international system that produce powerful incentives for states to adopt new military methods in order to compete effectively.[60]

Hypotheses derived from nonstructural arguments are summarized in Table 2.5.

CASE SELECTION AND CODING

This study provides historical perspective on the dilemmas facing U.S. strategic planners today by comparing the dynamics of strategy formation and threat assessment now with similar processes in the post–Crimean War and

Table 2.5. Hypotheses on nonstructural causes.

Effect of domestic politics on strategy

D1—Absent a clear threat, states shift resources from defense to social programs and emphasize long-term economic growth over military readiness, consistent with a strategy of reforming and reconstituting.

D2—Preferences of the dominant domestic coalition influence the implementation of strategy, not the choice of strategy.

    D2a—Internationalist coalitions prefer cooperative strategies.

    D2b—Statist coalitions prefer coercive strategies.

D3—Revolutionary regimes, which are more risk acceptant, adopt shaping strategies.

D4—Status quo regimes, which are more risk averse, adapt.

Effect of rapid technological change on strategy

T1—When the intentions of potential adversaries are unclear, technological threats become the focus of planning.

Effect of organizational and institutional tendencies on strategy

O1—In uncertain times, organizations rely on standard operating procedures, which result in incremental changes consistent with a strategy of adapting.

O2—In uncertain times, organizations adapt by mimicking the successful practices of other organizations.

Effect of cognitive limitations on strategy

C1—In uncertain times, strategy reflects recent, highly salient experiences, consistent with a strategy of adapting.

    C1a—In uncertain times, recent conflicts shape future projections.

    C1b—In uncertain times, militaries prepare for the last war.

C2—Absent external cues, individuals rely on planning shortcuts and rules of thumb (for example, hypothetical threats, two-war standard, two-power standard, and so on).

post–World War I eras. In all three periods, technological developments transformed the conduct of military operations. States also faced complex security environments characterized by the absence of a clearly defined or overarching enemy. Post-Crimea Russia faced a number of potential threats over the horizon. America in the 1920s faced no threats, even at a distance, while Great Britain at that time lacked major threats but faced a range of lesser problems and vulnerabilities. Today, the United States faces novel, diffuse, and qualitatively different types of threats in the near term and distant future. In all three periods, there was no general condition of peace, but there was a hiatus in great power rivalry.

The utility of the historical periods for the present lies in the fact that political and military leaders had to decide how to respond in the face of ambiguity about the identity and goals of potential adversaries, the time frame within which threats were likely to arise, and the contingencies that might be imposed on the state by others. In all three periods, rapid technological change further increased the complexity of the threat environment, posing a fundamental challenge for defense planners: how to leverage technological changes given great uncertainty about who one's future enemies would be and what type of war one would be compelled to fight. The first period overlapped with the technological innovations associated with the railroad, rifle, and telegraph revolutions; the second with the innovations in internal combustion, mechanization, radio, mobility, and air power; and the third with advances in range, strike, stealth, sensors, precision-guided munitions, microelectronics, computers, information processing, and biotechnology. Although September 11, 2001, marked the end of the post–Cold War period, uncertainty has not ended but has been compounded by the ability of shadowy networks of terrorists and other transnational groups to expose the vulnerabilities of the world's superpower and the most sophisticated military force in history.

This study employs the comparative case study approach and methods of within-case analysis like process tracing to examine the logic and consequences of strategy formation. The unit of analysis is the state-period, or specific periods of time in the histories of certain states that are relevant for illustrating and testing the proposed theory. I consider periods relevant when political and military leaders were uncertain because they faced a complex environment by virtue of multiple or unclear threats, high diversity of consequential security actors, and/or high interdependence.[61]

It is possible to identify periods that produce conditions of uncertainty. These periods emerge after intense conflict and rivalry when previous alignment patterns have dissolved and the security dilemma has been ameliorated. No systemic imperative exists to compel leaders down a particular strategic path. Even during such periods, state leaders may be convinced of the identity of the most probable enemy, as the French were after World War I. Though perceptions of threat will vary, the structural conditions that produce uncertainty can be identified and responses analyzed.

The start date for selecting cases coincides with the time when planning for the future became a routine governmental process. Although militaries have always been in the business of planning for the future, before the 1840s there were no military staffs or ongoing military planning. At the start of the nineteenth century, the Prussians created a general staff, the first regular planning instrument, with the express purpose of fashioning doctrine and planning future campaigns. Other European militaries followed suit, instituted planning procedures to cope with changes brought on by the Industrial Revolution. Prussian victories in 1864–1871 demonstrated the superiority of the German general staff system, and from that point on modern armed forces were continually concerned with planning for the future.

The book focuses on the strategic choices of Russia and Britain in the post–Crimean War period; Britain and the United States in the inter-world war period; and the United States in the current period. These are the formal units selected for intensive study, as indicated in Table 2.6. By selecting on the independent variable of relative state power, it examines rising powers, leading states, declining powers, and states in the trough of the power curve. The cases allow for longitudinal comparisons of the United States and Great Britain and for a more dynamic analysis of how states move from one strategy to another. The dependent variable, strategic response, also varies across the cases. Shorter discussions of other countries, or informal units treated less intensively, are included to demonstrate the applicability of the theory to nongreat powers.[62]

Each state's strategic posture is coded across three domains of strategy—military, diplomatic, and economic—with indicators that, while not exhaustive, are illustrative and functional for coding purposes. In the military domain, two indicators are used. Innovation-adaptation captures approaches toward innovation.[63] One can shape the technological landscape and secure "first move advantages" through innovation or be a "fast follower" and adopt

Table 2.6. Case selection.

Relative power	Post–Crimea era	Inter–world war	Post–cold war
Preeminent	Great Britain 1890–1905	None	United States
Rising	[Germany] [Meiji Japan]	United States 1919–1938 [Japan]	[China] [India]
Declining	[Late Ottoman Empire]	Great Britain 1919–1933	[Europe]
Trough	Russia 1856–1881 [Tokugawa Japan]	[Germany]	[Russia]

NOTE: *Italicized* cases are formal units of study. [Bracketed] cases are illustrative and not treated formally in this study.

(or adapt) innovations that have been successfully demonstrated elsewhere. The second indicator concerns the allocation of defense resources between the short term and long term, varying from readiness to modernization. If potential near-term threats appear serious, it makes sense to maintain capable forces in being. If potential long-run threats loom greater than short-run threats, it is more sensible to channel resources into long-term economic growth and research and development. This dimension captures the state's time horizon and the extent to which the state discounts the future.[64]

A key diplomatic indicator is level of flexibility. At one end of the spectrum, unilateralism maximizes flexibility to respond to unforeseen contingencies. In former Defense Secretary Donald Rumsfeld's words, "The mission determines the coalition." Ententes and alliances are more constraining; but, by tethering potential adversaries, they provide a way to manage strategic rivalries and reduce the range of scenarios for which the state must prepare.[65] Collective security imposes the most demanding obligations but is attractive when threats are ambiguous because it is not oriented toward a specific adversary.

Two economic indicators are useful for capturing differences in strategic posture. The first concerns the allocation of resources between defense and nondefense spending. The second concerns the economic posture the state adopts to improve its international relative standing.[66] Does it make sense to economically engage potential adversaries or to contain them?[67] In the international economic policy area, a key debate concerns trading with and transferring technologies to potential future challengers. Liberalizing trade with a potential future adversary may create a more powerful regional adversary or a more powerful future global challenger.[68] One's posture toward economic engagement logically should vary with one's relative power. Hegemons have an incentive to contain to minimize the war-making capabilities of potential rivals.[69] Rising powers and those in the trough of the power curve have an incentive to engage to increase their economic wealth and access to foreign technologies and to accelerate their rise. The logic for declining powers depends on whether the state is a declining hegemon.[70] Declining hegemons who still wield considerable power have a greater incentive to contain rising challengers to forestall their own decline, while declining challengers who never wielded preponderant power should want to engage to forestall their own decline. Because a state's international economic policy involves so many domestic interests and veto players, predictions based on structural theory are expected to be the least robust in this domain.

Table 2.7. Pure strategies.

Indicators	Strategic posture		
	Shape	Adapt	Reform and reconstitute
Military	Innovate	Emulate/adapt/fast-follower	Emulate/adapt/fast-follower
	Transform for the long term	Emphasize near-term readiness	Transform for the long term
Diplomatic	High flexibility	Status quo in diplomatic alignments	Moderate flexibility
	Radical change in diplomatic alignments		Diplomatic alignments sought to tether adversaries to minimize threats and allow for internal reform
Economic	Increase defense spending	Sustain defense spending	Reduce defense spending
	Contain to minimize potential adversaries' capabilities	Contain to minimize potential adversaries' capabilities	Engage and cooperate to increase access to foreign technologies and improve relative international standing
	Engage to increase access to foreign technologies[1] and improve relative international standing	Engage to increase access to foreign technologies and improve relative international standing	

[1] Meiji Japan is a good example. See Goldman 2006.

States can and do pursue mixed strategies. Table 2.7 specifies "pure" strategies across the three domains. This more detailed specification of the dependent variable allows for testing the causal implications of the theory through pattern matching. The theory of primary interest generates predictions or expectations on dozens of aspects of strategic choice. This allows the investigator to test the theory with degrees of freedom coming from multiple implications of any one theory.[71] One would not retain the theory unless most of these are confirmed.

Militarily, shapers try to leverage technology, innovate, and engage in big bets to define the terms of competition and dominate the playing field. Logically, they shift resources into research and development to meet unanticipated threats in the more distant future. Diplomatically, shapers prefer to maximize flexibility and minimize the chances of becoming mired in conflicts and contingencies that distract them from restructuring the system. Flexibility can be maximized in different ways: relying on ad hoc coalitions, creating new institutions that serve one's interests,[72] or defecting from institutions that no longer serve one's interests. Shapers are more likely to pursue radical realignments in their diplomatic posture. Economically, shapers maintain high defense spending. Because technology diffusion can erode one's position, innovators and technology leaders will be reluctant to transfer technology that may narrow the technological gap with future potential adversaries, although engagement in nonsensitive areas may positively shape an adversary's incentives and prevent a rising challenger from becoming a threat.

Militarily, adapters prefer a fast-follower strategy toward innovation, selectively adopting capabilities and practices to keep up while eschewing fundamental transformation. Diplomatically, adapters prefer the status quo in diplomatic alignments. Economically, adapters sustain current spending to meet near-term challenges and threats in the short to medium term, even if this comes at the expense of long-term modernization. Engagement is desired to increase access to foreign techniques to remain competitive without innovating. Declining hegemons, however, have an incentive to contain to prevent diffusion of economic and military capability, which will further erode their relative international standing.

Militarily, reform and reconstitute is geared toward internal reforms that allow the state to leverage new technologies more effectively in the future, while adopting innovations proven effective elsewhere. Resources are shifted from defense to nondefense spending to engage in deep social and economic reform. Diplomatic arrangements are sought to reduce the range of threats the state faces and define its most critical contingencies. States opting to reform and reconstitute should sacrifice diplomatic flexibility for the breathing room afforded by tethering peacetime alliances. States undergoing deep internal reform also have an incentive to foster peaceful external relations so they can focus inward on reform.[73] Economically, reform and reconstitute is premised on reducing current spending to reform and pursue long-term modernization. For declining powers and those in the trough of the power curve who are the most likely candidates for reform and reconstitute, economic engagement is important to gain access to foreign techniques.

The case studies that follow begin with an assessment of the state's relative power position and specification of the complexity of the state's external environment. Predictions are offered and evaluated based on evidence from the historical record. The case studies are structured to evaluate the extent to which relative power and complexity account for strategic choice. Correlation is not sufficient to establish causality, so the cases rely on causal process observations or evidence regarding the actual priorities of key political and military leaders during the decision-making process. John Gerring points out, "Often, the connections between a putative cause and its effect are rendered visible once one has examined the motivations of the actors involved. Intentionality is an integral part of causal analysis. . . ."[74] Evidence that is consistent with nonstructural causes is identified. Finally, the impact of different strategic choices on state power is assessed to establish the conditions under which different strategies preserved, augmented, or undermined state power.[75]

3 POST-CRIMEAN WAR PERIOD, 1856–1910

THE PERIOD BETWEEN 1856 AND 1914, from the end of the Crimean War up to the onset of World War I, was one of significant upheaval in economics, politics, and technology. The Industrial Revolution launched an economic and social transformation that expanded the reach of the state and laid immense resources and powerful new instruments of war at the feet of military planners. The second half of the nineteenth century witnessed equally momentous political changes in Europe. The power of nationalism unified Germany and Italy as it weakened the multiethnic Hapsburg and Ottoman empires. Prussia usurped France as Europe's leading military power. Germany and the United States challenged Britain's economic position. The Meiji Restoration launched Japan on its great power trajectory, which reached fruition with its defeat of Russia in 1905.

These economic and technological changes transformed warfare. The Crimean War was fought with weapons and tactics of the Napoleonic era, but contemporaries realized England and France won in part because they were modern and industrialized while Russia remained backward, inefficient, and agrarian.[1] Railroads, the electric telegraph, and rifling of muskets and artillery dramatically altered combat. On land, railway nets enhanced strategic mobility and allowed large armies to be sustained for longer periods of time and to continuously campaign. Rapid transmission of information by telegraph between leaders and field commanders, as well as among field commanders, supported rapid massing of forces and coordination of widely dispersed operations. Rifling improved the range and accuracy of musketry and artillery.

Continuing developments in artillery and the machine gun increased the volume, range, and accuracy of fire. Naval warfare underwent an equally dramatic revolution with steam propulsion, ship design changes, and improved armaments. Wooden ships powered by sail gave way to metal-hulled ships powered by turbine engines and armed with long-range rifled artillery:[2]

> Along with the American Civil War and the German wars of unification, the Crimean War was widely regarded as the victory of modern, industrialized militaries over those of more agrarian societies. If the Napoleonic Wars half a century earlier witnessed the transition to mass-conscription armies, confrontations like the Crimean War signaled the rising importance of mechanization, a mature manufacturing sector, and logistics.[3]

This chapter focuses on Russian and British responses to uncertainty about their strategic and technological environments. It examines their security environments and strategic choices. The chapter concludes by assessing the impact of relative power and complexity on strategic choice.

RELATIVE POWER AND STRATEGIC PREFERENCES

Russia was a defeated and recovering power in the trough of the power curve. Hypothesis P6 predicts that weakened powers will pursue a strategy of reform and reconstitute to strategically rebuild and reassert power and influence. Evidence indicates that Russian leaders were preoccupied with their relative weakness, feared imperial collapse, and were determined to regain strategic influence.

Russian leaders also faced a complex external security environment characterized by a large number of diverse and proximate threats, as well as adversaries who were developing and exploiting new military capabilities. Hypotheses E1 and E1a predict states with global interests and commitments that face numerous and diverse threats will adapt to a diverse range of missions and markets in response to near-term contingencies. For extremely weakened states, however, relative power position trumps incentives to adapt in response to the number and diversity of threats. Very weak powers, like post-Crimea Russia, should logically cut current defense spending and shift resources into long-term modernization and economic development, pursue a cooperative and accommodating diplomatic strategy that provides a peaceful environment for transformation and access to foreign technology for modernization, and join alliances that tether them to potential adversaries to narrow the spectrum of threats faced and reduce the range of military scenarios for which it must prepare.

Britain was a preponderant power, even if no longer a hegemon. It remained at the center of the global trading system, sterling was *the* reserve currency and currency of trade, and Britain was the hub of the global banking, communications, and insurance services industries. Britain's biggest economic challenger, the United States, was underdeveloped in all these areas. Britain's gross domestic product (GDP) even in 1913 was greater than that of any other country except the United States and Germany, both of which had larger populations, and Britain's GDP per capita exceeded that of any other European nation. Its share of world manufacturing exports was 30 percent, and it had more capital invested overseas than any other country.[4] Britain was the preeminent naval power and also possessed a limited war capability.

During periods of strategic pause, leaders either adapt, as predicted by Hypothesis P4, or shape, as predicted by Hypothesis P5. Britain's relative international standing created an incentive to adapt to preserve the current system. Global powers with expansive interests have an added incentive to adapt to prepare for a diverse range of missions, as predicted by Hypothesis E1a. But unlike Britain's situation after World War I, when a plethora of lesser problems across the empire required immediate attention, the late nineteenth century was a period of renewed imperial growth and what Nicholas Lambert calls "deep peace." Although potential great power threats loomed, like Germany's rise and French and Russian challenges to imperial interests, between 1870 and 1884 Britain expanded its empire by 4,750,000 square miles and 88 million people.[5]

British leaders were nevertheless sensitive to impending economic decline. In the 1880s, they perceived their economic lead to be slipping. War scares with Russia in 1884 and 1885, and with France in 1888, heightened perceptions of vulnerability.[6] Facing the prospect of relative decline, Britain opted to leverage its still formidable capabilities to shape in order to maintain strategic dominance, defend the empire, and prevent the emergence of more dangerous futures. The British exploited a period of strategic pause to develop the capabilities to protect its global interests against multiple unpredictable threats and to preserve the critical lynchpin of its power: naval mastery. In a close parallel to U.S. strategy at the turn of the twenty-first century, the British sought to preserve and extend their preeminent position by shaping their security environment through technological and doctrinal innovation.[7]

RUSSIA

The Security Environment

On the eve of the Crimean War, "the image of Russian military power still captivated European statesmen and generals."[8] The conflict disabused everyone of this perception. Russia had fallen behind economically and technologically. Its military system was discredited, and Russian leaders realized the empire needed sweeping reforms if it were to recover and reemerge as a great power. The war set into motion a process of strategic reassessment that resulted in far-reaching reforms to Russia's society, economy, and military.[9] The period from 1856 to 1874, the "era of Great Reforms,"[10] saw among other things the abolition of serfdom, extensive reform of civil and criminal legal codes, easing of press censorship, and establishment of elected local bodies (the zemstvo system). Key questions for Russian leaders were how to reinvent the state's military system and the economic and social systems that anchored it, what sort of new military system ought Russia to have, how to integrate modern military technologies into their armed forces, and how to finance the entire enterprise.

Each of these questions had to be answered against the backdrop of an array of potential adversaries including France, Britain, Austria, Prussia, and Turkey. A recurrent fear over the course of the entire period was that a coalition without parallel in history would arise against Russia, forcing it to disperse its forces and fight at a severe disadvantage. Russia's initial fear was a resuscitated Crimean coalition. By the late 1860s, it feared a coalition of Austria and Britain, assisted by Turkey and Sweden. The worst case posited France and Italy joining this opposing coalition. Britain was a persistent concern throughout the entire period, threatening intrusion through the straights and escalation of tensions over Asian colonies.

In the 1860s and 1870s, contingency planning also had to consider the requirement for large garrisons to ward off trouble on the Persian and Central Asian frontiers. The frontier provinces—Finland, the Baltics, Poland, Bessarabia, Transcaucasia, Armenia—could be picked off one by one, exposing Russia to territorial losses that would undo Russian history. In the words of Russian Foreign Minister Alexander Gorchakov, "Once despoiled of territory to the north, south and west, the Russian Empire would be degraded from its status as a major Western power to that of an Oriental backwater."[11] Russia faced a heretofore unimagined level of vulnerability to coalitions of wealthy industrialized states that risked unraveling the empire.

Up until 1870, a revived Crimean War coalition was the biggest concern. With the wars of German unification, Prussia emerged as a welcome counterweight to France, but eventually fear of a Crimean coalition gave way to concerns over Germany's rise, a German–Austrian alliance, and possible encroachment into the Balkans. Should Austria backed by Germany advance on the Balkans, Russian leaders believed they would have to engage. Perceived weakness would invite further challenges to the empire's detriment. Fears of an Austro-German combination arrayed against Russia waxed and waned depending on the status of diplomatic alignments like the Three Emperors' League. It climbed with Bismarck's resignation in 1890. Russia also feared that Germany would take up arms against France, compelling Russia to intervene to prevent German domination of Europe. Russia's alliance with France in 1894 forced this scenario to the fore, effectively focusing Russian planning around one dominant scenario—simultaneous war with Austria and Germany.

As a multinational state, Russia faced significant internal security problems. Non-Russian minorities lived overwhelmingly in the borderlands. Ethnic and nationalist groups were openly restless. The Poles were regarded as the most dangerous and disloyal. When planning for war, Russian military leaders simultaneously had to plan for defense of the Polish theater and more generally for threats from within as well as without.[12]

Over time, Russian strategy became increasingly Eurocentric while always cognizant of vulnerabilities in the East. Preoccupation with the Central European threat and defending the western empire led Russia to neglect preparations for other theaters and contingencies. Yet, nearly thirty-five years before Russia faced the Germanic powers, it fought a war against Turkey resulting in an "embarrassingly difficult victory over a third-rate power."[13] Ten years before World War I Russia took up arms against Japan and became the first European power to be defeated by a non-Western power.[14]

Strategic Responses

As a defeated and recovering power, we expect Russia to adopt a policy of reform and reconstitute. The evidence suggests this is precisely the course Russian leaders followed: They accepted the need for sweeping reforms to recover their standing as a great power. Reform and reconstitute was manifest in a number of developments: cuts in defense spending and standing military forces; far-reaching internal reforms that included replacement of the system of peasant slavery (serfs) with a labor market, adoption of universal conscription, reorganization of the government, modernization of the economy, liberalization of foreign trade regulations and foreign investment, and a policy of international diplomatic restraint and "peace in all her external relations" to implement those reforms.[15] Russia took advantage of a period of strategic pause to pursue a policy of self-examination and reform—or *recueillement*—most evident in Foreign Minister Gorchakov's diplomacy of the 1860s and Minister of War Dmitry Milutin's military reforms in the 1860s and 1870s. The French term, coined by Gorchakov in 1856, has been loosely translated as calculated introspection and improvement, self-contemplation and self-absorption. It found its deliberate expression in Russia's economic, military, and diplomatic policies.

Two key questions for formation of grand strategy are, What proportion of the nation's resources will be devoted to defense? And how will those defense resources be allocated?

The evidence shows that defense effort was cut, reflected most clearly in the proportion of military expenditures to overall budget expenditures.[16] Walter Pintner's analysis of the burden of defense in imperial Russia shows a steady decline in the proportion of military expenditures after the Crimean War until World War I. He argues that since army troop levels remained relatively steady, one would expect to see growth or at a minimum steady military expenditures. However, we see decline instead.[17] Part of the explanation lies in the economic boom of the 1880s and 1890s as well as the assumption by the state of new functions like railway construction. But neither is sufficient to account for the gradual decline in the military's total share of state expenditures.

Reduction in the overall level of defense effort was a deliberate decision consistent with a reform and reconstitute strategy. Persistent financial crisis confronted the tsarist government following the Crimean War, and Alexander II responded by reducing the number of men under arms to levels well below those of the 1840s. In 1873 Minister of Finance Mikhail Reutern placed budget caps on the War Ministry, judging that "prosperity, fiscal solvency, and a well-developed infrastructure were more beneficial to the national security than the possession of large arsenals of weapons."[18] Military expenditures were cut to safeguard the state's fiscal integrity and increase capital investment in private industry, commerce, and agriculture. Reutern, an advocate of private enterprise and market development, privileged a balanced state budget that would attract foreign capital, spur economic transformation, and underwrite a Russian resurgence.[19]

Expansion of the civilian economy was key to economic modernization and strengthening Russia's military power.[20] Railroad construction was critical to both. Absence of a national system of railroads linking industrial centers with battlefields in the south had been logistically and strategically disastrous. Russian leaders were acutely aware their country had failed to keep pace with Austria and Germany in this most important military development of the period. Railroads were also the backbone of a modern economy, necessary for trade, economic growth, and competitiveness, hence to stave off decline.[21] Under Reutern's stewardship, rail construction grew from 1,500 kilometers in 1860 to 21,000 kilometers by 1878.[22]

The logic of directing resources to the civilian sector and away from the military sector was based on a recognition that backwardness in Russian society and an outmoded socioeconomic system lay at the root of Russia's humiliating defeat in 1854–1855. Russian reformers

> understood that to immediately throw very limited resources into the purchase of new weapons, which would soon be made obsolete by fast improving technologies, would be a disastrous course.... Limited resources needed to be directed in areas that would enable Russia to produce new weaponry herself, or at least an economy that could support continual updating of the systems.[23]

Russian reformers believed the path to renewed great power status lay through economic, political, and social reform. They consistently strived to preserve the fiscal integrity of the state by reducing defense spending. Even with an economic boom in the late 1880s that increased government revenues and expenditures, the military did not benefit. Between 1888 and 1903, the Ministry of Finance imposed maximum budgets on the army, which reduced the military's relative share of the overall budget, even as absolute army outlays gradually increased.[24] As Table 3.1 shows, total military spending as a percentage of total government spending remained at 2 percent from the mid-1880s until the Russo-Japanese War.

Military policy is usefully viewed along two dimensions: the allocation of defense resources between the near term and long term, varying from readiness to modernization; and the related dimension of innovation-adaptation. We would expect defeated and recovering powers to sacrifice readiness for modernization and pursue adaptation rather than innovation. Evidence from the Russian case supports this hypothesis. Russian leaders focused on transforming the nation's military system for the long term and adopted a fast follower strategy toward innovation, emulating to the extent possible improvements introduced by other great powers.

Table 3.1. Russian military spending, 1856–1909.

Year	Total government spending (thousand rubles)	Spending on the army (thousand rubles)	Spending on the navy (thousand rubles)[1]	Total military spending (thousand rubles)[2]	Total military spending as percentage of total government expenditure
1856	619,000,000	23,3154		233,154	0.04
1857	348,000,000	101,848		101,848	0.03
1858	363,000,000	89,154		89,154	0.02
1859	351,000,000	106,692		106,692	0.03
1860	438,000,000	106,655		106,655	0.02
1861	414,000,000	115,965		115,965	0.03
1862	393,000,000	114,209		114,209	0.03
1863	432,000,000	155,632		155,632	0.04
1864	437,000,000	155,131		155,131	0.04
1865	428,000,000	140,019		140,019	0.03
1866	438,000,000	129,687		129,687	0.03
1867	460,000,000	127,250		127,250	0.03
1868	492,000,000	136,701		136,701	0.03
1869	535,000,000	147,702		147,702	0.03
1870	564,000,000	145,211		145,211	0.03
1871	557,000,000	159,257		159,257	0.03
1872	583,000,000	165,925		165,925	0.03
1873	612,000,000	175,033		175,033	0.03
1874	602,000,000	172,480		172,480	0.03
1875	605,000,000	175,432		175,432	0.03
1876	704,000,000	547,103		547,103	0.08
1877	1,121,000,000	618,980	9,799.5	628,779.5	0.06
1878	1,076,000,000	614,399	7,750.5	622,149.5	0.06
1879	812,000,000	308,020	7,926.3	315,946.3	0.04
1880	793,000,000	212,000	10,295.3	222,295.3	0.03
1881	840,000,000	212,000	9,872.5	221,872.5	0.03
1882	788,000,000	212,000	12,258.7	224,258.7	0.03
1883	804,000,000	212,000	11,000.2	223,000.2	0.03
1884	816,000,000	212,000	13,787.3	225,787.3	0.03
1885	913,000,000	212,000	10,146.1	222,146.1	0.02
1886	945,000,000	212,000	12,710.2	224,710.2	0.02

(Continued)

Table 3.1. Russian military spending, 1856–1909. *(Continued)*

Year	Total government spending (thousand rubles)	Spending on the army (thousand rubles)	Spending on the navy (thousand rubles)[1]	Total military spending (thousand rubles)[2]	Total military spending as percentage of total government expenditure
1887	931,000,000	212,000	11,350.6	223,350.6	0.02
1888	927,000,000	212,000	11,291.1	223,291.1	0.02
1889	963,000,000	229,100	11,365	240,465	0.02
1890	1,057,000,000	230,100	10,228.7	240,328.7	0.02
1891	1,116,000,000	231,100	9,646.5	240,746.5	0.02
1892	1,125,000,000	232,100	17,696.5	249,796.5	0.02
1893	1,061,000,000	229,359	16,921.2	246,280.2	0.02
1894	1,155,000,000	280,300	16,678.3	296,978.3	0.03
1895	1,521,000,000	285,444	14,889.1	300,333.1	0.02
1896	1,484,000,000	294,359	14,221.7	308,580.7	0.02
1897	1,495,000,000	293,789	9,540.5	303,329.5	0.02
1898	1,772,000,000	293,975	12,040.5	306,015.5	0.02
1899	1,785,000,000	333,579	25,490	359,069	0.02
1900	1,883,000,000	333,541	23,060.4	356,601.4	0.02
1901	1,874,000,000	379,081	93,046	472,127	0.03
1902	2,167,000,000	426,285	100,405	526,690	0.02
1903	2,108,000,000	355,679	113,936	469,615	0.02
1904	2,738,000,000	1,053,275	112,917	1,166,192	0.04
1905	3,205,000,000	1,516,874	116,694	1,633,568	0.05
1906	3,213,000,000	921,378	111,641	1,033,019	0.03
1907	2,583,000,000	591,425	87,711	679,136	0.03
1908	2,661,000,000	580,294	93,484	673,778	0.03
1909	2,608,000,000	555,674	92,224	647,898	0.02

SOURCES: Beskrovnyi, Lyubomir G. (1986) *Armiya I Flot Rossii v Nachale XXv.: Ocherki Voenno-Ekonomicheskogo Potentsiala (Russia's Army and Navy in the Beginning of the 20th Century: Narratives on the Military-Economic Potential).* Moscow: Nauka. Beskrovnyi, Lyubomir G. (1973) Russkaya Armiya I Flot v XIXv.: Voenno-Ekonomicheskii Potentsial Rossii (*Russia's Army and Navy in the 19th century: Military-Economic Potential of Russia*). Moscow: Nauka.

NOTE: Data for 1900 taken from Beskrovny 1986. Also, Beskrovny notes that during the 1880–1889 period, average annual spending on the army was 210 to 214 million rubles; 212 million was used as the average for this time period.

[1] Spending on the Navy: shipbuilding only; data start from 1877.

[2] Spending on the army plus spending on the navy. Only spending on the army presented when data on naval spending not available.

Russian military prowess since the time of Peter the Great had relied on a large standing army and navy; enserfment; conscription for common soldiers, which devolved into permanent military service; and an arms industry comprised of artisans.[25] The Crimean War highlighted two critical weaknesses. First, there existed no means for rapid large-scale expansion of the army in time of war to achieve the mobilization potential of the French nation in arms. Russia's recruitment practices were based on peasant conscription and could not match the effectiveness of the trained reserves being fielded by other European powers. Second, Russia's arms industry could not match the speed and scale of production of new technology that other European powers had achieved.[26]

In response to the manpower problem, Minister of War Dmitri Miliutin, who was appointed in 1861, submitted a comprehensive plan of reform in 1862. He reduced the term of service from fifteen years to eight years, thereby increasing reserves and cutting costs of what had become an expensive permanent establishment. His goal was a small peacetime army that could expand rapidly with trained reserves. Miliutin decentralized military administration by establishing a territorial district system to carry out supply and support functions separate from operational command, greatly enhancing the ability to coordinate operations. He reorganized the Ministry of War to create institutional links to military districts. He introduced military academies to elevate the level of officer education, created junker schools to compensate for officer shortages, and reformed the military justice system.[27] The reformed army proved to be more professional. Its structure, weaponry, and education were more modern and it outperformed the prereform army of the Crimean War. By 1870 army strength stood at 700,000 active duty and 500,000 reserves, substantial progress although still lagging behind the European powers.[28] (See Table 3.2.) John Bushnell argues the Russian army should have achieved an easy victory over Turkish forces in 1877–1878. Its failure to do so was a function of underfunding, outmoded tactics, and an imperial patronage network that the autocracy refused to replace with a system of advancement based on professional competence.[29]

The technology problem went to the heart of the economic foundations of military power. Russia was simply unable to innovate to match the latest technologies coming from Europe. Defeated and recovering powers have an incentive to maximize access to foreign technology. Russia actively worked to assimilate new technologies in areas like shipbuilding, emulating innovations that were underway in the West and purchasing steamships from England,

Table 3.2. Size of the army and navy in Russia, 1856–1914.

	Army			Navy		
Year	Generals and officers in the army	Troops in the army	Size of the army (generals, officers, and troops)	Admirals, generals, and officers in the navy	Sailors in the navy	Size of the navy (admirals, generals, officers, and sailors)
1856				3,838	125,769	129,607
1857				3,836	85,067	88,903
1858				3,833	52,022	55,855
1859				3,761	51,663	55,424
1860				3,683	53,054	56,737
1861				3,340	55,216	58,556
1862				3,131	49,405	52,536
1863				3,114	40,708	43,822
1864	31,704	904,145	935,849	3,086	47,134	50,220
1865	30,507	798,151	828,658	3,142	40,336	43,478
1866	29,843	749,414	779,257	3,168	37,343	40,511
1867	29,196	727,600	756,796	3,154	31,892	35,046
1868	28,429	704,010	732,439	3,148	28,184	31,332
1869	28,140	683,246	711,386	3,124	23,496	26,620
1870	27,841	733,761	761,602	3,122	20,986	24,108
1871	28,076	732,068	760,144	3,160	24,195	27,355
1872	28,394	726,903	755,297	3,101	25,130	28,231
1873	28,431	738,194	766,625	2,823	26,081	28,904
1874	29,174	742,456	771,630	3,111	24,498	27,609
1875	29,359	737,528	766,887	3,114	25,623	28,737
1876	31,239	1,005,825	1,037,064	3,150	25,795	28,945
1877	35,614	1,512,998	1,548,612	3,145	25,739	28,884
1878	37,231	1,111,218	1,148,449	3,187	28,920	32,107
1879	36,414	894,094	930,508	3,209	26,683	29,892
1880	34,917	858,275	893,192	3,135	26,064	29,199
1881	33,050	812,484	845,534	3,154	26,327	29,481
1882	30,831	819,769	850,600	3,196	26,288	29,484
1883	30,889	798,908	829,797	3,339	26,087	29,426
1884	30,390	807,009	837,399	3,322	24,726	28,048
1885	30,655	824,762	855,417	3,285	24,994	28,279
1886	31,196	840,568	871,764	3,177	24,665	27,842

(Continued)

Table 3.2. *(Continued)*

Year	Army			Navy		
	Generals and officers in the army	Troops in the army	Size of the army (generals, officers, and troops)	Admirals, generals, and officers in the navy	Sailors in the navy	Size of the navy (admirals, generals, officers, and sailors)
1887	32,086	853,589	885,675	2,954	25,778	28,732
1888	32,644	820,484	853,128	2,764	25,317	28,081
1889	33,023	831,740	864,763	2,657	25,654	28,311
1890	33,545	842,580	876,125	2,533	25,965	28,498
1891	34,244	852,149	886,393	2,385	25,906	28,291
1892	34,794	863,290	898,084	2,325	27,322	29,647
1893	35,332	926,777	962,109	2,302	28,813	31,115
1894	35,500	940,413	975,913	2,284	30,152	32,436
1895	36,568	954,239	990,807	2,304	32,340	34,644
1896	37,621	972,082	1,009,703	2,304	34,560	36,864
1897	38,008	995,145	1,033,153	2,344	36,016	38,360
1898	38,616	1,013,012	1,051,628	2,273	38,952	41,225
1899	39,138	1,024,268	1,063,406	2,307	44,651	46,958
1900	38,908	1,005,292	1,044,200	2,331	48,730	51,061
1901	38,908	1,005,292	1,044,200			57,300
1902	39,630	1,029,985	1,069,615			58,200
1903	40,538	1,042,455	1,082,993			59,600
1904	41,871	1,053,190	1,095,061			61,400
1905	32,879	1,032,136	1,065,015			40,400
1906						41,400
1907						44,400
1908						39,100
1909						41,100
1910						40,000
1911						42,400
1912						46,100
1913						47,200
1914						53,400 (95,000)[a]

[a] Size of the navy after mobilization; data for 1901–1914 converted from rounded numbers (originally, data were in thousands).

even risking a repeat of British stranglehold on procurement that had materialized on the eve of the Crimean War.[30] In critical technology areas like engines, single copies of the latest models were ordered from private British firms to feed a prototype system where Russian yards used foreign models to develop their own production lines. Investment in intelligence assets increased to gather information on the latest British shipbuilding and production techniques.[31] British engineers and shipwrights were also recruited to train Russians. Each of these methods of emulation is consistent with a fast follower strategy. They allowed the Navy ministry to rapidly move from foreign purchase to domestic construction of ironclads by 1863, albeit heavily reliant on foreign know-how and materials.[32]

In response to economic backwardness and technological inferiority, and consistent with a strategy of reform and reconstitute, the Russian navy sacrificed readiness for modernization. The Navy Ministry decommissioned sailing ships and demobilized surplus personnel to increase the share of budget resources for procurement of new ships.[33] "In 1850 the empire had 100,000 men and over 40 ships-of-the-line in its two fleets, but by 1860 those figures had declined to 54,500 men and eight ships-of-the-line in one fleet."[34] Although the navy's size declined in the post-Crimea period, it made the transition from sail to steam-screw propulsion by 1860.[35] The Navy Ministry relied primarily on private firms but also reformed government dockyards. It emancipated admiralty serfs and replaced the large number of conscript workers with a permanent skilled labor force that could be expanded with unskilled laborers when required.[36]

The strides in naval modernization made between 1863 and 1867 were an exception to the fiscal austerity of the post-Crimea period. By 1867, the ministry's budget was cut, and shipbuilding came to a halt. Advances had been made in areas where Russia could easily assimilate new technologies from abroad, copy foreign technology, and harness private enterprise. As technologies became more advanced and production costs rose—for steam engines and artillery, for example—dependence on the state became necessary, but resources were not available. Defense was cut across the board, and resources were shifted to the civilian sector. Expansion of the civilian economy was made a priority as the key to economic modernization and regaining international position.[37] When it came to military expenditures, the army received the lion's share. Shipbuilding declined, private yards went bankrupt, and construction projects were stretched out. Russia's ironclads were obsolete by the time they came on line.[38]

The strategic level provides further insight into how a weak and recovering Russia tried to manage a complex environment. The navy's chief reformer, Grand Duke Konstantin Nikolaevich, faced a less daunting problem than his army counterpart because Russia was not a traditional naval power. Geographic limits prevented Russia from concentrating its naval assets and relegated the navy to second-class status. In assessing the purpose, size, and composition of Russia's fleet, Konstantin realized it was futile to attempt to match the first-ranked fleets of France and Britain. He concluded,

> Our fleet ought to be such that we will always be stronger than our weak neighbors, and such that the first-time naval powers, in the event of war between them, will prize our alliance or neutrality, and such that our shores will be secure from sudden attacks by several ships.[39]

Russia's naval strategy was a minimalist and defensive strategy of calculated inferiority designed to prevail over the navies of Turkey, Sweden, and Persia and to deter surprise attack by Britain and France.

Army reform was more complicated because the army could not afford to limit itself to one or two threat scenarios. Throughout the 1860s, strategic planning was almost exclusively oriented toward the defense. It was reactive and situation specific, based on the belief that it was premature to draft long-term plans given the need for internal reform and instability in European and domestic politics.

The magnitude and speed of France's defeat by Prussia in 1870 shocked the Russian military establishment. Miliutin became convinced that a revolution in warfare had occurred; that the disparity in technology, logistics, and doctrine between Russia and its potential European rivals was growing with each passing decade; and that Russia was in great jeopardy. Russia had to establish some consistent national security priorities rather than continue with an ad hoc approach to military planning.

The first wave of army reform was complete, troops were being rearmed, and the empire was now organized into military districts. Strategic planning took a new turn with Miliutin's Strategic Conference in 1873, the first attempt in Russian history to commit the entire government to a long-term plan for the defense of the empire for fear of being "wiped from the earth by history."[40] Chief of the General Staff Nikolai Obruchev argued that the armed forces in their present condition could not defend the empire. If war broke out in Europe in the near future, Russia would probably face a coalition of enemies that included Austria-Hungary and Germany. Russia's ability to mobilize and field a larger number of troops had improved since the mid-1860s, but Austria-Hungary and Germany could mobilize and concentrate their forces more rapidly because they had better railway nets. Miliutin called for a crash program of military railway construction, fortifications for Poland, and a partial redeployment of the army to plug gaps in Russia's western defenses.[41] Although Russia continued to face potential security threats on all its borders, Miliutin argued that the Central European situation was so ominous that all other dangers—Central Asia, nationalism in the Balkans, coastal defenses on the empire's southern border—though not to be ignored must not drive planning. It was better to arm thoroughly against the most serious threat than to dissipate the empire's defense efforts among multiple threats and theaters.

William Fuller observes that threat assessment was based on technical considerations rather than political ones.[42] The War Ministry was not making political judgments about the sorts of wars that were more or less probable. Rather, the recommendation that Russia should concentrate on a single European war scenario and downplay other scenarios was based on the comparative offensive capabilities of potential enemies. Austria-Hungary and Germany were the countries that could do greatest harm, regardless of whether or not they had malign intentions.

Miliutin's arguments failed to sway the Ministry of Finance. The notion that Russia must take emergency action to prop up its security lest it be wiped from the face of history seemed grossly exaggerated given fiscal constraints and the likelihood that military expansion would derail internal reform. Miliutin's strategic plan to prevail in a short European war, which depended on acquiring modern weapons, improving fortifications, and laying a strategic railway network, was not funded. The War Ministry's budget was capped, so a substitute strategy not to win but to avoid defeat was adopted. Forward deployed troops and cavalry would have to compensate for the lack of fortifications and railroads.

Technological underdevelopment, which was never adequately addressed, coupled with low military budgets meant Russia would surely be defeated in the near term if war came with a first-rate power. The shock was that Russia barely defeated second-rate Turkey. Still, the emperor remained sympathetic to Ministry of Finance pleas for continued austerity given the fiscal crisis in the 1880s. Military pleas for weaponry and railway construction fell on deaf ears, so planners were forced to devise a new approach to technological backwardness, one based on a higher state of readiness than neighboring powers to the west and greater emphasis on collection of reliable intelligence about adversary innovations and mobilization plans. Russia would have to fight smarter through foreign espionage. According to Fuller, "Intelligence collection was one of the motors that drove Russian war planning from the 1880s until the outbreak of WWI."[43]

As a weak and recovering power with serious resource constraints, Russian strategy relied heavily on diplomacy to compensate for military weakness, protect gains made in 1815, and provide breathing room to reform and reemerge as a formidable power. Russia adopted a cautious, nonprovocative diplomacy that allowed it to sit aside and modernize its socioeconomic and military systems.[44] The chief purpose of post–Crimean War diplomacy was "to foster the process of internal reform [and internal regeneration] by shielding the country from distractions from abroad. Russia consequently needed a careful, risk-adverse foreign policy compatible with its internal occupations."[45] "Peace in all her external relations" would provide time and space to reform and modernize.[46]

To ensure peaceful relations and prevent resurgence of the Crimean War coalition, Russian followed a flexible diplomatic strategy, allying with different members of the coalition off and on over the period. Loose alliances that tethered Russia to potential adversaries minimized the contingencies for which Russia needed to prepare. Collectively, these diplomatic efforts allowed Russia to focus on the strategic priority of internal reform.

The clearest example of a "tethering" strategy was the Three Emperors' League. Germany's unification and defeat of France in 1871 posed a formidable threat. Relations with Vienna and Constantinople were tense over Balkan issues, while relations with London were strained over Russia's expansionism in Central Asia. France was of little concern at this time, as it was recovering from defeat by Prussia. Fearing *most* an Austro-German block, Russia joined Austria and Germany in the Three Emperors' League in 1873.[47] All agreed to mutually consult in cases of divergent interests and third-party aggression. The agreement stipulated the three would not seek new alliances and would promote a common foreign policy line in cases of threat. Russia had tethered itself to potential adversaries, neutralizing near-term threats and extending its strategic planning horizon.

War with Turkey once again exposed grave internal problems. As in the 1860s, Russia was determined avoid clashes with other great powers and compensate for military weakness with diplomacy. Russia renewed the Three

Emperors' League to escape diplomatic isolation, avoid war, and secure German loans to finance military reform.[48] Eventually, Russia entered into an entente with France in 1890 to keep Austria and Germany in check; then subsequently it entered into an entente with Britain. Always the intent was to manage or narrow the spectrum of threats to which Russia was exposed.

In Central Asia, Russia preferred restraint lest it antagonize Britain. Russia exercised imperial expansion chiefly for strategically defensive reasons.[49] If Russia did not secure Central Asia, the empire's frontier would be plagued by constant bandit invasions. Facing a military manpower crisis, Russia lacked sufficient troops to police a vast Asiatic border. Moreover, the Ministry of War allocated few resources to defend Central Asia, believing Europe must come first. Imperial expansion promised to curtail the demands of frontier security, but it had to be executed cautiously so as not to provoke London and risk the outbreak of war in Asia, which would detract from European priorities. For similarly defensive reasons, Russia pursued imperialism in the Far East and Pacific, yet in a more unrestrained fashion:

> Japan and the European Powers were on the march in the Pacific. If Russia declined to play the game of imperialism in Asia, it not only needlessly impoverished its future, but also risked eventually losing such Asian territories as it already had.[50]

Conclusions

Reconstructing Russian military power in the post-Crimea period was a daunting undertaking:

> Overcentralized administration, inferior munitions, and the manpower crisis resulting from the antiquated conscription system enfeebled defense efforts. At the same time the War Ministry's obligation to prepare for the possibility of simultaneous conflicts in multiple theaters, each poor in roads and railways, each separated from the others by thousand of miles—all severely taxed the ingenuity of Russia's strategists, who also had to keep a precarious financial position in mind.[51]

Russian policy across this time period spanned two interwar periods: 1856–1877 and 1878–1904. The first period saw social reforms in response to the Crimean defeat—the so-called era of Great Reforms—and military reforms spearheaded by Minister of War Miliutin. Russia engaged in a long-term strategy by carrying out deep internal social, economic, and military reforms to regain its power. These reforms represented an investment in organizational capabilities to increase military strength, improve the economy, and mobilize resources more effectively for the future. The second period is framed by the Russo-Turkish War of 1877–1878 and the Russo-Japanese War of 1904–1905. Russia had more resources at its disposal during the second interwar period, but its strategic approach remained the same. Evidence shows the hallmarks of a reform and reconstitute strategy: defense cuts, resources migrated to the civilian economy, significant social and economic reform, a nonprovocative diplomatic strategy, tethering to potential adversaries to provide time to reform and reconstitute, emulation of military inventions abroad, and emphasis on intelligence capabilities and building organizational capacity.

Russian statesmen viewed empire building as one of the main purposes of military power and a primary strategic goal. After the devastating Crimean defeat, they were determined to hang on to what they had acquired. Though appreciative of their country's military debility, they would not moderate imperial ambitions or resign themselves to any diminution in international standing and prestige. Russian strategy was designed to reserve the nation's right to play in European great power politics, and they succeeded.

GREAT BRITAIN

The Security Environment

The lynchpin of Britain's power and strategic influence was its naval supremacy. In the decades immediately following the Crimean War, no state posed a serious threat to British power. The continental European powers lagged behind in industrial development. Neither alone nor in combination did they pose a threat to the homeland, colonies, or maritime lines of communication. Britain could ensure fleet supremacy in home waters and command of the seas abroad with relative ease. There were alarmist claims made about Russian designs on British territories, but it was unrealistic to expect a post-Crimea Russia to launch a "war of conquest from Central Asia against the British possessions in India."[52] All potential great power opponents were weak, allowing the British to focus on colonial expansion.[53] Trade with Asia, Africa, and the Western Hemisphere increased tremendously as did control over extra-European territory.[54]

By the 1880s, trends were beginning to shift, and British global dominance was receding. New competitors in its home market and traditional world markets, new patterns of world food and industrial production, and new distributions of power and naval capabilities emerged in the 1890s and early 1900s. "The Pax Britannica in the 1890s seemed to be more secure than at any time in the preceding 100 years, but deterioration in the 'informal empire' forced Britain to make deft adjustments to maintain commercial security and profitability under rapidly changing conditions." Exports were shifted to the overseas empire and the American hemisphere was ceded to the United States. Profits were sustained, but the "British hold on leading economic sectors and global security slipped away."[55]

By the late 1890s and early 1900s, Germany's increasing military and economic power could not be ignored. Germany had been a close commercial partner in the British world system between 1870 and 1890. In the 1880s, Germany imported British textiles and manufacturers and exported food supplies to Britain. By 1900 the roles had reversed. Germany by then was a vital exporter of beet sugar to Britain, and by 1913 Britain had become dependent on German supplies of chemicals, coal, cloth, machinery, and ironware. Britain's economic and naval superiority were under assault and its world market shares declining relative to Germany.[56]

Economic developments enabled France, Russia, and later Germany to build large navies. As other European powers gradually strengthened their navies, the price of retaining British naval supremacy rose. The cause of decline in Britain's naval dominance, according to Nicholas Lambert,[57] was due less to the technological innovation and increasing military strength of other powers and more to the increasing costs of technological innovation and capital depreciation. In essence, the cost of maintaining the same level of British superiority over other navies kept growing. As the nineteenth century came to a close, Britain faced the prospect of a hostile continental coalition with combined naval resources equal to or exceeding those of the Royal Navy. It was no longer possible to dismiss the threat of invasion to the homeland and colonies or assaults on commercial lines of communication. By 1900 Britain was experiencing "a crisis of its world leadership."

Over the course of the post-Crimea period, the nature of the threat changed. For the duration of the nineteenth century, Russia was the most pressing concern for England. Absent a continental peer competitor with nefarious intent, the security of India and routes to and from attained primacy in British strategic thinking. England's tussling with Russia focused on the Bosphorus and Dardanelles and on keeping Russia's fleet bottled up in the Black Sea to ensure "the short route to India" across the Suez isthmus, first by rail and later (after 1869) by canal. Between the Treaty of San Stefano (1878) and the Treaty of

Berlin (1885), Britain was concerned most about the safety of the Suez Canal lest Russia gain control of it. By 1884 Russia had conquered substantial territories in Asia, causing alarm about possible invasion of India. Toward the end of the century, focus shifted from the sea routes to India to land encroachment of Russian influence through Afghanistan.

The Treaty of Berlin in 1885 confined Russia's fleet to the Black Sea. Russia's willingness to make concessions to appease British interests in Asia and the Far East—consistent with Russia's reform and reconstitute strategy—assuaged concerns over Russian expansionism. The defeat of Russia in 1905 largely eliminated concerns over Russian imperialism and eastern expansion while Anglo-French entente in 1904 reduced fears of a combined Franco-Russian naval threat.

Germany thus emerged as Britain's primary naval challenger after the turn of the twentieth century.[58] Germany's merchant ship and naval buildup weakened British naval superiority while German banks, industry, and science and technology threatened Britain's economic and cultural standing.[59] In 1894, Admiral Alfred von Tirpitz proposed his "risk theory" to deter Britain. Germany "should be strong enough at sea to be able to damage seriously the world's most powerful fleet—even in a losing battle."[60] Tirpitz elected to concentrate Germany's naval forces in the North Sea, arguing that

> ... commerce raiding and transatlantic war against England is so hopeless because of the shortage of bases on our side and the superfluity on England's side. Assaults upon the peripheries of the British Empire, pinprick attacks upon that power's vast floating commerce, offered little chance of success: a direct threat to Britain's coastal waters did, for it would not only deter a British attack but it would also make London conciliatory and amenable in world affairs.[61]

The greater the risk to the Royal Navy and Britain's naval dominance, the more Britain would appease Germany.

In 1898, the German Reichstag voted for a radical expansion of the fleet. The British fleet at the time had twenty-nine modern battleships with twelve more on the stocks. Germany possessed thirteen and five respectively, all a third smaller than their British counterparts. The Fleet Law called for construction of seven battleships and two heavy cruisers. After decommissioning older warships, Germany would possess nineteen battleships, twelve heavy cruisers, and thirty light cruisers by 1903, the end of the five-year period covered by the law.[62] Germany's goal was to build three capital ships per year. Dan Van der Vat describes the British reaction as one of "genuine puzzlement" and inertia. Britain did not respond immediately to the Fleet Law; neither did it perceive the law as a threat. Concerns about the Franco-Russian alliance continued to drive British military policies until the early 1900s, just as Britain's Naval Defense Act of 1889 had been directed at France and Russia. Neither Germany nor the United States was considered a likely enemy at the time.[63]

Views on the origin and implications of Anglo-German tensions diverge. Some trace the beginning of the rivalry to the 1898 German naval law.[64] Others contend Britain began treating Germany as the primary rival only after the 1905 Morocco crisis, which led to improved relations with France. Up until then, the Admiralty believed the Royal Navy was strong enough to interdict German oceanic trade and compel Germany to sue for peace. Britain harbored no aggressive intentions and had no specific war plans against Germany and so adopted a "wait and see" strategy.[65]

In 1902, Britain's Committee on Imperial Defense outlined the empire's strategic priorities: defense of the United Kingdom from invasion, defense of India from invasion, and defense of the route to India through the Mediterranean. France was the source of the first threat, Russia the culprit in the second scenario, and both posed a threat to maritime lines of communication. Imperial rivalries were identified as the key strategic challenge. By 1905, these receded with Japan's destruction of Russia's navy. Germany remained Britain's chief naval rival although shifting power dynamics on the continent complicated strategic calculations. So long as a Franco-Russian alliance—established in 1894—balanced German military power, Britain could set a European commitment aside and focus on the graver threat to India from Russia and to Egypt from France. Germany's naval ascendance and Russia's naval defeat introduced the possibility of a three-power naval coalition of France, Russia, and Germany that could simultaneously threaten Britain European and extra-European interests.[66] Notably, Britain had not abandoned its distrust of Russia and France entirely. The 1906 naval maneuvers were aimed at developing strategies to protect trade in case of war with any possible combination of France, Germany, and Russia. The maneuvers represented the prevailing complexity in Britain's strategic environment. The question was, given increasing financial constraints, how Britain should preserve the naval supremacy so critical to defending it global interests.

Over the course of the post-Crimean period, England would first neglect its navy, then strive for naval dominance, and finally struggle to maintain naval preeminence over its rivals. These strategic oscillations occurred against the backdrop of rapid technological change. The second half of the nineteenth century witnessed more changes in naval technology than the previous ten centuries combined.[67] Innovations included improvements in gunnery, torpedoes, and mines as well as introduction of the submarine, radio, and oil-powered turbine engine.[68]

The Crimean War showed the efficacy of steam power and ironclad ships in naval warfare, and in response England launched its first modern battleships, HMS *Warrior* and HMS *Black Prince*, in 1860. Each carried forty guns in an iron hull, displaced over 9,000 tons, and could reach fourteen and half knots.[69] Gunnery technology underwent momentous changes. The traditional muzzle-loading, smoothbore, broadside cannons became breech-loading, rifled, armored, and turreted guns that grew to calibers of sixteen or more inches. The projectiles fired from these guns changed from solid shot (solid iron balls) to elongated, explosive shells. The rapid tempo of development had three results. First, crews constantly had to undergo training on new equipment and gunnery techniques. Second, ships were frequently pulled out of service to update the guns. Third, absent live combat with a peer to evaluate weapons and tactics, all serious theories regarding the development and use of guns had to be entertained. The result was a constant state of heterogeneity in weapon systems on British warships up until the twentieth century and the "bizarre, ill-assorted vessels of the late 1860s, 1870s and early 1890s."[70]

The submarine torpedo had important consequences for naval strategy. The French built up large squadrons of small torpedo boats in the Channel and in the Mediterranean in the hopes of delivering a single mortal blow to a first-class battleship. In actuality, the torpedo was still in its infancy, and the vast majority malfunctioned, missed their target, or simply sank. But the threat was taken seriously by British naval leaders, who rebuilt naval installations with breakwaters to prevent night raids by torpedo boats. Static operations had become very dangerous, so blockading enemy ports, a staple of British strategy, had to be reconsidered. Finally, the British developed a fast, slightly larger ship to deal with the enemy torpedo fleets—the modern destroyer.

The personnel who manned British warships also underwent rapid changes during this period. Before the 1850s England's warships were occupied by "impressed" seamen (forced conscripts), who were supplemented in times of crisis by additional "hire and fire" sailors. The Crimean War marked the end of this system and the beginning of the modern force of "bluejackets."[71]

Sustaining this new all-volunteer force required improvements in pay and living conditions.[72] Sailors' duties changed as well from traditional roles for which they could be quickly trained—swarming in the rigging, firing broadsides of cannon, and boarding with cutlasses—to newer roles that required a much higher level of training. The boilers required engineers and well-trained tenders. The guns, whose range began to be measured in miles rather than yards, required personnel trained in mathematics and technical precision. Highly trained personnel could not be easily replaced, and the Navy had to compete with the private market for skilled labor. Larger ships also required more men at a time when personnel costs were rising. The Navy struggled by the 1890s to put all of its first-line ships to sea for lack of seamen.[73]

British naval planners were determined to create and sustain the most capable navy in the world. In the absence of a peer competitor, it was difficult to decide how many ships were needed, what type they would be, and how they would be armed. Outside of actual combat experience, arguments concerning weapons and tactics remained strictly hypothetical.

In sum, the heady advances in naval technology including steam power, all-metal hulls of ships, iron and steel plating, rapid advancements in guns in the decades between the Crimean War and World War I were astounding. With this cascade of innovation, ships literally became obsolete before they were launched. Rapid technological change prevented homogeneity among warships, leaving planners uncertain of the actual capabilities of their forces while rising personnel costs prevented the British from manning the ships they had built. The prospect that a revolutionary technology would nullify contemporary systems and allow competitors to start on equal footing was a real possibility. The British had to balance how many ships would be needed in the short term with waiting until technology reached a plateau. One would be hard pressed to imagine a more complex technological environment for planners trying to construct a force to ensure naval supremacy well into the future.

Strategic Responses

Two key questions for the formation of grand strategy are what proportion of the nation's resources should be devoted to defense and how those defense resources should be allocated. Britain was a leading power facing a complex and shifting strategic environment. Its strategy had to be able to adapt to changes in the most probable opponents and combination of opponents including France, Russia, Germany, and Austria-Hungary. From the 1880s until World

War I the British adopted several shaping strategies designed to maintain strategic dominance.

In the decades immediately after the Crimean War, the British allowed their navy to fall into disrepair and obsolescence, with few consequences.[74] John Beeler points out that

> ... from 1856 to the passage of the Naval Defense Act [in 1889] there was very little from which the Empire or British commerce required defending. For most of the era the actual foreign threat to the countries of the Empire and to the sea lines of communication which connected them was virtually non-existent.[75]

A searing series of critical articles in 1884 in the *Pall Mall Gazette* sparked a panic concerning the decline of the Royal Navy.[76] A second panic ensued in 1888 following French naval increases. In response, Parliament passed the Naval Defense Act in 1889, "a five year building program that nearly doubled the effective battleship and cruiser strength of the Royal Navy."[77] The act provided for construction of seventy new warships and reinforced Britain's commitment to maintaining naval supremacy. The act called for modernization, efficiency, increased recruitment, and faster construction over the five-year program period. It stipulated a ratio of five battleships to three in any possible hostile combination of foreign navies—the famous two-power standard—with a generous margin to protect the worldwide empire at the same time. The two-power standard was chiefly for budgetary planning purposes. Naval requirements were defined as a fleet of battleships strong enough to defeat the combined fleets of the next two ranking naval powers. This standard of British naval production remained constant no matter how the diplomatic situation varied. For most of the period, the two navies in question were France and Russia. Even as late as 1912, in the midst of a naval race with Germany, planning was still couched in these terms.[78] Absent a peer competitor, judging actual capabilities was difficult, particularly with no military engagements to serve as a proving ground: Was a battleship launched two years ago "equal" to a foreign battleship launched this year? How should one assess the value of new destroyer class ships if the vessels had never seen combat? Still, in a swirl of changing diplomatic ties, planning against capabilities provided a way to sustain in peacetime the defense spending deemed critical to ensuring naval supremacy.

This fast-paced building effort was aimed at dissuading France and Russia from launching ambitious naval programs, but the intended result did not materialize. The combined French and Russian navies continued to have a greater rate of ship building than Britain, laying down twelve battleships compared to Britain's ten between 1889 and 1893.[79] Given the growth of the German and Japanese navies, by the 1900s "it was even doubtful whether the [Royal] Navy could command the seas against the most likely combination of its European adversaries."[80] Britain had little choice but to plan for an even larger fleet. By 1899, the annual naval budget had grown to twice the size it had been a decade earlier and it continued to grow over the next six years.[81] (See Table 3.3.)

By 1904, mounting popular pressure to reduce defense spending reached a climax. Fifteen years of naval expansion, coupled with the fiscal burden of a colonial war in South Africa (1899–1902), had become politically unsustainable. With a public clamoring against higher taxes and rising deficits, the government cut the Admiralty's budget, a decision that happened to coincide with the outbreak of war between Russia and Japan in 1904. Japan destroyed Russia's navy but not before a Russian fleet mistakenly fired on British fishing vessels, bringing the two countries to the brink of war. Crises like these could erupt again in the future but would have to be met with a fleet potentially weakened by budget cutbacks. The possibility also existed of a hostile three-power coalition of France, Russia, and Germany threatening Britain in European and extra-European waters simultaneously.[82]

By 1905, the British understood that their approach to strategic dominance had become financially untenable. They could no longer guarantee a two-power standard let alone a three-power standard. So the Royal Navy, under the leadership of Admiral Sir John Fisher, embarked on a new solution to achieve its strategic goal. The Royal Navy would exploit technological innovations to create a new type of force that could unilaterally defend Britain and her empire at an affordable cost. Economy and operational effectiveness would be achieved by replacing a strategy of mass with a strategy of maneuver.[83] Lambert argues Fisher deliberately implemented a "revolution in military affairs" that proposed a radically different approach to the allocation of defense resources—another indicator of strategic response under uncertainty.[84]

How defense resources are allocated is usefully viewed along two dimensions: the balance between the near term and long term, varying from readiness to modernization; and the related dimension of innovation-adaptation. During the 1880s and 1890s, when defense expenditures were rising, the Admiralty adapted rather than innovated reasoning that innovation would be

Table 3.3. Great Britain's naval expenditures, 1889-1914.

Years	Gross naval expenditures	Spending on shipbuilding, repairs, maintenance	Percentage of gross	Spending on personnel	Percentage of gross
1889/90	15,588,502	6,460,001	41	6,374,311	41
1890/91	18,061,816	6,676,628	37	6,640,375	37
1891/92	18,150,638	6,746,216	37	6,912,539	38
1892/93	17,402,741	6,635,612	38	7,116,460	41
1893/94	16,327,641	6,357,457	39	7,343,120	45
1894/95	18,595,685	9,113,968	49	7,588,186	41
1895/96	21,264,377	10,934,554	51	7,934,887	37
1896/97	23,886,177	13,215,564	55	8,234,668	34
1897/98	22,547,844	11,239,225	50	8,594,869	38
1898/99	26,145,598	13,462,803	51	9,355,440	36
1899/00	28,478,842	15,043,853	53	9,771,314	34
1900/01	33,302,260	18,411,543	55	10,147,182	30
1901/02	34,994,553	19,114,676	55	10,511,508	30
1902/03	35,525,731	18,573,040	52	10,971,611	31
1903/04	40,503,873	22,360,630	55	11,683,599	29
1904/05	41,696,313	22,575,297	54	12,275,095	29
1905/06	38,175,045	19,059,433	50	12,012,387	31
1906/07	35,693,850	17,658,932	49	12,047,839	34
1907/08	33,950,169	16,368,536	48	12,247,174	36
1908/09	34,775,752	16,974,653	49	12,043,061	37
1909/10	37,385,460	19,784,032	53	13,055,683	35
1910/11	43,903,499	24,064,361	55	13,414,318	31
1911/12	46,793,789	25,242,570	54	13,903,589	30
1912/13	48,742,182	27,419,414	56	14,390,697	30
1913/14	52,920,960	29,792,872	56	15,235,171	29

SOURCE: Jon Sumida, *In Defense of Naval Supremacy*.

detrimental to Britain's strategic advantage. This is compelling logic for a preponderant power because rapid innovation shortens the effective life of any weapon system. Lambert argues that British policy prohibited even experimenting with the submarine and contact mines so as "not to justify or encourage" other navies developing them. However, once naval intelligence warned that a rival power had perfected some new weapon system, Britain followed suit. The Admiralty was content to let others set the pace and direction of naval innovation, counting on Britain's superior financial and industrial strength to catch up and overtake when necessary.[85]

This strategy, which underlay the two-power standard, was problematic for several reasons. First, it was very costly. Britain could not afford to expand its fleet in response to every new innovation introduced by rival naval powers. Second, Britain could not sustain the skilled personnel to operate a growing number of battleships and armored cruisers. Third, technological developments in torpedoes and submarines had made battleships into large targets.[86] Fisher believed there was a far more economical and effective way to maintain naval supremacy than a battleship-centered fleet. "Rather than react to innovation and allow foreign rivals to set the pace of progress, Fisher wanted to promote and direct change to achieve strategic advantage."[87]

Britain's chief rivals—France and Russia—were most likely to target Britain's trade routes rather than her fleet or homeland in order to strangle her economy. Fisher believed the Navy's chief mission must be to safeguard British commerce and interdict enemy trade, thereby compelling France and/or Russia to sue for peace.[88] Fisher's vision hinged on exploiting the technological innovation of stealth (that is, the submarine) and superior mobility, communications, and accuracy in targeting (that is, battle cruisers directed by radio and equipped with advanced methods of gunnery) to achieve sea denial in home waters and sea command abroad. By using wireless, telegraph, coaling stations, and powerful turbine engines, the Navy could create a rapid reaction force that could be supplemented with littoral-denial forces made up of submarines, torpedo boats, and floating mines.[89]

On being appointed first sea lord in 1904, Fisher launched a series of reforms that transformed the Royal Navy in important ways: nucleus crew system, scrapping obsolete ships, redistributing the fleet, and all big-gun battleships and cruisers. These reforms worked together as a system. Nucleus crews were an attempt to deal with shortage of personnel. Scrapping obsolete vessels was aimed at reducing maintenance costs and wasted labor. Fleet distribution was designed to focus on fast, uniformly effective fleets. All big-gun ships were designed to facilitate effective fire control and maximize damage inflicted.

Facing impending reductions in naval expenditures, Fisher also proposed replacing the conventional battleship and first-class cruiser with the battle cruiser. This new type of capital ship was faster and more powerful than the armored cruisers the French had been laying down since the 1890s as they strived to remain a first-class naval power and challenge the Royal Navy on the cheap. French armored cruisers were designed for commerce raiding, an asymmetrical approach to offset Britain's superior battle fleet. According to Lambert, Fisher's

> ... battlecruiser concept was an attempt to build a multi-role warship capable of performing the functions of both cruisers and battleships. Although individual units would be more expensive, the cost of building a single multi-role warship instead of two specialized types—a battleship and an armored cruiser—offered the Royal Navy potentially huge savings in money and especially manpower.[90]

Fisher's programs helped reduce naval expenditures by approximately four to five million pounds per year between 1905 and 1910.[91]

Battle cruisers enabled by advanced communication systems would protect oceanic trade and the outer reaches of the empire and allow Britain to abandon its costly station fleet system. The navy no longer needed to be deployed in force everywhere at once because wireless telegraphy coupled with the exploitation of naval intelligence would allow the navy "to replace the numerous assortments of cruisers scattered around the globe with a centrally located force of modern long-range, high-speed vessels that could be vectored toward any commerce raiders at large."[92] The British would exploit the information communications revolution that was underway by fitting all warships with wireless sets and constructing navy-owned shore stations—in effect building a communications grid that would give British commanders a clearer picture of situations than their counterparts.

By 1903, the Admiralty had already begun to establish intelligence centers to report "the dispositions and movements of foreign ships of war, details of trade routes, together with a study of probable enemy shipping."[93] In 1904, the system was expanded to cover the Far East. All intelligence data were routinely passed to London, where a big picture was developed.[94] In 1905, Fisher

> ... directed the Trade and Intelligence Divisions to poll their efforts and track *daily* the movements of every warship in the world (British and foreign), plus about 100 liners and fast cargo ships that conceivably might be converted into auxiliary cruisers, plus any other "merchantmen" of interest to the Admiralty.[95]

These efforts, together with the establishment of the naval secret intelligence service in 1906–1907, which provided information by clandestine means, collectively helped the British achieve information superiority and dominant battle space awareness.[96] Lambert argues that what Fisher envisaged

> ... went far beyond utilizing the benefits of wireless to enhance strategic warning. It was the first attempt made by any naval power to make systematic use of intelligence and apply it strategically. . . . The Admiralty now possessed the ability to vector centrally located warships towards specific targets, and thus respond to threats with precision and economy of force.[97]

Deployability was critical because it would bring economies without sacrificing capability. Fisher's "preferred capital ships were highly mobile multi-purpose warships that could be moved rapidly by wireless in response to new intelligence . . . no one characteristic should be exaggerated at the expense of any other so that the craft built should retain maximum flexibility of deployment."[98] A strategy of forward presence—simultaneous concentration of numerically superior conventional forces at all potential points of engagement, based on the sailing ship technology of the past—could be supplanted by a strategy of maneuver—use of greater mobility and other qualitative advantages to achieve decisive superiority wherever and whenever needed based on the technology of the present.[99]

Fisher's proposed reconfiguration of Britain's fleet made the radical call for sea denial in home waters rather than sea control. "Flotilla defense" was based on his belief that the submarine had made the narrow European seas unsafe for any large warship. "Infesting the narrow seas with an ever present mosquito fleet of flotilla craft" would protect the homeland from invasion and the British Isles from blockade in place of a far more costly battle fleet while freeing up the rest of the armored fleet for operations in distant seas where "rapid intelligent deployment would enable them to do the work that would have required many more battleships and cruisers."[100]

Fisher's strategy included a novel economic dimension—an industrial policy called "plunging." Fisher wanted to use technology and industry as strategic weapons to ensure that budget cuts did not compromise research and development and jeopardize his revolution. Leveraging technological advancements and pipeline (shipbuilding) speed would ensure Britain could trump foreign navies' force structures.[101] As Fisher wrote in one of his letters, "Whatever type the French have, we must go one better, and that is a principle which will always keep us safe, and, if we built as quickly as we ought to build, we ought always to commence after they are well advanced and have the more powerful vessel afloat beforehand."[102] He established a close relationship with Britain's top four private armaments firms. They would receive an effective monopoly on big ship contracts. In return, the firms would retain current levels of research and development investment and also maintain spare manufacturing capacity for critical path components to ensure new weapon systems could be developed on time and on demand.[103]

Plunging's success was limited by service resistance and the inability to coordinate private industry effectively. In the years following the 1889 naval reform, up to 50 percent of naval building had to be contracted out to private yards.[104] Fisher worked to establish a close relationship with private firms, but he struggled to effectively control the release of technical innovation in a strategic manner. British naval architecture was largely run on an apprentice system, one lacking in formal education and made up of (quoting Derek Arnoldson) "'practical tinkerers' who were reluctant to depart from 'rule of thumb' methods and were 'proud of the fact that they carried out little original research or employed few technicians.'"[105] Such a force could hardly be relied on to systematically conduct the basic research required for a true plunging strategy. Moreover, although the Royal Navy wanted a large potential for rapid shipbuilding, it did not have the budget to consistently supply all of the private yards with contracts. So it encouraged yards to take on foreign contracts, which inevitably led to the diffusion of England's technological edge. Despite confrontations with Russia during the crisis over Poland in 1863 and the Russo-Turkish war, Britain continued to supply Russia with naval technology and allowed recruitment of its engineers to oversee the construction of Russia's navy. Economic historian Clive Trebilcock's examination of British armament firms in Russia and Spain shows that

> Under these agreements [signed in 1905] the British firms would make available to the Russian constructors their designs, their guarantee of quality and of expert supervision, and any patents relevant to the work in hand. The most modern shipbuilding knowledge was thus made available to Russian industry.[106]

This was a development inconsistent with predictions that, economically, shapers will be reluctant to transfer technology that might narrow the technological gap with potential adversaries.

Preserving Britain's comparative strength in naval technologies was the lynchpin of Fisher's strategy, and it had some unanticipated positive results. In 1905, Fisher introduced to all-big-gun type battleship—the dreadnought—

which unexpectedly disrupted rival naval programs. The dreadnought had a uniform-caliber armament (twelve-inch guns) to reduce the amount of ammunition and spare parts needed and a new engine type that increased the ship's speed. Fisher was widely criticized for introducing the dreadnought on the grounds that it rendered all existing battleships obsolete, thus doing away with Britain's overwhelming superiority of about three to one over Germany in predreadnoughts.[107] In one stroke, it swept away British naval preponderance and gave the Germans a level, or near level, start in the competition for naval supremacy. Many believed conservatism in naval design was more appropriate.[108] Fisher countered that the Japanese and the Germans were already contemplating dreadnought-type ships and that the United States was planning on building one as well. Britain needed the jump on its competitors. Moreover, the disruption to foreign warship construction that resulted was a positive development. Fisher envisioned Britain periodically introducing into service new models that incorporated a cluster of innovative systems that would deliberately render rival fleets obsolescent whenever Britain wanted. Through plunging, Britain could exploit its financial and shipbuilding superiority to not only take and hold the technological lead over rivals but to "[shape] and [direct] technological change to achieve long-term strategic advantage."[109]

Toward the end of his tenure as first sea lord, Fisher proposed a novel approach to imperial defense, one designed to protect all imperial interests in the Far East. At the Imperial Defense Conference of 1909, the Admiralty proposed the "fleet unit" concept. The British would reestablish a large fleet presence in the Pacific—belying claims that concerns about imperial interests had been entirely squelched by the German threat—to protect Far Eastern interests in coordination with Dominion naval forces that were being developed with the Japanese threat in mind. The British recognized that, absent an overarching construct, the Dominions would build inefficient "twopenny-halfpenny navies" that would provide no positive contribution to defense of the empire.[110] The fleet unit concept would closely link Dominion naval development to the Royal Navy. It required interchangeable personnel and doctrine. "Interchangeability was the key to efficiency. The Admiralty proposed that any nation 'desirous of creating a navy should aim at forming a distinct fleet unit' built around a battle cruiser and supported by twelve smaller warships of specific types."[111] The fleet unit concept was an effort to integrate the empire into a defense system, producing a fleet "collective security" of sorts. The Dominions had local maritime interests to protect. If Britain would not assist, the Dominions would do it themselves. Accordingly, the British realized they could leverage Dominion naval forces to enhance broader imperial security. But Fisher's fleet unit concept went one step further by proposing an integrated system to develop Dominion capabilities that would significantly augment British power. Toward that end, the British were willing to give Australia cutting-edge materiel and include them in the intelligence network. In 1913, First Lord of the Admiralty Winston Churchill abandoned the fleet unit policy for financial reasons and over concerns about the German threat.[112]

The strategic logic behind Fisher's reforms has been hotly debated by historians. For Arthur Marder, these reforms worked together toward a hard core of effective ships with no fat in the system. Strategically, they were a response to Germany's incipient rise and the changing systemic landscape:

> The redistribution of the Fleet to meet strategical ("and not sentimental") requirements was the crowning stroke of all. The distribution had been determined in the sailing-ship era, when sea voyages were long and when squadrons to protect trade had to be distributed widely. There were nine squadrons or fleets in 1904. The advent of steam and cable communications, later the wireless, lessened the need for many isolated foreign squadrons. The entire distribution system was rendered wholly obsolete by the Japanese Alliance (1902), the French Entente (1904), the excellent relations with the United States and Italy after 1898, and by the fact that, since the Autumn of 1902, the Admiralty had looked upon the German Navy as the potential opponent of the Royal Navy. No special effort was made to conceal the fact that the rearrangement of naval forces in home waters was due principally to the German Navy menace.[113]

For Nicholas Lambert, the Edwardian naval reforms were instituted in response to fiscal concerns and innovations in communications technology.[114] Strategically they were not a response to a rising Germany but rather designed to deal with imperial rivals France and Russia.[115]

It is safe to say that sometime between 1900 and 1905 Fisher saw the main threat shifting from imperial rivals to Germany. The alliance with Japan (1902), the Entente Cordiale with France (1904) and the decimation of the Russian fleet in the Russo–Japanese War (1904–1905) all served to ease fears regarding the maintenance of the empire. Though some posit the shift coming as early as 1900 or 1902, while others hold off until 1906[116] or later (Lambert), it is clear Britain was planning for a war with Germany by 1905. Regardless of which competitor one thinks was dominant in the minds of British strategists, the shaping strategy was designed to maintain naval supremacy, forestall the rise of a peer competitor, and prolong Britain's preeminent position on the world stage.

Throughout this period, the standing army was repeatedly denigrated in favor of the navy and also mistrusted. Any efforts to increase or update the command structure of the army were received with cries of militarism and images of the English Civil War. The result was maintenance of outdated practices, including buying of officer commissions and promotions (until 1871), refusal to create a general staff (until 1904), and the commander in chief answering directly to the sovereign instead of the secretary of state for war (until 1870). The influence of the army and its leaders in the sphere of policy making was limited in the time period from the Crimean War to the First World War. A number of civil-military and strategic issues help explain this phenomenon and the resulting consequences for the state of army readiness and modernization.

The Crimean War exposed the weaknesses of the British army as an antiquated and poorly led field force. In the wake of that conflict, however, few measures were taken to improve or expand the organization, and it was left to decay into a second-rate service. Three reasons explain the continued neglect of the army: geography, relations with Parliament and the monarch, and the nature of its organization.

England's island geography greatly influenced the development of the army. The physical reality of an island allowed planners a "cushion zone" of time that they would not have with contiguous neighbors. The time needed for an attacker to amass and transport its forces would allow the British time to create the necessary defense forces without depending on a large standing army. Naval advocates, on the other hand, could lobby for a larger share of limited resources because of their prominence in the pantheon of English history. Simply put, the British were willing to bear the tax burden for a large navy but not a large army.

The army's relationships with the Parliament and the monarch also help explain their role in grand strategy. The constant enmity between the army advocates and the Parliament, specifically the House of Commons, and the close ties between the soldier and the Crown are the defining themes in this area. The lingering effects of the English Civil War produced the permanent specter of militarism even through the nineteenth century. The rise of the militarist state of Prussia, whose very existence was inimical to liberal English ideals, provided a vivid example. Though the Prussian system was the model of success, many felt the risks of authoritarianism outweighed the gains in efficiency. To highlight this, the very existence of the British army was subject to yearly sufferance, a tradition going back to the Mutiny Act of 1689. This yearly ritual of addressing the army's very legitimacy shows how strained the relationship was between the two institutions.

The army responded to this disdain with disdain in turn. The officers and troops felt that their loyalty extended to the Crown and the flag but not to the politicians. The dynamic of this antagonism produced uneven organizational development in the army. The practice of commission purchasing for officers, for one, continued through most of the nineteenth century and extended up to the regimental level (rank of lieutenant colonel). Above that, appointment was the result of a mixture of seniority and patronage, maintaining the gentry and wealthy merchant classes as the pool for the officer corps. This was seen as a safeguard against military coups by linking the interests of the two groups, even if it resulted in an inefficient fighting force. The purchase system was thrown out during the Cardwell Reforms of 1871, but its imprint remained. Another feature was the lack of a British General Staff until the Esher Commission created one in 1904. Until that time, the army and the monarchy fought to maintain a "commander in chief" officer who conferred directly with the monarch and who frequently slighted Parliament.

From the Crimean War to the outbreak of World War I, the army's use was limited to wars at the periphery of the empire. On the Continent, the army was threatened but never used. The reasons were deficiencies in size and technology. The field army establishment was determined by Parliament each fiscal year. In the wake of the Crimean War, this number dipped as low as 157,000 but averaged a little over 200,000. In addition to the regular army were two other forces that could be drawn on for troop numbers—the militia and Indian army. The militia (English, Scottish, and Irish) totaled an average of 150,000 troops. These were of dubious fighting quality, and a political uproar resulted from attempts to force the militias to serve abroad. A second source of personnel was the Indian army, which was transferred from private to royal control in 1859. Two events served to dispel illusions about India as a troop resource. In 1857, the Sepoy Mutiny (native troops fighting for the British), which required regular forces to quell, showed that India could be a liability instead of an asset. An even more disturbing event was the White Mutiny of 1859, which resulted from problems of integration of white Indian army personnel into the regular army. This reinforced the belief that only the tiny regular army was wholly trustworthy.

Consequently, the size of the British army squelched any ideas about action against European powers. After leaving forces to defend the homeland, the largest conceivable expeditionary force would be no greater than 50,000. In the event of deployment to the continent, the British would be dwarfed by the magnitude of any single opponent. Greater populations, fewer colonial responsibilities, and conscription ensured that Prussia, France, Russia, and Austro-Hungary would each be able to field more than a million troops.

Advances in military technology were also problematic. Breech loading and rifling advancements proceeded at a rapid clip during the late nineteenth century. The first modern British small arm, the Martini-Henry rifle (small bore, internal hammer, greater range and accuracy) was first introduced in 1869. Its domination in colonial wars gave the British a false sense of modernity in terms of its military. Artillery was a particular problem. Guns rapidly progressed from brass to iron to steel and from muzzle to breech loading. With budgetary constraints, the army was often far behind its continental peers. In truth, the primitive opponents faced during this period did not provide a true test of the British army or its weaponry and deficiencies were painfully laid bare during the Anglo–Boer War (1899–1902). Unsurprisingly, the British army's size and stage of technological development affected the way it was perceived as a tool of grand strategy. Policy makers were forced to contend with the paradox of maintaining the role of empire builder and continental arbiter while equipped with limited military resources.

Though there were distinct ideological differences between the Liberal and Conservative parties of the period, there was much continuity in decisions to use force throughout the second half of the nineteenth century. The Liberal Party of the post-Crimean period received its support from Whig gentry and landowners who championed prosperity through free trade and intellectual radicals who favored negotiation over force of arms. The Liberal Party hoped to see all of Europe embrace the Republican spirit and renounce autocratic ways. The Liberals were against forceful colonial policies that might paint England as a hypocritical oppressor, trusting to free trade to civilize the colonies and enrich England through new markets. Under Liberal administrations, army budgets suffered more than usual, as it was seen as an accouterment of authoritarianism. The use of the army was also eschewed for these ideological reasons. The Conservative Party was an amalgamation of aristocracy

Table 3.4. Distribution of British defense expenditures by department, 1904–1914 (in millions of pounds).

Fiscal year	Total defense expenditure	Navy total	Navy percentage of total	Army total	Army percentage of total
1904/5	72.2	35.5	49.2	36.7	50.8
1905/6	66	36.8	55.8	29.2	44.2
1906/7	62.2	33.3	53.5	28.9	46.5
1907/8	59.2	31.4	53	27.8	47
1908/9	58.2	31.1	53.4	27.1	46.6
1909/10	59	32.2	54.6	26.8	45.4
1910/11	63	35.8	56.8	27.2	43.2
1911/12	67.8	40.4	59.6	27.4	40.4
1912/13	70.5	42.9	60.9	27.6	39.1
1913/14	72.5	44.4	61.2	28.1	38.8

SOURCE: Mitchell, *British Historical Statistics*.

and working class. Both were united under sentiments of nationalism and assertive expansion of English interests around the world. Yet, despite the desire for a stronger military, the army had to compete with the navy for limited defense budgets and often came up short. (See Table 3.4.)

Despite party and personality, British foreign policy displayed unmistakable continuities in regards to the army, characterized as "permanent braggadocio" or speaking loudly while carrying a small stick. Use of the army was often threatened but rarely used due to its prohibitively small size. In the Schleswig-Holstein Affair of 1864, the Seven Weeks War of 1866, and the Franco-Prussian War of 1870, England protested but remained inactive. Military weakness combined with diplomatic visibility defined England's role on the Continent during the second half of the nineteenth century. It was not until the rise of Germany at the turn of the century that Britain's perception of the role of the army changed. The army began to prepare for military contingencies on the continent, and its primary role became to participate in European operations.[117] To quote John McDermott,

> The anti-German, Eurocentric military strategy which had been adopted by January 1906 improved the position of the army: it had found a role it could play without drastic reorganization and it established a strategic dominance over the Admiralty which was to last throughout the First World War.[118]

Britain's diplomatic strategy during the period displayed a preference for flexibility and avoiding military commitments to diplomatic partners. Treaties were desired that allowed, but did not require, intervention. Republican political structures were often used as an excuse (the changing of parties in power) to stay out of binding treaties.

On the continent, England wanted to play the part of an interested but nonaligned caretaker. Britain's traditional foreign policy objectives were a balance of power in Europe, independence of the Low Countries, and security of its trade routes and overseas interests. As long as German military power was balanced by the Franco-Russian alliance of 1894, Britain could eschew European commitments and maintain neutrality in European affairs while also retaining global preeminence and naval supremacy.[119]

The Russo-Japanese War left Germany the leading power in Europe and forced Britain to become more entangled in European affairs. Tension with Germany originated over commercial and colonial rivalries, but Russia and France had traditionally been greater concerns. Russia threatened to expand in Central Asia toward India while Anglo-French rivalry on the Upper Nile had almost led to war during the Fashoda incident of 1898. Control of the sea enabled Britain to defy European opinion during the Boer War (1899-1902), but the growing burdens of empire led Joseph Chamberlain in a 1902 Colonial Conference to compare Britain to "a weary titan under the too vast orb of its fate."

Tirpitz's risk strategy in 1899, among other things, triggered a reorganization of British defense policy. To avoid provoking American antagonism, the Hay-Pauncefote Treaty of 1901 recognized American supremacy in the Caribbean. Britain agreed to America building and fortifying the Panama Canal. The Alaskan boundary dispute was resolved to the advantage of the Americans and at the expense of Canadian claims in 1903.

Fears that the Royal Navy would be unable to match a Franco-Russian naval combination in the Far East led Britain to conclude an alliance with Japan in 1902, formally ending its "splendid isolation." Britain and Japan agreed to maintain the status quo of China and Korea, to hold peacetime conversations between military and naval commanders to develop plans for joint action, and to support the other if it was attacked by more than one power.

Aware of the ramifications of isolationism and reasons for improved relations with other continental powers, Britain sought ententes in Europe. Chamberlain turned first to Russia in 1898, but Russia refused. He then approached Germany, but Germany also refused. Each saw more advantages in diplomacy with the other than with Britain. The most Britain secured was the Anglo-German Convention in August 1898 on the partition of the Portuguese colonies.

The Anglo–Japanese alliance necessitated an entente with France to prevent Britain from being drawn into a conflict as a result of its newfound relationship with Japan.[120] Also, the Admiralty had always assumed British ships would be able to move freely through the Straits of Gibraltar. This depended on British possession of Gibraltar and a compliant kingdom in Morocco, the latter of which was called into question by France's policy of "peaceful penetration" of Morocco:

> If a strong naval power such as France occupied the coastline, Britain's naval position in the Mediterranean would be seriously jeopardized. London had either to prevent this development or to reach an accord with Paris . . .[121]

An entente with France was reached in April 1904. The Anglo-French accord on Morocco and Egypt established mutual diplomatic support between England and France. Both agreed to recognize each other's respective dominant interests in Egypt and Morocco. Although initially conceived as a strictly colonial settlement, the entente had European and Anglo-German connotations and took on greater significance once Britain began to consider a European role for its army.[122] So, for example, an attempt by Germany to exploit Russian weakness in defeat in 1905 by pressuring France over Morocco led to Anglo–French staff talks on what might be done in the event of war.[123] By 1904 Britain planned to shift the focus of its navy to the North Sea and leave protection of the Mediterranean to the French.[124]

Anglo–French rapprochement created fertile soil for Anglo-Russian reconciliation. The Anglo–Russian entente has been described as an "alliance of restraint." Russia and Britain wanted to keep each other in check. Britain wanted to ensure Russia did not expand further into the Middle East and gain full control of the Straits. Russia wanted to ensure Britain did not seize control of Middle Eastern affairs by replacing France as the Ottomans' traditional ally.[125]

The benefits to Indian defense to be gained from an entente with Russia were also clear.[126] Britain's army could not defend India and South Africa. British despair regarding Indian defense was based on the numerical superiority of the Russian army and the inferiority in numbers and organization of the British army. "Intelligence reported that Russia could at any time send 50,000–60,000 men to Afghanistan (fully expanded up to 200,000 men), supported by continuous reinforcements at a rate of 20,000 men a month."[127] The entente with Russia meant Britain could stop allocating part of the British Expeditionary Force for operations in India.[128]

For Russia, British support increased its security in Asia, while Russia's defeat by Japan diminished the threat to British Far Eastern interests.[129] Finally, Britain and Russia shared a mutual animosity toward Germany, and the entente strengthened Russia's position with respect to Germany and Austria. Entente eventually led to an agreement in 1907 that settled Anglo-Russian colonial disputes in Asia.

Ententes with France and Russia did reduce flexibility when compared to Britain's traditional policy of splendid isolation. However, they committed Britain only to giving diplomatic support. To be sure, military and naval practicalities required prior planning if diplomacy were to be backed by armed force. But overall Britain succeeded throughout the period in minimizing tight commitments and maximizing flexibility in response to a diverse and shifting security environment.

Conclusions

Jon Sumida has observed that

> Global interests are difficult to protect because they require the distribution of large amounts of force capable of dealing multiple threats whose character, magnitude and timing are difficult to predict. Democracies are generally unwilling to maintain standing forces that are strong enough to execute a strategy of mass, and this is especially the case in times of international tranquility. When the military and naval authorities of representative governments are confronted with severe fiscal limitation during such periods while burdened with the responsibility for maintaining the security of global interests, one attractive option is resort to a strategy of maneuver based on radical technological innovation that allows smaller and more capable forces to do the work of much larger and therefore more expensive conventional formations.[130]

At the turn of the century Britain faced challenges from Germany, France, and Russia. Her traditional strategy could no longer address these challenges, and Fisher's reforms provided a coherent vision to respond to them. Although his vision never fully became a reality, the emphasis on emerging technologies in a period of rapid change helped sustain British naval preeminence into the twentieth century:

> The years from 1889 to 1918 may, therefore, be seen as a distinct stage of British naval history—the heyday of the Royal Navy in the industrial era, when

EVALUATION OF HYPOTHESES ON SOURCES OF STRATEGY

The Russian and British experiences in the post-Crimea period lend some support to nonstructural arguments about strategic choice in a complex environment. First, organizational factors often undermined the coherence of strategy. The Russian government was fragmented, and ministries operated at cross-purposes. Threat analysis was decentralized, based on the military district system, and each district had an incentive to exaggerate the threat, resulting in the maximization of threat perception.[132] Nevertheless, prior to 1905 foreign and finance ministers were generally in agreement that Russia should pursue a cautious foreign policy and limited imperial expansion to assure Russia's immediate international security and prevent collapse of the domestic economy.[133]

After its defeat by Japan in 1905, Russia appeared open to implementing any reforms to address external threats, but Parliament was deadlocked due to disagreements over resource allocation and the substance of reforms. Deadlock characterized the Duma for most of the time from its creation in 1905. Institutional changes fragmented Russia's decision making, and it seems that, after the creation of the Duma, political institutions and politically relevant organizations came to bear significant and direct influence on Russia's foreign policy making. Furthermore, during this period, interministerial tensions climbed. There was no unified strategy and implementation because ministries worked at cross-purposes. Due to lack of coordination, Ministries of War, Finance, and Foreign Affairs frequently subverted each other's policies.[134] Contending political interests and institutional diffusion of political power contributed to subsequent inconsistencies and lack of cohesion in the mobilization of financial, military, and political resources, which undermined unified and consistent military decision making. A phenomenon accompanying the political changes was the emergence of a powerful voice for the press, which publicized political debate and reinforced factional divisions among the elite.[135] Bruce Menning notes that, after 1905, the government had a clear mandate for substantial military reform yet

> . . . a variety of factors ranging from lack of unifying purpose to financial constraint came to exert a strong mitigating influence on the forces of

thorough-going change. The result was that St. Petersburg translated lessons learned from recent defeat only imperfectly into preparation for future war. Other important lapses in institutional adaptation and anticipation, including faulty war planning, marked the route to recurring catastrophe.[136]

Organizational factors also compromised the coherent implementation of Fisher's reform policy in Britain. Fisher failed to overcome political and service opposition to his reformist vision or to convince more conservative naval peers of the virtue of his vision. The battle cruiser system was never fully implemented. His plunging plans for twenty-eight knot cruisers in 1908 were scuttled by the Admiralty.[137] Fisher was determined that England "plunge" naval technology to foil rivals' attempts to challenge British naval dominance. Plunging was only a limited success due to service resistance. In addition to failing to overcome political and service opposition, the navy's relationship with private industry and economic realities outside his control precluded the type of technological edge necessary for true "plunging."

Domestic political factors also influenced Fisher's initiatives in important ways. Fisher chose to fight political, interservice, and intraservice rivalries in the public eye, introducing a new player into the equation—public opinion. This not only engendered public outcry over abandoning the battleship but also caused many naval officers to side against Fisher because he was seen as a threat to naval tradition. Fisher's "go public" strategy also produced a reciprocal response from his opponents. Fisher had whipped up fervor for a "big navy-blue water" school to the public but failed to sell his nuanced view of strategy to go along with it or to replace the mantra of "battleships" with "battle cruisers and flotilla defense."[138] Popular support was critical for a big navy but only for one that captured the public's imagination. Cruisers, submarines, and torpedo craft did not sell nearly so well as large fleets of massive battleships. Even Winston Churchill, who was won over by the theories of Fisher in private, realized the political necessity of the battleship race. By securing public support, Fisher ensured a large navy, just not the flavor he had hoped for. Yet for all the shortcomings, Fisher was very successful in maintaining British naval preeminence in the face of declining relative power.

The cases also lend some support to cognitive explanations about strategic choice under uncertainty. In Russia, to discriminate among threats, the central government tended to project the experience of the immediate past into the future. So, up until 1870, fear of a revived Crimean coalition dominated planning. After 1870, Russia prepared for war in Central Europe. Obsession with the German menace led Russia to try to compensate for German advantages by prepositioning troops in Poland and forging an alliance with France; but, in 1877, Russia stumbled into war with Turkey. After the Russo-Japanese War in 1905, defense efforts were reoriented around Asia, only to hamper Russian strategy in World War I.

Technological hypotheses also find some support in military planning tendencies. Russian planners tended to focus on military capabilities, not political intentions.[139] British planners likewise judged that the most effective response to the uncertainties they faced was to create standard-based ratios of capabilities instead of planning against specific adversaries.

The overarching contours of Russian and British strategy are most consistent with the interpretation that strategic responses to a complex security and technological environment reflect concern with relative international position. Russia, a country in the trough of the power curve, strived to create time and space to internally reform and reconstitute its international power and position. The Treaty of Paris, signed in 1856, undermined Russia's imperial position and international prestige. It exacerbated the discrepancy between Russia's traditional aspirations for a great power status and its backward social and economic conditions. With Russia bankrupt after the Crimean War, agricultural, trade, and commercial reforms were pursued to restore economic solvency and great power status.[140] The broad contours of Russia's behavior in the international arena were driven by the desire to maintain the empire and great power status through domestic reforms. The pattern of change within Russia's military was consistent with this reformist strategy—incremental, not revolutionary, with Russia following a step behind the technological progress of the Western powers.[141] Britain, for its part, the leading power of the day, endeavored to sustain its preeminent position and extend its lead, delaying as much as possible the time when others could rise to challenge the supremacy of the Royal Navy, lynchpin of Britain's strategic position.

4 INTER-WORLD WAR PERIOD, 1918-1939

IN THE YEARS BETWEEN THE TWO WORLD WARS, Europe and Asia experienced significant political upheaval. On the Continent, once great powers that had sustained tremendous human losses now faced huge war debts and the daunting task of physical reconstruction. A vanquished Germany, bound by the Versailles Treaty, confronted revolutionary attacks from the left and right. Revolution and civil war challenged Russia. The Ottoman Empire was destroyed and dismembered. Great Britain, France, and Italy, with few resources to spare, struggled to defend their weakening hold on foreign territories. The United States, by contrast, emerged from war virtually invulnerable, while in Asia Japan was poised to continue its rise along the trajectory set by the Meiji Restoration and cemented by its defeat of Russia in 1904–1905.

Technological changes were reshaping the battlefield in equally significant ways. Improvements in internal combustion engines, aircraft design, radio, and radar vastly enhanced their military utility. The great powers experimented with different ways to use these technologies, making possible the tactics of blitzkrieg, carrier aviation, modern amphibious warfare, and strategic aerial bombardment. Entirely new kinds of military formations appeared, like the panzer division, carrier battle group, and long-range bomber force.[1] Over a twenty-year period, the nature of conflict changed significantly, but the course of transformation was far from clear at the time. Debate over the role and mix of armor, infantry, mechanized infantry, and artillery assets in ground operations; of fighters, bombers, and ground support aircraft in air operations; and of aircraft carriers, surface combatants, and submarines in naval warfare raged vigorously up until the Second World War. So too were the operational concepts governing their use and the proper integration of ground, naval, and air power hotly contested.[2]

Periods of strategic pause, coupled with rapid technological change, increase complexity and raise uncertainty for political and military leaders. This chapter examines how British and U.S. leaders responded to uncertainty in their strategic and technological environments and the extent to which relative power and complexity shaped those choices. The first task is one of describing strategic choices. The second task is one of assessing and explaining the influence of relative power on strategic choice. It requires that we first establish the relative power of Britain and the United States and the strategic preferences hypothesized to follow.

RELATIVE POWER AND STRATEGIC PREFERENCES

There is an unresolved debate over Britain's relative power in the twentieth century and the extent to which Britain had declined.[3] The concept of decline began to appear in the 1880s and 1890s with concerns over educational standards and the need for reform.[4] During the 1890s, debate shifted to business decline and Britain's loss of relative market share. Yet, in military terms, after World War I Britain had more trained troops and more extensive stocks of materiel than any other state.[5] The Royal Navy possessed more battleships, cruisers, and destroyers than any other navy and was the strongest it had ever been.[6] Britain had clear advantages in intangible sources of power such as intelligence capabilities and continued to play a central role in the global commercial, banking, and financial infrastructure.

Between 1870 and 1900, Britain's gross national product and national per capita income were rising.[7] Although the economy was growing in absolute terms, by the late nineteenth century Britain was also experiencing *relative* economic and industrial decline. "Its share of world trade was 23.2 per cent in 1880 and 14.1 per cent just over thirty years later. In 1880 it could boast 22.9 per cent of total world manufacturing output; in 1913 only 13.6 per cent."[8] In terms of productivity growth, Britain's less-than-spectacular performance in the twentieth century can partly be explained by a relatively high level of productivity in the late nineteenth century.[9] Still, by the 1890s, the United States had overtaken Britain in aggregate GDP per person, and U.S. labor productivity in manufacturing was roughly twice Britain's.[10]

Paul Kennedy writes,

> In retrospect one can assert, "From 1870 to 1970 the history of Britain was one of steady and almost unbroken decline, economically, militarily and politically, relative to other nations, from the peak of prosperity and power which her industrial revolution had achieved for her in the middle of the nineteenth century"; but there is also a danger of exaggerating and anticipating the pace of that decline and of ignoring the country's very considerable assets.[11]

The Continental giants that had posed threats to Britain in the past were weak and recovering. The United States showed signs of a return to isolationism, while Britain remained an economic and military power to be reckoned with. Still, the British knew they had been overtaken industrially by the United States and Germany, that they could not defend imperial commitments, and that they faced increasingly "intense competition in commercial, colonial, and maritime spheres."[12] The British had already scaled back their presence in the Far East by forging a defensive alliance with Japan in 1902. Although they gained territory as a result of Germany's defeat in the First World War, they recognized the mismatch between their capabilities and commitments. Sir Henry Wilson, chief of the Imperial General Staff, expressed to the cabinet in June 1920, "I cannot too strongly press on the Government the danger, the extreme danger, of his Majesty's Army being spread all over the world, strong nowhere, weak everywhere, and with no reserve to save a dangerous situation or avert a coming danger."[13] Although some claim financial stringency and adoption of the 1919 Ten Year Rule were signs of British confidence in their international position,[14] the emphasis on economic strengthening dominated all other strategic considerations because the British knew they must shore up their economy to maintain their international position.

Despite weakness of the Continental powers and America's postwar diplomatic retreat from Europe, we can safely code Britain as a declining power in relative terms. Britain should have tried to arrest further decline by adapting as Hypothesis P2 predicts. Britain had not declined far enough that we would expect them to exploit the strategic pause to reform and reconstitute as Hypothesis P3 predicts.[15] The nature of complexity is relevant, but Britain faced countervailing pressures. As a defensively advantaged state vis-à-vis other great power contenders, Britain could opt to transform for the long term, a choice consistent with a strategy of reforming and reconstituting as Hypothesis B1 predicts. But defensively advantaged states are also prone to neglect innovation, as Hypothesis B3 predicts, because they lack the urgency that persistent border pressure creates. Low border pressure allows a state to adopt a wait-and-see approach and adapt incrementally or to exploit windows of opportunity by investing to improve future competitiveness and relative position. We may see reductions in defense effort and little innovation or investment in new capabilities because the state has the luxury to focus on the future.

Innovation becomes a more attractive path when leaders can identify a strategic focus. For an imperial power with extensive global interests, no strategic focal point existed. Hypothesis E1 predicts that states with global interests and commitments will face a large number and wide variety of security challenges as well as more near-term security demands. In a resource-constrained environment, resourcing for near-term demands invariably comes at the expense of preparing for the future. The high number and high diversity of threats the British faced created pressures to respond to near-term problems. This prevented the British exploiting a strategic pause in great power rivalry and a window of opportunity offered by newly emerging technologies to transform for the long term. We should expect to see evidence that the British adapted: by adopting a fast-follower strategy toward military innovation; by reacting to new strategic conditions as they arose; and by trying to minimize near-term risk rather than maximize long-run advantage. The evidence shows adaptation in military terms, coupled with reduced defense effort overall—a weak combination for deterring and defending against future strategic challenges. Cuts in defense spending meant that any available resources would be channeled to near-term requirements.[16]

The United States possessed immense resources relative to the devastated powers of the day. Rising powers like the United States have an incentive to pursue a shaping strategy, as predicted by Hypothesis P1, to maximize influence and control of the environment. The United States was also defensively advantaged. According to Hypothesis B1, defensively advantaged states face fewer threats and so should be able to exploit periods of strategic pause and rapid technological change to shape their environment to compete more effectively in the future. Hypothesis B3 cautions, however, that defensively advantaged states might logically neglect innovation because they lack the urgency that defensively disadvantaged states possess. Once again, low border pressure allows a state to strategically relax, reduce defense spending, and neglect innovation. It also allows a state to exploit windows of opportunity to maximize long-run advantage. The British had global interests and so lacked a strategic focus, but the United States was an emerging great power that faced few strategic challengers. The most prominent was Japan, whose designs in the Pacific could curtail America's regional aspirations. The United States faced a less diverse, although still uncertain, security environment. Rapid changes in technology introduced great uncertainty, as interwar debates within the United States show, but the number and diversity of threats were less for the United States than for Great Britain. A high number and high diversity of threats facing a declining Britain produced adaptation in response to near-term demands, while the low number and low diversity of threats facing a rising United States supported a strategic response of shaping. The United States had more latitude to exploit the strategic pause in great power rivalry and a window of opportunity offered by newly emerging technologies to prepare itself to compete for influence in the future.

The case studies that follow describe how British and U.S. leaders understood their security environments and analyze the strategic choices they made. The chapter evaluates the extent to which the evidence supports predictions based on relative power and complexity and the extent of support for predictions based on nonstructural variables like domestic politics, organizational interests, and cognitive constraints of individuals operating under uncertainty.

GREAT BRITAIN

The Security Environment

In the aftermath of World War I, the British confronted no overriding or imminent threat although they did foresee potential long-term strategic problems with each of the great powers—Russia, Germany, France, the United States, and Japan—as well as with various combinations of powers—Russo-German-Japanese or Russo-German-Turkish.[17] There was wide-ranging opinion over how to manage the balance of power in Europe given potential threats to postwar stability from Germany, Russia, and France. France might establish hegemony in Europe, but Germany and Russia could unite to overthrow the order. There was also debate over whether American or Japanese policies were more inimical to Britain's Far Eastern interests. Japan might threaten Britain's Far Eastern Dominions, but the United States seemed bent on achieving maritime supremacy.

Each of these great power threat scenarios was in the distant future. Europe was hardly quiescent after the armistice as Russia plunged into civil war and revolution; the newly emancipated countries of Eastern Europe clashed over disputed boundaries; and Greeks fought Turks. British civilian leaders nevertheless judged the nation's interests in Europe to be secure, certainly by comparison to the challenges to imperial authority they faced in India, Afghanistan, Mesopotamia, Palestine, and China,[18] places where Russia posed the greatest threat.[19]

With the Continental giants weakened from war, the center of gravity for security shifted to India and the Middle East, where a series of upheavals occurred between 1918 and 1923. The British had extended commitments to Persia, Mesopotamia, and Palestine to curtail Soviet and German involvement. By June 1921, they had withdrawn from Persia. In March 1921, Mesopotamia (soon to be Iraq) was handed over to King Faisal, although Britain retained responsibility for internal order. Palestine continued to pose a heavy burden, while internal upheavals and frontier disputes in India demanded continued engagement. In 1922, Turkish nationalist forces threatened to invade Chanak on the Asiatic shore of the Dardanelles, seize Constantinople, and deprive Britain use of the straits.[20] In what has been called the gravest military test of the 1920s, the Chanak crisis revealed Britain's inability to fulfill major imperial policing requirements and to count on the unquestioned cooperation of the Dominions. The British also faced violent nationalist forces in Ireland.

In the eyes of an influential group of British policy makers and strategists,[21] imperial security was Britain's biggest strategic problem and the group "was not likely to give to the European theatre any larger priority than it could help."[22] Confronted with a range of lesser strategic contingencies on the heels of the armistice, on February 17, 1922, the British cabinet assumed,

> We need not now contemplate fighting a European enemy equipped with all the latest mechanical appliances for war. We should now visualize a situation in which we might have to fight Indians and Arabs. This involved military operations of a very different class.[23]

A consensus developed that Britain should be planning for small wars, peacekeeping operations, and policing duties rather than for a great power war against a technologically sophisticated adversary.[24] Army modernization suffered most because the service was ordered not to prepare for great power war. The Royal Air Force fared better once it made the case for "substitution of mechanical devices for manpower in Imperial policing."[25] The Royal Navy fared best because its strength was judged against the U.S. Navy.

Britain was experiencing relative economic decline yet had expanded its imperial concessions and responsibilities with the collapse of the Ottoman Empire. It faced severe budget problems at a time when cutting social policy expenditures was tantamount to political suicide.[26] Competing visions of the future great power threat coexisted with immediate demands for imperial policing. Recognizing the need to lower defense expenditures, British leaders chose to minimize short-term risks and respond to near-term threats to imperial security rather than maximize long-run gains against a hypothetical future great power threat. They adopted a strategic posture of adapting based on a belief that the country possessed the military stocks, economic strength, and organizational capacity to respond to any great power threat with sufficient warning.

Strategic Responses

The proportion of national resources devoted to defense and how defense resources are allocated provide a window into how British leaders understood their security environment between the wars. The British cut defense effort, which was reflected in expenditures and manpower levels.

Total military expenditure as a percentage of government expenditure less debt servicing (Table 4.1, column H) shows a significant drop in the level of defense effort in postmobilization years (1923 onward) from the levels of defense effort sustained before World War I.[27] Prior to the war, defense expenditure averaged about 44 percent of government expenditure. From 1923 until 1938, it averaged 23 percent, hitting a low point of 18.7 percent in 1933. Total military expenditure as a percentage of GDP (Table 4.1, column J) shows defense effort averaging 2.7 percent of GDP, a level remarkably similar to the period of "profound peace" in the 1890s when no real war with another great power was likely.[28]

Gross spending figures however are not adjusted for inflation. Post–World War I inflation distorted relative prices to such an extent that spending levels are virtually meaningless. Comparing spending figures before World War I with those after the war can be misleading, although leverage can be gained by examining defense spending from 1921 onward.

A crude alternative data set is manpower levels. The skill sets before World War I were quite similar to those after the war, so it makes sense to compare prewar and postwar manpower levels. Prior to World War I, manpower levels

Table 4.1. Great Britain's defense spending, 1910–1939 (in millions of pounds).

Years	A Total government expenditure	B Debt servicing	C Government expenditure less debt servicing	D Army expenditures	E Navy expenditures	F Air force expenditures	G Total military expenditures (army + navy + air force)	H Total military expenditures as a percentage of column C	I GDP	J Defense expenditure as % of GDP
1910	156.9	20.8	136.1	27.2	35.8	-	63	46.29	2,043.00	3.08
1911	167.9	20.4	147.5	27.4	40.4	-	67.8	45.97	2,128.00	3.19
1912	174.1	20.1	154	27.6	42.9	-	70.5	45.78	2,242.00	3.14
1913	184	19.9	164.1	28.1	44.4	-	72.5	44.18	2,322.00	3.12
1914	192.3	19.3	173	28.3	48.8	-	77.1	44.57	2,347.00	3.29
1915	559.5	21.7	537.8	28.9	51.6	-	80.5	14.97	2,676.00	3.01
1916	1,559.20	60.2	1,499	-	-	-	-	0.00	3,176.00	0.00
1917	2,198.10	127.3	2,070.8	-	-	-	-	0.00	3,951.00	0.00
1918	2,696.10	189.9	2,506.2	-	-	-	-	0.00	4,770.00	0.00
1919	2,579.30	270	2,309.3	-	-	-	-	0.00	4,992.00	0.00
1920	1,665.80	332	1,333.8	395	156.5	52.5	604	45.28	5,688.00	10.62
1921	1,188.10	342.3	845.8	181.5	88.4	22.3	292.2	34.55	4,601.00	6.35
1922	1,070.10	323.2	746.9	95.1	80.8	13.6	189.5	25.37	4,027.00	4.71
1923	812.50	324	488.5	45.4	56.2	9.4	111	22.72	3,830.00	2.90
1924	748.80	307.3	441.5	43.6	52.6	9.6	105.8	23.96	3,960.00	2.67
1925	750.80	312.2	438.6	44.8	55.6	14.3	114.7	26.15	4,242.00	2.70
1926	776.10	308.2	467.9	44.3	59.7	15.5	119.5	25.54	4,030.00	2.97
1927	782.40	318.6	463.8	43.6	57.6	15.5	116.7	25.16	4,262.00	2.74

(Continued)

Table 4.1. Great Britain's defense spending, 1910–1939 (in millions of pounds). (*Continued*)

Years	A Total government expenditure	B Debt servicing	C Government expenditure less debt servicing	D Army expenditures	E Navy expenditures	F Air force expenditures	G Total military expenditures (army + navy + air force)	H Total military expenditures as a percentage of column C	I GDP	J Defense expenditure as % of GDP
1928	773.60	313.8	459.8	44.2	58.1	15.2	117.5	25.55	4,280.00	2.75
1929	760.50	311.5	449	40.5	56.9	16.1	113.5	25.28	4,420.00	2.57
1930	781.70	307.3	474.4	40.5	55.8	16.8	113.1	23.84	4,356.00	2.60
1931	814.20	293.2	521	40.5	52.6	17.8	110.9	21.29	3,948.00	2.81
1932	818.60	289.5	529.1	38.5	51.1	17.7	107.3	20.28	3,833.00	2.80
1933	833.00	282.2	550.8	35.9	50	17.1	103	18.70	3,933.00	2.62
1934	770.50	216.3	554.2	37.6	53.5	16.8	107.9	19.47	4,192.00	2.57
1935	784.70	211.7	573	39.7	56.6	17.6	113.9	19.88	4,376.00	2.60
1936	829.40	211.5	617.9	44.6	64.8	27.5	136.9	22.16	4,625.00	2.96
1937	889.10	210.9	678.2	54.8	81.1	50.1	186	27.43	4,913.00	3.79
1938	909.30	216.2	693.1	77.9	102	82.3	262.2	37.83	5,124.00	5.12
1939	1,005.70	218.7	787	121.4	127.3	133.8	382.5	48.60	5,297.00	7.22

SOURCES:
1. "Statistical Abstract for the United Kingdom for each of the fifteen years from 1911 to 1925" (1927). V.70. London: Great Britain Board of Trade.
2. "Statistical Abstract for the United Kingdom for each of the fifteen years from 1913 and 1918 to 1931" (1930). V.76. London
3. "Statistical Abstract for the United Kingdom for each of the fifteen years from 1913 and 1924 to 1937" (1966; Reprinted). V.82. London
4. "Annual Abstract of Statistics, 1935–1946" (1970; Reprinted). V. 84. Kraus Reprint (Central Statistical Office)
5. Feinstein, C. H. 1972. *National Income, Expenditure and Output of the United Kingdom, 1855–1965*. Cambridge, UK: Cambridge University Press
6. Mitchell, B. R., Deane, Phyllis. 1971. *Abstract of British Historical Statistics*. Cambridge, UK: Cambridge University Press

of the Royal Navy and Royal Marines averaged around 130,000 (Table 4.2). After 1921, they dropped almost 25 percent, bottoming out in 1933 at 89,773. The regimental strength of the regular army stood at six to eight divisions, or approximately 250,000, before World War I (Table 4.3). After demobilization, army strength stabilized at about 205,000 until 1927 and thereafter at 195,000. At its lowest level in 1930, army strength dropped to 188,460. The decline in manpower levels by the late 1920s no doubt reflected the financial crisis that was facing the British government.

Table 4.2. Great Britain's naval manpower, 1912–1938.

	Personnel				
Years	Officers, men, and boys serving in Royal Navy	Royal Marines (ashore and afloat)	Coast Guard	Other divisions	Total numbers borne
1912	113,512	17,165	3,038	—	133,715
1913	118,569	17,817	3,038	—	139,424
1914	173,419	24,840	1,910	848	201,017
1915	197,815	26,086	2,455	24,776	251,132
1916	251,748	30,099	2,781	43,519	328,147
1917	283,000	30,517	2,986	52,045	368,548
1918	335,370	37,290	4,281	30,375	407,316
1919	220,281	29,920	3,087	14,823	268,111
1920	113,335	16,547	3,210	6	133,098
1921	105,022	15,107	3,206	—	123,335
1922	104,649	13,622	2,969	—	121,240
1923	90,090	9,899	2,180	43	102,212
1924	89,128	9,936	—	262	99,326
1925	89,529	10,288	—	287	100,104
1926	89,850	10,463	—	312	100,625
1927	90,764	10,774	—	383	101,921
1928	91,096	10,511	—	405	102,012
1929	89,506	10,147	—	415	100,068
1930	86,841	10,002	—	453	97,296
1931	83,898	9,707	—	442	94,047

SOURCES: For years 1911–1918:
"Statistical Abstract for the United Kingdom for each of the fifteen years from 1911 to 1925" (published in 1927; No. 70) (See *Pp. 102–103, Table No. 84. – Number of Officers, Men and Boys borne on the Books of His Majesty's Ships, at the Royal Marine Divisions*).

(Continued)

88 INTER-WORLD WAR PERIOD, 1918–1939

Table 4.2. Great Britain's naval manpower, 1912–1938. *(Continued)*

	Personnel				
Years	Officers, men, and boys serving in Royal Navy	Royal Marines (ashore and afloat)	Coast Guard	Other divisions	Total numbers borne
1932	81,498	9,637	—	556	91,691
1933	79,876	9,338	—	559	89,773
1934	81,021	9,274	—	809	91,104
1935	82,529	9,398	—	382	92,809
1936	87,350	9,962	—	889	98,201
1937	91,615	10,270	—	890	102,776
1938	100,870	10,940	—	868	112,678

SOURCES: For years 1919–1939:
"Statistical Abstract for the United Kingdom for each of the fifteen years 1913 and 1918 to 1931" (published in 1933; No. 76: 1913 and 1918–1931) (See *Pp. 126–127, Table No. 103. – Number of Officers, Men and Boys Borne on the Books of His Majesty's Ships, at the Royal Marine Divisions*; tables adapted; numbers as of March of each year) London: Great Britain Board of Trade.
"Statistical Abstract for the United Kingdom" (Reprinted in 1966 by Kraus Reprint LTD; No 82: 1913 and 1924–1937) (*P. 166, Table No. 141. – Number of Officers, Men and Boys Borne on the Books of His Majesty's Ships, at the Royal Marine Divisions*); London: Great Britain Board of Trade.

Several caveats must be made when examining manpower levels of the navy and army. First, in 1921 the Royal Air Force (RAF) was created, and all aviators from the navy and army were transferred to the RAF. So part of the decline in numbers could reflect loss of aviators. (See Table 4.4.) Still, even when RAF numbers are included (Table 4.5) there is a noticeable decline in total numbers, which averaged 387,000 before the war and steadily dropped after demobilization to bottom out at about 325,000 in 1933.

Second, the numbers do not reflect British troop levels in India. Data for British troop levels in the Indian Army are not available after 1920, but they averaged 74,000 before the war and had already dropped to 60,000 by 1920 (Table 4.6). It is conceivable that some British postings abroad were redefined as Indian postings, but this only suggests a further reduction in British defense effort.

By 1925, with the "triumph of Treasury control," in John Ferris's words, economic strength came to be seen as the most critical element of national power to the detriment of the strength of the armed forces. The Foreign Office

> ... defined Britain as a status quo power and supported the Treasury's views on the role of finance in strategic policy. Although Britain needed armed

Table 4.3. Great Britain's army manpower, 1911–1937

Years	Cavalry	Royal artillery	Royal engineers	Infantry	Royal army service corps	Colonial corps	Indian native troops borrowed	Other arms	All arms
1911	21,288	49,785	9,648	149,656	6,748	3,977	4,833	8,374	254,309
1912	21,098	48,508	9,661	148,322	6,504	3,876	7,054	8,739	253,762
1913	19,990	47,533	10,013	143,232	6,505	3,825	7,069	9,083	247,250
1914	92,745	174,976	36,201	926,750	34,358	3,915	7,063	51,364	1,327,372
1915	120,220	352,944	150,126	1,492,111	173,032	3,983	5,343	177,105	2,475,764
1916	130,310	470,227	220,022	1,932,176	265,024	4,073	5,994	306,971	3,343,797
1917	104,357	527,638	336,062	1,888,835	313,434	4,212	3,877	704,602	3,883,017
1918	78,075	537,474	359,964	1,737,497	326,770	18,363	1,375	778,747	3,838,265
1919	27,695	123,012	94,269	516,251	86,479	4,830	1,347	210,080	1,064,743
1920	17,676	45,013	17,638	159,381	20,478	10,071	131,880[a]	32,588	434,725
1921	16,412	40,804	10,140	134,706	17,336	6,388	42,467	28,645	296,948
1922	13,661	37,292	8,798	117,628	10,950	2,344	1,684	25,130	217,477
1923	12,530	34,277	7,871	115,360	8,740	2,523	1,497	22,297	205,095
1924	13,186	35,227	7,676	118,278	7,258	2,305	724	22,498	207,152
1925	13,304	34,781	7,442	121,551	6,736	2,292	886	22,399	209,391

[a] Troops of the Indian Army borrowed from India and employed on garrison duties in China, Singapore, and so on.

SOURCE: P. 128, Table No. 105—*Regimental Strength of the Regular Army, by Arms, All Ranks, on 1st October in each year* (in the 1933 publication) *Statistical Abstract for the United Kingdom for each of the fifteen years 1913 and 1918 to 1931* (published in 1933. London: Great Britain Board of Trade.

(Continued)

Table 4.3. Great Britain's army manpower, 1911–1937 (Continued)

Years	Cavalry	Royal artillery	Royal engineers	Infantry	Royal army service corps	Colonial corps	Indian native troops borrowed	Other arms	All arms
1926	12,579	34,666	6,902	120,719	6,536	2,343	895	21,118	205,758
1927	12,137	33,294	6,769	121,216	6,625	2,263	2,831	20,781	205,916
1928	11,553	33,317	6,770	118,270	5,766	1,152	954	22,036	197,818
1929	11,899	33,273	6,521	113,480	5,408	1,136	885	21,424	194,026
1930	11,558	33,506	6,348	109,002	4,957	1,099	902	21,088	188,460
1931	11,928	32,309	6,172	113,043	5,287	1,228	919	22,053	192,939
1932	11,749	32,522	6,280	112,994	5,472	1,169	943	21,548	192,677
1933	11,380	31,961	6,446	116,228	5,463	1,222	972	21,584	195,256
1934	11,405	32,230	6,667	116,698	5,457	1,152	964	21,262	195,845
1935	11,382	33,098	7,258	114,993	5,552	1,375	1,110	21,369	196,137
1936	10,917	32,441	7,815	110,627	6,209	1,449	1,115	21,752	192,325
1937	10,325	31,636	7,939	107,758	6,675	1,781	942	23,774	190,830

Table 4.4. Great Britain's Royal Air Force numbers, 1920–1939.

Years	RAF (thousands)	RAF reserves	All RAF	Years	RAF (thousands)	RAF reserves	All RAF
1920	27,664	4,865	32,529	1930	32,989	11,892	44,881
1921	27,528	5,682	33,210	1931	32,469	11,390	43,859
1922	29,502	6,492	35,994	1932	32,287	10,120	42,407
1923	29,883	5,041	34,924	1933	31,202	8,763	39,965
1924	31,429	6,782	38,211	1934	30,500	9,124	39,624
1925	32,642	6,927	39,569	1935	32,145	10,058	42,203
1926	34,015	7,174	41,189	1936	45,804	9,927	55,731
1927	30,035	10,249	40,284	1937	56,163	11,348	67,511
1928	30,467	12,045	42,512	1938	69,500	17,000	86,500
1929	31,070	12,621	43,691	1939	112,500	55,700	168,200

SOURCES:
1. "Statistical Abstract for the United Kingdom for each of the fifteen years from 1911 to 1925" (1927). V.70. London: Great Britain Board of Trade.
2. "Statistical Abstract for the United Kingdom for each of the fifteen years from 1913 and 1918 to 1931" (1930). V.76. London: Great Britain Board of Trade.
3. "Statistical Abstract for the United Kingdom for each of the fifteen years from 1913 and 1924 to 1937" (1966; Reprinted). V.82. London: Great Britain Board of Trade.
4. "Annual Abstract of Statistics, 1935–1946" (1970; Reprinted). V. 84. Kraus Reprint (Central Statistical Office). London: Great Britain Board of Trade.

forces to speak "with authority," their cost might hamper the economy, the basic element in British strength. Without our trade and finance, we sink to the level of a third-class Power.[29]

With an economy severely damaged by war and a shortage of investment funds, but ample stocks of defense materiel, devoting scarce resources to defense, the British believed, would leave them in too precarious a position when real dangers arose. British governments "consistently subordinated service policies to social, financial and diplomatic considerations; they deferred programmes for Britain's security until threats actually became imminent."[30]

Churchill dominated the formulation of British service policies in 1922. He wanted the minimum necessary for deterrence and imperial policing and a nucleus for expansion. The Churchill Committee called for maintenance of the essential elements of the fighting services to ensure national security, reduction in the peacetime defense establishment and reconstitution after a rupture of relations with another power, and adequate provision for research and development.[31] Convinced that peace existed, that it would be the state

Table 4.5. Great Britain's military manpower totals, 1912–1939.

Years	All navy	All army	All RAF	Total
1912	133,715	253,762		387,477
1913	139,424	247,250		386,674
1914	201,017	1,327,372		1,327,573
1915	251,132	2,475,764		2,726,896
1916	328,147	3,343,797		3,671,944
1917	368,548	3,883,017		4,251,565
1918	407,316	3,838,265		4,245,581
1919	268,111	1,064,743		1,332,854
1920	133,098	434,725	32,529	600,352
1921	123,335	296,948	33,210	453,493
1922	121,240	217,477	35,994	374,711
1923	102,212	205,095	34,924	342,231
1924	99,326	207,152	38,211	344,689
1925	100,104	209,391	39,569	349,064
1926	100,625	205,758	41,189	347,572
1927	101,921	205,916	40,284	348,121
1928	102,012	197,818	42,512	342,342
1929	100,068	194,026	43,691	337,785
1930	97,296	188,460	44,881	330,637
1931	94,047	192,939	43,859	330,845
1932	91,691	192,677	42,407	326,775
1933	89,773	195,256	39,965	324,994
1934	91,104	195,845	39,624	326,573
1935	92,809	196,137	42,203	331,149
1936	98,201	192,325	55,731	346,257
1937	102,776	190,830	67,511	361,117
1938			86,500	
1939			168,200	

of affairs for the foreseeable future, and that there would be plenty of warning time to reconstitute, the British took a strategic gamble. They cut service spending to assist economic growth, hoping to sustain security on the cheap.

The performance of British armored forces against the Italians in the desert in 1940 suggests "that the lack of resources in the 1930s is not the only explanation for operational and tactical weaknesses."[32] Treasury policy in the

Table 4.6. Strength of the Indian army, 1910–1921.

Years	Total army	British infantry	British other	British total	Indian total
1910	205,933	53,205	21,454	74,659	131,274
1911	205,837	53,735	20,889	74,624	131,213
1912	205,875	52,733	20,910	73,643	132,232
1913	204,890	53,057	20,321	73,378	131,512
1914	200,649	53,746	21,829	75,575	125,074
1915					119,985
1916					139,976
1917					191,242
1918					341,458
1919					229,713
1920		37,425	23,187	60,612	
1921					440,351

SOURCES: *Statistical Abstract Relating to British India. From 1903–04 to 1912–13*. Forty-eighth number (London: His Majesty's Stationary Office, 1915); *Statistical Abstract Relating to British India. From 1910–11 to 1919–1920*. Fifty-fifth number (London: His Majesty's Stationary Office, 1922)

1920s is overmaligned to the extent that it has shouldered nearly all the blame for British performance in the early days of World War II, yet financial stringency did not prevent planning for the conversion of industry and personnel to military purposes[33] or for the acquisition and stockpiling of vital raw materials, preparations that "played a major role in the speed with which British industry caught up and surpassed German production for such critical weapon systems as fighter aircraft early in the war."[34] David Edgerton challenges the reigning historical consensus that Britain had retrenched severely by 1932, arguing the British spent nearly as much as any other country on warfare in the 1920s and 1930s and possessed the strongest navy and air force in the world.[35] Of critical importance during periods of uncertainty are decisions about *how* to allocate scarce defense resources and what types of contingencies to plan for, another aspect of the military domain of strategy.

Military policy can be conceived to vary along two dimensions: the allocation of defense resources between near-term readiness and long-term modernization, and the related dimension of innovation-adaptation. In critical ways, the British focused on near-term contingencies at the expense of long-term transformation to meet unanticipated threats in the future.

The emphasis on planning for the near term is clearest in the British cabinet's 1919 directive that the services draw up their annual budgets with the assumption that "the British Empire will not be engaged in any great war during the next ten years." The Ten Year Rule explicitly instructed the War Office not to prepare for the contingency of a major Continental war. From 1920 until 1925, the services either ignored the Ten Year Rule or used it to support their building programs by interpreting it to mean they must be prepared for war *by* 1929. The services were able to rearm in support of diplomatic policies against the French, Americans, and Japanese up until 1925 when the Treasury finally succeeded in using the Ten Year Rule to control service spending.[36]

The Ten Year Rule was not "an essay in prophecy, but a working hypothesis intended to relieve the Chiefs of Staff from the responsibility of preparing against contingencies which the Government believed to be either remote or beyond the financial capacity of the country to provide against."[37] Consistent with government directives, the chiefs of staff in their First Annual Review of imperial defense policy in 1926 stated their assumptions for sizing and structuring the armed forces: to meet the requirements of imperial security, not those of a general war in Europe.

The other 1919 principles—that the Royal Navy should not build against the American navy, that imperial policing should be the primary mission of the services, and that all efforts should be made to substitute technology for manpower—were more influential than the Ten Year Rule in shaping strategic policy. The principles assigned a preeminent role to imperial policing and imperial security. "The principle functions of the Military and Air Forces is [sic] to provide garrisons for India, Egypt, the new mandated territory and all territory (other than self-governing) under British control, as well as to provide the necessary support to the civil power at home."[38] The underlying assumption was that Britain would not be threatened for many years and only after a lengthy warning period. The challenge in the Treasury's view was to balance risks and the financial risks facing Britain dwarfed all others.

After World War I, the British army quickly demobilized and "plunged without a break into world-wide garrison, occupation and police duties."[39] In contrast to the prewar army, which was assigned two roles—imperial policing and insurance against major threats—the postwar army was forbidden by the 1919 principles to prepare forces for major wars.[40] Frederick Lambart, Commander of the Imperial General Staff from 1922 to 1926, reasoned in a memo to the chiefs of staff in 1924:

> Under existing world conditions we require no plans of campaign (except for small wars incidental to our Imperial position) . . . We must concentrate on Imperial defence. There is no need to try and justify our existence by wasting our time and energies in the compilation of elaborate plans for war against hypothetical enemies.[41]

Without a mission in Europe, the army's focus became imperial defense.

Planning for imperial defense was complex and required different organization, equipment, and training than a Continental conflict against a great power adversary. The army's 1934 edition of *Training Regulations* described the challenge of planning for the diverse operational environments the army faced:

> In a world-wide Empire the Army may be called upon to fight in developed or underdeveloped countries, and under every condition of climate and ground. In India, and in certain of the other parts of the Empire, the garrisons are faced with specific military problems, but, broadly speaking, there is no single predominant objective towards which the training of the Army can be categorically directed.[42]

Most of the immediate postwar emergencies had died down by 1923, leaving the British Army in India as the largest commitment. Given that the traditional problem of the North West Frontier dominated military thinking in India, Major B. C. Dening, an advocate of army reform, lamented in 1928,

> We thus have a situation in which the greater portion of the British Army is regulated by the conditions prevailing on a portion of one of the frontiers of one of the Empire's constituent parts.[43]

The defense of India created serious obstacles to the army's ability to modernize for several reasons. First, the Indian Army was a backwater in ideas and equipment. Imperial policing and peacekeeping in India did not require mechanized forces, and the majority of senior officers there were loathe to substitute machines for infantry and cavalry. Second, internal security measures required breaking up battalions into small detachments, which inhibited training for combat. This all "complicated the process of mechanization; militated against the creation of an Expeditionary Force in peacetime; and prevented a radical redistribution of imperial garrisons in response to changing strategic conditions."[44] Third, defense of India reinforced the Cardwell system and the army force structure on which the system was based. The Cardwell system linked battalions at home and abroad to maintain a regular flow of replacements and reliefs, so training and equipment at home could not vary too much from that overseas. Under the Cardwell system, the army's role and equipment was shackled to problems of internal security and frontier warfare. It was impossible to modernize (that is, mechanize) the army at home and have it be interchangeable with units of an unmechanized army in India or to devote more resources to armored and mechanized forces.[45]

Army leaders were not reactionary intellectuals, unable to understand the capabilities of armored forces. They judged correctly that "aircraft and mechanized forces alone could not surmount widespread colonial disorders" that Britain faced.[46] Military intellectuals remained preoccupied with conventional European warfare,[47] but no resources were allocated to that contingency. Failure to secure an Anglo–American guarantee of French security removed any possible incentive to maintain a Continental capability. As late as 1937, the Cabinet continued to define the army's roles as imperial defense and home defense against air attack.[48]

At sea, the Admiralty wanted an ambitious naval policy to prevent U.S. maritime supremacy and any dependence on the United States. The Royal Navy's building programs were approved but only temporarily to support a diplomatic agenda vis-à-vis Japan and the United States. Growing financial pressure reigned in the Admiralty. In addition, a larger proportion of a smaller pool of resources was shifted to the new procurement-intensive RAF at the expense of naval procurement and the naval industrial complex.

Britain nevertheless remained a great naval power.[49] In 1935, the British had the same number of battleships as the Americans, and all fifteen were refitted in the 1930s. They possessed more aircraft carriers than any other navy, although fewer aircraft.[50] The Royal Navy was also a technical leader in electronic technology. But in key respects the British left it to the Americans and Japanese to set the pace of innovation.[51] Although the Royal Navy was the most advanced in carrier design and development at the end of World War I, the first to assign aircraft to ships on a regular basis, and the inventors of the aircraft carrier, it lost that lead in the interwar years. Compared to the U.S. Navy's visionary program to produce 1,000 naval aircraft by 1931, Admiralty plans were modest. The Royal Navy also privileged readiness with the average squadron spending eighty days per year at sea. Fuel bills suggest the U.S. Navy sustained a much lower level of readiness, an indicator of the relative importance placed on near-term versus future requirements.[52]

Although relatively complacent in carrier innovation when compared to their American and Japanese counterparts, the impact of air power on land dramatically harmed Britain's strategic situation. For the first time since Napoleon, the British Isles were vulnerable to direct attack. The British had never regarded European battle as the final arbiter of fate, but air power altered that calculus. Between 1924 and 1932, RAF procurement expenditure increased while naval and army procurement expenditures fell. Twenty different types of aircraft were ordered in numbers greater than one hundred, dispelling the myth that the RAF failed to reequip between the world wars.[53] The British aircraft industry became a major exporter of military aircraft and remained large in comparison to those of Germany and France, although not when compared to the United States.

Debate on Britain's relative decline continues, with revisionists mounting convincing evidence to challenge the view that defense forces and defense industries fell to dangerously low levels by 1932. Nevertheless, innovation is as much if not more about how weapon systems are used as it is about the acquisition of hardware. There is little dispute that the British fell behind in applying the new technologies of warfare on land and at sea.

As a declining power, the goal of Britain's diplomatic strategy was to preserve the nation's strategic position and maintain the status quo. Various options were considered, including a security guarantee for France, an entente with the United States, disarmament conferences, and strategic isolation. A preference for flexibility, wide latitude, and few entangling commitments reflected uncertainty about allies in both Europe and the Pacific. Illustrative of this uncertainty over allies, in 1922 the British had approved or were on the verge of approving military programs against nearly all their former allies: battleships against the United States, the Home Defense Air Force (HDAF) against France, and the Singapore base against Japan. The British debated whether diplomatic commitments to France and Japan would strengthen or undermine their power and position.[54] Even internationally minded statesmen viewed the post-1919 international scene with "caution and noncommitment" lest a diplomatic guarantee jeopardize imperial unity among self-governing dominions that were pressing for greater independence.[55] Maximizing flexibility may make sense given diverse and competing requirements but also precludes the use of diplomacy to reduce the range of threats for which one must prepare militarily.

In Europe, the British hoped to use their diplomatic leverage to reduce the mutual animosity between France and Germany, to persuade the French to curtail military programs (submarines and air power) and entangling commitments in Eastern Europe that could draw France into war, and to accommodate

Germany's moderate demands to revise the Versailles Treaty. Up until 1925, arguments were marshaled both for and against an alliance with France, but the British ultimately would not commit without a U.S. guarantee.[56] Those opposed to an alliance feared being drawn into a European war, freezing an unsatisfactory status quo, emboldening the French to pursue more aggressive and provocative policies, and, in the end, securing very little diplomatic leverage in return. Those supporting even a limited commitment saw it as the only way to persuade the French to alter their alliance strategy in the east and prevent the Germans from overthrowing the European order. Revealing of Britain's diplomatic preferences, Germany's offer to France and Britain of a nonaggression pact based on binding arbitration, though absent an enforcement mechanism, was all the British needed to retreat from any type of commitment to French security. "The CID, believing that Britain could gain its aims without a specific commitment to France, thus reconsidered the dangers of any commitments at all."[57]

The Locarno guarantees were Britain's most specific commitment to European security.[58] Twelve ministers debated a variety of European security guarantees in 1925—formal alliance with France, mutual security guarantees, mere pledges of assistance, regional security pacts for specific emergencies, nonaggression treaties, and commitments under the auspices of the League. In the end, the Locarno Pact established nonaggression treaties among France, Belgium, and Germany, with Britain agreeing to defend any signatory attacked by any other. In theory, the British assumed very precise military obligations in Europe: to guarantee the German–Belgian and German–French frontiers against aggression from either side and to maintain the demilitarization of the Rhineland. But military leaders never developed any plans for implementing the guarantees.[59] No military forces were devoted to the mission; nor did the British engage in joint planning for combined operations with allies.[60] "Britain retained wide latitude for deciding when and how to act and accepted this commitment in the expectation that it would never have to be honoured."[61]

The result is not surprising given the strategic priorities expressed by the chiefs of staff in 1926. Their assumptions for sizing and structuring the armed forces were to meet the requirements of imperial security, not a general war in Europe:

> Though the Expeditionary Force, together with a limited number of Air Force Squadrons, constitute the only military instrument available for immediate

use in Europe or elsewhere outside Imperial territory in support of foreign policy, they are so available only when the requirements of Imperial Defense permit. It follows that so far as commitments on the Continent are concerned, the Services can only take note of them.[62]

In the end, the Locarno obligations were undertaken in the belief that the treaties themselves demonstrated that Europe had become more stable, and the British never designed the forces or plans to meet their Locarno obligations. The chiefs of staff remarked in their 1930 annual review, "This country is in a less favorable position to fulfil the Locarno guarantees than it was, without any written guarantee, to come to the assistance of France and Belgium in 1914."[63]

In the Pacific, the British weighed the advantages of allying with the United States or Japan. The Far East was an anomaly because the British had already abandoned splendid isolation by entering into an alliance with the Japanese in 1902 to raise the stakes for France and Russia should they go to war in the Far East. The Royal Navy saw no real operational purpose in the alliance, and it had certainly not increased the number of units in home waters.[64]

The rise of the United States as a formidable Pacific power forced the British to reconsider the relative advantage of the Anglo–Japanese alliance, which was due for renewal in 1922. Tensions were escalating between Japan and the United States, and the Japanese were using the alliance to pursue an imperialist agenda. British debates about whether to stand by Japan resembled debates about whether to stand by France. The fear was that allying with Japan and France might embolden those states while antagonizing the United States and Germany, both of whom were viewed as unreliable. America was unpredictable, undependable, and subject to the whims of a fickle public opinion. Germany had revisionist aspirations. The British considered a range of options from an Anglo–American entente directed against Japan to renewal of the alliance with Japan.[65] The British preferred a multilateral arrangement, but failing that and believing an entente with the United States unlikely, they were prepared to renew the Anglo–Japanese alliance. In the end, the Washington treaty negotiations produced the Four Power Treaty, a nonaggression pact according to which Great Britain, the United States, Japan, and France agreed to respect one another's Pacific interests, insular possessions, and insular dominions and to refrain from alliances, force, and collusion. This suited Britain's near-term goals of preserving the status quo in the Pacific.[66]

Conclusions

Between the world wars, Britain faced several different threats. All of them eventually materialized.[67] The services and Treasury advanced their own distinctive yet competing visions of Britain's strategic future. The Treasury feared economic collapse and demanded that any rearmament not undermine long-term economic health. The army focused on policing the empire and preparing an expeditionary force for the continent. The RAF focused on the air threat from Europe, arguing that land-based air power was also the best method to defend imperial bases. The Admiralty concentrated on defending the empire's vulnerable sea lines from Japan and also kept an eye on the possible reemergence of a German naval threat. World War II proved that all these strategic visions were correct, but they represented a multiplicity of risks that the British could not effectively meet without unacceptable cuts in social programs.

The British army could reasonably expect to engage in four broad types of military activity: imperial policing, minor peacekeeping, major expeditions that would involve a Territorial Army, and a national war involving full mobilization.[68] Within the empire, the army also confronted a wide array of conditions and opponents, which "presented a near-impossible problem to those responsible for devising training appropriate to all the conditions likely to be met by imperial troops."[69] The navy faced different operational conditions across the Mediterranean and Pacific. Requirements for operating in the Mediterranean conflicted with efforts to develop an offensive maritime air power capability for the Pacific. George Peden asks,

> What economic and financial factors prevented Britain from creating and maintaining an air force equal to any other within striking distance of the United Kingdom? Or maintaining a navy capable of defending Britain's interests in the Far East from the 1920s, while also dealing with the German and Italian navies from 1935 and protecting Britain's worldwide trade routes? Or creating an army capable of co-operating with European allies, while also defending Britain's overseas territories and interests?

He laments, "Merely to list Britain's defence requirements is to show that not all could be met, and that therefore strategic choices would be necessary."[70]

As a global power facing a diverse array of problems across the Empire, the British judged the near-term risks to imperial security to be greater than the long-term risks of a great power threat. Defense effort was put toward the colonial warfare mission, with clear opportunity costs for conventional war making. The army found it more difficult than the navy or air force to keep pace with its modernizing counterparts because it had to "find a balance between technology and tactics appropriate for major wars, on the one hand, and for limited wars, on the other."[71] The regular army was crippled. The Royal Navy remained in a high state of readiness but lost its edge in naval aviation. The RAF had to make the case for its relevance to imperial security because of the absence of any plausible enemy within range of Britain between 1919 and 1933. Peden summarizes:

> By May 1939, the navy doubted its ability to fulfill plans, dating from 1920, to send out a fleet to the Far East adequate to meet the Japanese fleet, and Bomber Command doubted its ability to carry out the strategic air offensive that Air Staff doctrine laid down for it. From February 1939 the army was being belatedly prepared for a conventional commitment that it had been told throughout the previous twelve months not to prepare for.[72]

There is always a tension between responding to near-term challenges and preparing for the future, of staying abreast of rapidly changing technologies while simultaneously sustaining readiness levels to respond to near-term operational demands. For global powers like interwar Britain—and contemporary America—those tensions are unavoidable, and capability gaps cannot be avoided. What can be avoided is the trap of projecting present threats into the future and making strategic decisions based on them.

THE UNITED STATES

The Security Environment

After World War I, the United States faced no serious threats, had no imperial commitments, and was burdened with few peacetime demands on strategic resources. The oceans remained safe defenses. World War I proved that technological and economic capacity would be crucial to success in future wars, and America's economic and industrial potential was overwhelming:

> In 1919, the human, material, and fiscal resources of the nation were intact and the United States had become the world's creditor nation. In the late 1920s, the United States remained an industrial giant, producing an output of manufactures larger than that of the other six major powers—Great Britain, Germany, France, the Soviet Union, Italy, and Japan—combined.[73]

> . . . The country remained self-sufficient in most mineral resources; by the latter 1920s even the anxieties over oil supplies had largely faded.[74]

Between 1918 and 1933, U.S. planners saw no major threats to the nation's security. The British were focused on imperial security. The French remained preoccupied with Continental security and a potential German threat, distracted by rebellious overseas possessions and domestic recovery. The Europe of pre-1933 was of little military concern. To the extent U.S. leaders thought about Europe, it was chiefly in economic terms.[75]

The Japanese posed a problem because their wartime acquisition of the former German Pacific islands placed them astride the U.S. fleet's line of communications. Defense of the Philippines had become virtually impossible. It was also in the Far East that a naval race threatened to erupt between the United States, Japan, and Great Britain. In July 1920, the Japanese Diet adopted their eight-eight plan to give the Imperial Navy a fleet of eight superdreadnought battleships and eight giant battle cruisers by 1927. The British responded by announcing in March 1921 their intention to initiate naval construction to retain Britannia's rule of the waves. The Washington and London naval arms control treaties circumvented the naval race, but the balance of naval power in the western Pacific remained a preoccupation for U.S. leaders because the treaties left the United States without a well-equipped base there.[76]

Although Japan was America's most natural enemy in the 1920s, a significant degree of diplomatic compromise and naval cooperation was achieved between the two. Up until the unification of China in 1928, U.S.–Japanese relations were stable and mutually profitable—politically and economically. Tokyo's Far Eastern ambitions and policies were more an irritant than a serious concern, and outright distrust of Japan was perceived by most observers as a ploy by big-navy lobbyists to secure funds in budget battles. If hostilities with Japan were to erupt, it was assumed they would result from a clash over Japanese expansionism in China. But it was not clear that U.S. policies in China would lead to a clash with Japan.[77]

Although the United States had the gross resources to act as a global power after World War I, it did not think of itself as one. Security still meant the ability to protect U.S. territory, the Panama Canal, and U.S. overseas possessions and interests in China and to uphold the Monroe Doctrine. Armed forces were seen as a form of insurance. The question is, With no clear enemy, insurance against what?

U.S. Strategic Choices

We would expect the United States, as a rising great power contender, to adopt a shaping strategy; and, in key respects, it did. Contrary to the received conventional wisdom of a withdrawn great power, the United States did shape, but it did so regionally. It was in the Far East and western Pacific that U.S. diplomacy paved the way for arms control to stem a naval arms race. The United States prepared to prosecute a war there by developing innovative capabilities to project power across the vast expanses of the Pacific and embraced the doctrine of amphibious assault, which others had dismissed as futile. U.S. planners anticipated strategic challenges to their interests in the distant future and carefully considered a range of contingencies. The evidence shows that economically, militarily, and diplomatically, the United States pursued a regional shaping strategy between the world wars.

A key dimension of economic strategy is the allocation of resources between defense and nondefense. Resources for defense were cut but not to prewar levels and not as drastically as they had been in Great Britain.

If we look at total military expenditure as a percentage of government expenditure less debt servicing (Table 4.7, column G), we see a decline from the prewar level of 45 percent to between 23 percent and 25 percent until 1932. Thereafter, military expenditure as a percentage of total expenditure steadily drops off, but this no doubt reflects a dramatic rise in social and public works spending in response to the Great Depression. One sees a similar drop in total military expenditure as a percentage of GDP (Table 4.7, column I). Prewar levels of 0.8 to 0.9 percent drop to 0.7 percent throughout the 1920s. Expenditures, however, can be misleading, and so it is important to look also at manpower levels.

If we look at manpower levels (Table 4.8) we see that the army averaged between 90,000 and 100, 000 in the years before World War I. After demobilization, army levels stabilized at 135,000 to 140,000 and remained at those levels from 1922 until 1935. In the navy, numbers were around 50,000 in the years preceding the war and stabilized after demobilization at around 95,000. Again, navy manpower levels were similarly consistent between 1922 and 1935. The marines show the same pattern: averaging around 10,000 prior to mobilization for war and stabilizing at about 20,000 after demobilization. Whereas postwar British troop levels dipped well below prewar levels, in the United States postwar numbers stabilized well above prewar levels.

Manpower levels for the navy, in particular, shed light on U.S. strategy. The Washington Naval Treaties prevented the United States from increasing the total tonnage of naval combatants and hence the number of units that could be built. With personnel stable, the gradual rise in naval spending in the late 1920s suggests that the United States was investing in technology.

Table 4.7. U.S. defense spending, 1910–1939 (data in thousands of dollars).

Years	A Total government expenditure	B Debt servicing	C Government expenditure less debt servicing	D Army expenditures
1910	693,617.00	21,343	672,274.00	189,823
1911	691,202.00	21,311	669,891.00	197,199
1912	689,881.00	22,616	667,265.00	184,123
1913	714,864.00	22,899	691,965.00	202,129
1914	725,525.00	22,864	702,661.00	208,349
1915	746,093.00	22,903	723,190.00	202,060
1916	712,967.00	22,901	690,066.00	183,176
1917	1,953,857.00	24,743	1,929,114.00	377,941
1918	12,677,359.00	189,743	12,487,616.00	4,869,955
1919	18,492,665.00	619,216	17,873,449.00	9,009,076
1920	6,357,677.00	1,020,252	5,337,425.00	1,621,953
1921	5,061,785.00	999,145	4,062,640.00	1,118,076
1922	3,289,404.00	991,001	2,298,403.00	457,756
1923	3,140,287.00	1,055,924	2,084,363.00	397,051
1924	2,907,847.00	940,603	1,967,244.00	357,017
1925	2,923,762.00	881,807	2,041,955.00	370,981
1926	2,929,964.00	831,938	2,098,026.00	364,090
1927	2,857,429.00	787,020	2,070,409.00	369,114
1928	2,961,245.00	731,764	2,229,481.00	400,990
1929	3,127,199.00	678,330	2,448,869.00	425,946
1930	3,320,211.00	659,348	2,660,863.00	464,854
1931	3,577,434.00	611,560	2,965,874.00	486,142
1932	4,659,182.00	599,277	4,059,905.00	476,305
1933	4,598,496.00	689,365	3,909,131.00	434,621
1934	6,644,602.00	756,617	5,887,985.00	408,587
1935	6,497,008.00	820,926	5,676,082.00	487,995
1936	8,421,608.00	749,397	7,672,211.00	618,587
1937	7,733,033.00	866,384	6,866,649.00	628,104
1938	6,764,626.00	926,281	5,838,345.00	644,244
1939	8,841,224.00	940,540	7,900,684.00	695,296

SOURCE: 1. *The Statistical History of the United States From Colonial Times to the Present.* New York: Basic Books, 1976.

Table 4.7. U.S. defense spending, 1910–1939 (data in thousands of dollars). *(Continued)*

E Navy expenditures	F Total military expenditures (army and navy)	G Total military expenditures as percentage of column C	H GDP	I Total military expenditure as percentage of GDP
123,174	312,997	45.13	35,300,000.00	0.89
119,938	317,137	45.88	35,800,000.00	0.89
135,592	319,715	46.34	39,400,000.00	0.81
133,263	335,392	46.92	39,600,000.00	0.85
139,682	348,031	47.97	38,600,000.00	0.90
141,836	343,896	46.09	40,000,000.00	0.86
153,854	337,030	47.27	48,300,000.00	0.70
239,633	617,574	31.61	60,400,000.00	1.02
1,278,840	6,148,795	48.50	76,400,000.00	8.05
2,002,311	11,011,387	59.54	84,000,000.00	13.11
736,021	2,357,974	37.09	91,500,000.00	2.58
650,374	1,768,450	34.94	69,600,000.00	2.54
476,775	934,531	28.41	74,100,000.00	1.26
333,201	730,252	23.25	85,100,000.00	0.86
332,249	689,266	23.70	84,700,000.00	0.81
346,137	717,118	24.53	98,100,000.00	0.73
312,743	676,833	23.10	97,000,000.00	0.70
318,909	688,023	24.08	94,900,000.00	0.72
331,335	732,325	24.73	97,000,000.00	0.75
364,562	790,508	25.28	103,100,000.00	0.77
374,164	839,018	25.27	90,400,000.00	0.93
353,768	839,910	23.48	75,800,000.00	1.11
357,518	833,823	17.90	58,000,000.00	1.44
349,373	783,994	17.05	55,600,000.00	1.41
296,927	705,514	10.62	65,100,000.00	1.08
436,266	924,261	14.23	72,200,000.00	1.28
528,882	1,147,469	13.63	82,500,000.00	1.39
556,674	1,184,778	15.32	90,400,000.00	1.31
596,130	1,240,374	18.34	84,700,000.00	1.46
672,722	1,368,018	15.47	90,500,000.00	1.51

Table 4.8. U.S. military numbers data, 1900–1939.

Year	Grand total	Army			Navy			Marine Corps		
		Total	Officers	Enlisted	Total	Officers	Enlisted	Total	Officers	Enlisted
1900	125,923	101,713	4,227	97,486	18,796	1,683	17,113	5,414	174	5,240
1901	112,322	85,557	3,468	82,089	20,900	1,742	19,158	5,864	171	5,694
1902	111,145	81,275	4,049	77,226	23,648	1,822	21,826	6,222	191	6,031
1903	106,043	69,595	3,927	65,668	29,790	1,893	27,897	6,658	213	6,445
1904	110,129	70,387	3,971	66,416	32,158	2,014	30,144	7,584	255	7,329
1905	108,301	67,526	4,034	63,492	33,764	2,079	31,685	7,011	270	6,741
1906	112,216	68,945	3,989	64,956	35,053	2,133	32,920	8,218	278	7,940
1907	108,375	64,170	3,896	60,274	36,119	2,238	33,881	8,086	279	7,807
1908	128,500	76,942	4,047	72,895	42,322	2,463	39,859	9,236	283	8,953
1909	142,200	84,971	4,299	80,672	47,533	2,630	44,903	9,696	328	9,368
1910	139,344	81,251	4,535	76,716	48,533	2,699	45,834	9,560	328	9,232
1911	144,846	84,006	4,585	79,421	51,230	2,886	48,344	9,610	328	9,282
1912	153,174	92,121	4,775	87,346	51,357	3,074	48,283	9,696	337	9,359
1913	154,914	92,756	4,970	87,786	52,202	3,273	48,929	9,956	331	9,625
1914	165,919	98,554	5,033	93,5511	56,989	3,405	53,583	10,386	336	10,050
1915	174,112	106,754	4,948	101,806	57,072	3,593	53,479	10,286	338	9,948
1916	179,376	108,399	5,175	103,224	60,376	4,022	56,354	10,601	348	10,253
1917	643,883	421,467	34,224	387,243	194,617	8,383	186,234	27,749	776	26,973
1918	2,897,167	2,395,742	130,485	2,265,257	448,606	32,631	424,975	52,819	1,503	51,316
1919	1,172,602	851,624	91,975	759,649	272,144	19,357	252,787	48,834	2,270	46,564

Table 4.8. U.S. military numbers data, 1900–1939. *(Continued)*

Year	Grand total	Army			Navy			Marine Corps		
		Total	Officers	Enlisted	Total	Officers	Enlisted	Total	Officers	Enlisted
1920	343,302	204,292	18,999	185,293	121,845	10,642	111,203	17,165	1,104	16,061
1921	386,542	230,725	16,501	214,244	132,827	9,979	122,848	22,990	1,087	21,903
1922	270,207	148,763	15,667	133,096	100,211	8,334	91,877	21,233	1,135	20,098
1923	247,011	133,243	14,021	119,222	94,094	8,410	85,684	19,674	1,141	18,533
1924	261,189	142,673	13,784	128,889	98,184	8,651	89,533	20,332	1,157	19,175
1925	251,756	137,048	14,594	122,454	95,230	8,918	86,312	19,478	1,168	18,310
1926	247,396	134,938	14,143	120,795	93,304	9,091	84,213	19,154	1,178	17,976
1927	248,943	134,829	14,020	120,809	94,916	9,440	85,476	19,198	1,198	18,000
1928	250,907	136,084	14,019	122,065	95,803	9,401	86,402	19,020	1,198	17,822
1929	255,031	139,118	14,047	125,071	97,117	9,434	87,683	18,796	1,181	17,615
1930	255,648	139,378	14,151	125,227	96,890	9,540	87,350	19,380	1,208	18,172
1931	252,605	140,516	14,159	126,357	93,307	9,849	83,458	18,782	1,196	17,586
1932	244,902	134,957	14,111	120,846	93,384	9,967	83,417	16,561	1,196	15,365
1933	243,845	136,547	13,896	122,651	91,230	9,947	81,283	16,068	1,192	14,876
1934	247,137	138,964	13,761	124,703	92,312	9,972	82,340	16,361	1,187	15,174
1935	251,799	139,486	13,471	126,015	95,053	10,115	84,938	17,260	1,163	16,097
1936	291,356	167,816	13,512	154,304	106,292	10,247	96,045	17,248	1,208	16,040
1937	311,808	179,968	13,740	166,228	113,617	10,367	103,250	18,223	1,312	16,911
1938	322,932	185,488	13,975	171,513	119,088	10,739	108,349	18,356	1,359	16,997
1939	334,473	189,839	14,486	175,353	125,202	12,023	113,179	19,432	1,380	18,052

SOURCE: *The Statistical History of the United States from Colonial Times to the Present* (New York: Basic Books, 1976), p. 1141, Series Y 904–916. Military Personnel on Active Duty: 1789 to 1970 (table adapted).

In addition, between the wars the U.S. fleet was in an extremely low state of readiness, as evidenced by spending on fuel as reported in the secretary of the navy's annual reports. In contrast to the Royal Navy's high state of readiness, the U.S. fleet was rarely at sea. Again, these are telltale signs of different strategic approaches: adapting and focusing on the near term in the case of Britain and shaping and focusing on the more distant future in the case of the United States. The U.S. army and navy remained larger and more powerful between the wars than they had ever been in peacetime,[78] despite a domestic political climate that was hostile to defense spending.[79]

In this study, military strategy is assessed along two dimensions: the allocation of defense resources between the near term and long term, varying from readiness to modernization, and the balance of effort between innovation and adaptation. For the United States, the long term trumped the near term, and innovation trumped adaptation, particularly in the Far Eastern theater.

Between the wars, no serious attempt was made by civilian leadership to develop a national strategic doctrine or to link foreign policy and military planning.[80] Even absent overarching guidance, the services consistently planned for future rather than immediate contingencies (of which there were few relative to Great Britain) and more specifically for major conventional war. The navy and marines developed strategy and doctrine to prosecute a new type of war that involved projecting power across a vast ocean expanse without a fortified base. The army focused on mobilization planning for large-scale war. Strategic thinking assumed a long-term horizon as distinct from the adaptive approach and near-term focus of British strategy. The adoption of a skeleton regular army is a case in point. It served as a foundation for expansion but provided no prompt readiness, even for relatively small emergencies. Only in 1930 did work on an Instant Readiness Force begin, yet civilian leadership still refused to increase the regular army to provide for a contingency response capability.[81] The navy also remained at a low state of readiness between the wars.

Consistent with U.S. planning efforts during this time of strategic uncertainty were the color plans—war plans with potential enemies designated by color,[82] which gave military planners valuable insights to use when developing the more realistic Rainbow Plans that addressed real strategic problems in 1939. The focus in the 1920s and early 1930s was on limited contingencies and hypothetical training exercises. Many of the plans remained outside the realm of political reality but provided valuable training for coping with a range of wartime contingencies. The only color plan that carried any immediate prospect of being carried out was Plan Orange for war with Japan.

The color plans addressed three sets of problems: immediate contingencies with forces actually available; remote dangers to gain an appreciation of more complex strategic, logistical, and force generation requirements; and major war against a hostile coalition to train officers to raise and direct forces on the scale deployed during World War I. The categories were not mutually exclusive. "A realistic plan for the defense of the Panama Canal Zone, for example, would fit into a broader plan for a Pacific Ocean war. A war plan dealing with the Pacific would, with modifications, become a [sic] element in a two-ocean war scenario."[83]

The pre–World War I focus was on single color plans—Black against imperial Germany and Orange against Japan. After 1919, the focus was on real contingencies that might arise even in the benign environment of the 1920s and on large-scale problems designed as training exercises.[84] White focused on domestic unrest; Brown focused on insurrection in the Philippines; Violet signified intervention in Central America; Tan signified intervention in Cuba to maintain the Monroe Doctrine and U.S. hegemony in the Caribbean; Green focused on protecting U.S. interests during a Mexican insurrection. Brown, Violet, and Green were politically plausible, though Violet and Green, if waged at higher levels of conflict, were barely within the nation's military capabilities. Brown, Violet, Tan, and Green reflected traditional missions of implementing the Monroe Doctrine, guarding American overseas possessions, and protecting U.S. lives and property abroad.[85]

Yellow signified intervention in China to protect the interests, privileges, and citizens of foreign powers from local government and warlord factions. Plan Yellow was the only color plan that contemplated U.S. forces acting in conjunction with other powers because the size of Chinese political and warlord factions demanded a coalition size response.

Plan Red, for war against the British Empire, and Plan Orange, against Japan, received the most attention, even though Red was known to be politically implausible, while conflict with Japan was unlikely so long as the Washington and London Naval Treaties remained in effect—which they did until Japan's withdrawal from the treaty regime in 1935. Naval officers were the impetus behind Pacific campaign planning, while army officers were the force behind Red (and Red-Orange) as the basis for their Basic Mobilization Plan.[86]

Individually, Red and Orange were very useful training exercises. The adversaries were major powers with large armed forces and extensive global reach. "A hypothetical war with either power compelled planners to deal with the problems of national policy, hostilities on a vast scale, generation of massive forces, economic mobilization, and wartime diplomacy."[87] Red provided useful training for large-scale operations in the Western Hemisphere and Atlantic and for the complexities of an Atlantic-centered war. Orange provided planners with an appreciation for the complexities of a Pacific war, which the plan presumed would begin with a surprise offensive by the Japanese, possibly an attack on Pearl Harbor. Orange predicted a long and difficult fleet advance across the Pacific but never the speed and extent of the Japanese offensive, the nature of the U.S. counteroffensive, or the efforts required to defeat Japan.[88]

The Washington Naval Conference of 1921–1922 supplanted the Anglo-Japanese Alliance and made a Red-Orange war politically implausible. For planning purposes, however, Red-Orange focused attention on the "immense problems posed by its hypothetical enemy combination,"[89] fighting on two fronts and prosecuting a global war. Red was defined as the more demanding threat because of its military power, industrial potential, and geographic proximity to vital U.S. industrial regions. U.S. military leaders planned to defeat Red first and retain a defensive posture in the Pacific. Once the fate of Red was sealed, resources would shift to the Pacific. Although planning for a two-ocean war on a global scale against a hostile coalition was envisioned only as a training exercise, hypothetical dangers became distinct possibilities in the late 1930s. Red-Orange's "Europe-first strategy" formed the basis for U.S. grand strategy in World War II.

With the Color Plans as the planning paradigm, "U.S. strategic thought from 1919 to 1938 was largely oriented towards the Pacific and the problems arising out of possible Japanese aggression against American interests or territory there."[90] The Harding administration permanently stationed the Navy's fastest and most modern battleships in the Pacific and rapidly improved facilities at Pearl Harbor. The greatest advances in technology, tactics, and doctrine occurred in areas most relevant to the Pacific: amphibious warfare and carrier aviation.[91]

World War I dramatically altered the strategic position of the United States. The Treaty of Versailles gave to Japan Germany's Pacific islands, and these lay astride U.S. supply routes to the Philippines. The Washington naval treaties then restricted the fortification of insular possessions in the western

Pacific, denying the U.S. Navy advanced bases from which to operate land-based aircraft. Lacking adequate power projection capabilities, the U.S. Navy could not defend the nation's Far Eastern commitments.[92] Fleet aviation based on the carrier concept offered a way for the United States to remedy its deficiency in bases within treaty constraints. The navy's conviction that it must be able to project power across the Pacific despite a loss of bases motivated it to develop weapon systems and their support elements—long-range submarines, long-range patrol bombers, and the fleet train, comprised of flotillas of logistics ships and mobile floating docks to repair and maintain warships and keep them stocked with food and supplies—along with the doctrine to operate carriers in the Pacific.

With the advanced base mission at the forefront of American military planning,[93] the navy revised War Plan Orange to capture bases in the Caroline and Marshall Islands currently occupied by the Japanese.[94] Revised Orange gave the marine corps a critical role. The Washington treaties placed no limits on mobile forces that could seize and defend advanced bases, so the marines created the units, developed the doctrine for amphibious landings, and provided an island-hopping capability to overcome loss of the Philippines early in a war. Britain's amphibious assault on Turkish defenses in 1915 at Gallipoli had been a huge disaster, convincing many that amphibious landings in the face of heavy opposition could not succeed. But the navy's War Plans Division could see no way to prosecute Plan Orange other than by amphibious assault.

Corps Headquarters officially embraced the base seizure mission as part of its repertoire in 1920 and began in-depth analysis at marine corps schools.[95] Studies revealed that flaws in the Gallipoli operation could be corrected, and training exercises in 1923–1924 and 1925 demonstrated that seizing advanced bases was possible. By 1931, the corps had committed itself to serving the fleet in wartime by seizing bases for naval operations and preparing in peacetime for the successful execution of that wartime function. Theoretical instruction at marine corps schools was overhauled, and three years later a detailed manual entitled "Tentative Manual for Landing Operations" was adopted as official doctrine. From this point forward, a series of Fleet Landing Exercises (FLEXes) provided continuous practical training for the marines to test and refine their doctrine.[96] In 1933, the marine corps created the Fleet Marine Force, a permanent unit composed of base defense and amphibious assault units, and adopted the amphibious assault mission as the service's new core task.[97]

The navy, for its part, assumed it would have to take the offensive into the Pacific and so adopted the strategy of "progressive advance," retaking the Philippines by way of the Marshalls, Truk, and the Marianas.[98] In solving the problems of transoceanic passage, the navy introduced a new offensive role for the aircraft carrier to overwhelm the enemy's combined fleet and shore-based air force.[99]

Key to the intellectual breakthroughs that transformed the role of the aircraft carrier were simulations conducted at the U.S. Naval War College.[100] The problems of a Pacific campaign drove realistic simulation exercises against a tactically superior Orange. Numerical inferiority in battleships was compensated for by air superiority. Simulations highlighted the importance of the carrier as an independent offensive striking force and the need to mass aircraft for strikes, rather than assigning aircraft to scout for each battleship.[101]

The Pacific situation also shaped the fleet exercises that demonstrated the value of carrier mobility and led to the recommendation that carrier admirals be given complete freedom of action in employing carrier aircraft.[102] The United States entered World War II with the carrier still subordinate to the battleship line, largely due to carrier vulnerabilities and technical limitations of aircraft.[103] But the groundwork for a profound transformation in naval warfare had been laid.

In contrast to the strides made in warfare at sea, progress in mechanization and armored warfare was minimal. General John Pershing articulated the army's primary mission in 1919: defense of the American continent against invasion.[104] In his view, tanks had no role to play in continental defense. Based on Pershing's testimony, Congress disbanded the Tank Corps as an independent organization in 1920 and placed it under the chief of infantry.[105] There was broad support among the army leadership for mechanization,[106] but continental defense undercut any strategic rationale for an aggressive mechanization policy.[107]

For an insular nation with no great powers contiguous to its borders and no imperial commitments, this defensive mission made perfect sense. But operating on the American continent did require mobility.[108] The problem was that tank doctrine had evolved in a static warfare situation. U.S. ground forces were in the war too short a time to conduct extensive tests and accumulate sufficient combat data, so the army accepted British and French concepts of tank use. These linked the tank to trench warfare, as a siege weapon in close support of the infantry.[109] Tanks were judged to be largely irrelevant to the army's postwar mission of continental defense,[110] and a separate tank service was deemed too expensive.[111] Some experimentation did take place, but the reorganization placed major constraints on tank development. In 1928, the army organized the first Experimental Mechanized Force to serve as a technical and tactical laboratory,[112] and a board of general staff officers recommended creation of a follow-on Experimental Mechanized Force. But tank modernization was low on the priority list of War Department leaders searching for ways to maintain the army with limited funds. Between 1925 and 1939, the average allotted to tank development was approximately $60,000 per year. In 1931, the cost of a single Christie tank, without armor, engines, guns, or radios, was $34,500; and seven years later, the Ordnance Department estimated the cost of a medium tank to be $50,000. Only one experimental model could be built in any one year.[113] The second Mechanized Force was constituted in 1930 with obsolete equipment and was disbanded in 1931, halting further experimentation in armored warfare.

America's geographic position also made it difficult to justify strategic bombing, unless the United States were to wage all-out war with Mexico or Canada, an inconceivable scenario. What role was there for bombers beyond coastal defense?[114] What was the role for nonnaval air power against Japan? The U.S. had a strong civil aviation industry that could have supported innovation in strategic bombing, but no "bolt from the blue" national psychosis ever took hold. When a real threat did emerge, however, the United States with sufficient warning and industrial prowess mobilized its latent economic strength for the air battles over Central Europe.

Mobilization planning provides another set of indicators of America's strategic orientation between the wars. In the 1920s, studies of the nation's war industrial capacity demonstrated that industrial plants could not meet many of the essential requirements of the army's 1924 General Mobilization Plan.[115] Over the course of a decade, "A radical change had taken place in the thinking of the army's command structure. It had finally accepted army dependence on the civilian economy in order to fulfill the military mission."[116] By 1936, with the Protective Mobilization Plan (PMP), war plans were finally based on industrial potential.

Economic planning for the national economy proved to be more daunting, but the Army Industrial College (AIC) was established to train officers in industrial mobilization and to promote service-industry cooperation and interservice planning. Logistics and mobilization planning came to be seen as equally important as strategy and tactics.[117] A Planning Branch in the Procurement Division of the Office of the Assistant Secretary of War (OASW) became the focal point for industrial mobilization planning. By 1929, it produced the first official economic blueprint for war—the Industrial Mobilization Plan of 1930 (IMP).[118] The scope of political problems involved in directing such a large economy remained underappreciated[119] and the production needs of the civilian population were not included in planning;[120] but, despite these shortcomings, the army had come to recognize the importance of economic planning and close coordination with civilian agencies during war.[121]

Between the world wars, few international pressures compelled army leaders to focus on mobilization planning. Potential great power competitors had been vanquished or were consumed with reconstruction. A climate of public indifference if not hostility toward any measures that could be described as "preparation for war," the remoteness of American involvement in any future conflict, and preoccupation with peacetime pursuits made it difficult to arouse public interest in planning for a hypothetical future war, let alone secure the appropriations and staff to conduct those efforts.[122] Yet the army made important intellectual strides by 1929 due to its focus on fighting another peer competitor.[123]

In the diplomatic domain, U.S. leaders exhibited a preference for maximum flexibility and independence but coupled with significant diplomatic engagement. The country was anxious to return to "normalcy," but its leaders remained concerned with developments abroad. The nation may have clung to neutrality but not isolationism. The conventional wisdom of a nation turned inward, isolationist, retreatist, and noninternationalist is a caricature rooted solely in the absence of a U.S. military commitment to Europe. U.S. leaders were unwilling to enter into binding commitments, refusing to ratify the Versailles Treaty and join the League of Nations. Yet the United States was hardly isolationist. Steven Ross summarizes,

> The United States was, in fact, quite willing to participate in world affairs, rejecting only permanent or entangling commitments. Washington actively sponsored naval disarmament conferences, took the lead in attempting to resolve the issue of German reparations, and acted vigorously to settle a wide range of Far Eastern problems.[124]

Business leaders engaged in international economic life, and diplomats participated in the major international conferences of the period. "Both the Washington Conference and the Kellogg-Briand Pact resulted from American initiative, and they stand as testimony to the continuing, though cautious, activity of the United States in the world arena."[125] U.S. engagement abroad between the world wars has been underestimated by those who focus exclusively on Europe and the absence of security agreements there. In the 1920s, the nation was engaged abroad, even in Europe.

Up until 1933, when the Depression sapped the nation's economic and financial power, U.S. leaders worked to shore up European stability, despite Senate rejection of the League of Nations and a refusal to commit to defense of the Versailles settlement. Melvyn Leffler develops a very persuasive case for the fact of U.S. involvement even in European affairs continuously, though not always successfully, up until 1933.[126] That involvement was primarily economic in nature. Its distinct economic caste was intimately linked to U.S. perceptions of its own economic strength and geographic distance from Europe, coupled with more plausible real threats to U.S. interests in the Far East. Leffler continues,

> In their efforts to implement a foreign policy based on "prosperity and peace," American policy makers recognized the overriding importance of reconciling Franco-German differences in particular and of restoring European economic stability in general. . . . Indeed, the deterioration of European financial, political, and social conditions in the early 1920's alarmed many Americans and convinced them that the interests of the United States and Europe were "indissolubly united."[127]

The United States used financial leverage, particularly private capital, to stabilize Europe and strengthen Germany's economy.[128] Business leaders and government officials "assumed that the stabilization and economic rehabilitation of Europe would generate worldwide economic growth, would stimulate total world demand, would contribute to world peace and social order, and would benefit American commercial interests."[129] European economic stability and peace depended on an economically prosperous, republican, contented Germany.

Security commitments, on the other hand, meant support for France, preservation of the status quo, and ultimately French hegemony over Germany. John Braeman points out,

> Diplomatic and military commitments meant in the context of the time support for France against Germany. Although regarding a strong France as indispensable for a European balance of power, Washington did not accept

Paris' definition of what constituted French security. American officials were convinced that the French hard line on reparations, their refusal to meet Germany's legitimate grievances, and their efforts to keep Germany down were self-defeating by undermining the possibility of a prosperous, satisfied, republican Germany.[130]

Preserving the status quo was not the goal in Europe. Any political-military involvement or security guarantees designed to support the status quo were avoided.

In the Far East, U.S. civilian leaders pursued naval arms control and economic cooperation with all the great powers, including Japan. Economic cooperation would lead to a strong and stable China, a bulwark for peace and assured access to lucrative markets. The Four Power Treaty that resulted from the Washington Conference of 1921–1922 established a modus vivendi among the United States, Britain, Japan, and France in the Far East, committing the signatories to "discuss fully and frankly the most efficient measures to be taken" in the event of any "aggressive action" in the Far East. It fell far short of committing the United States to an alliance.[131] The Nine Power Treaty enshrined the open-door policy and America's commitment to preserve China's territorial and administrative integrity as a source of stability in the region. But legitimate Japanese interests in China were acknowledged to avoid confrontation with Japan. In the Far East as in Europe, the United States sought a "stable international economic and financial environment in which American industry and commerce could grow and prosper,"[132] a logical strategy for a rising power.

Conclusions

Between the wars, U.S. strategists and planners were farsighted in their thinking about the future security environment. They studied a range of scenarios, learned from simulations, and closely scrutinized lessons from the First World War—all in an effort to prepare for a future conflict of that magnitude, perceived as remote in time, given postwar devastation, and distant in space.

The navy came to appreciate the nation's emergence as a global naval power and the need to project power to protect vulnerable interests in the Far East.[133] Rigorous war gaming transformed a transit itinerary into a doctrine of progressive transoceanic offensive operations.[134] In the early 1920s, a Pacific campaign was envisioned as swift, offensive, and decisive; by 1928, a protracted war of attrition dominated planning. The emphasis was on evolving carrier doctrine, the fleet train and oceanic logistics, joint operations with the army, coalition operations, air superiority, and large-scale amphibious assault that would develop into the serial amphibious process of island hopping by the marine corps. With few duties in peacetime and little prospect of aerial attack from nearby hostile territory, the United States could devote more air assets to maritime matters than could Britain,[135] producing greater strides in the technologies, tactics, and doctrine for offensive carrier warfare.

All of these advances were made in anticipation of a rising competitor in the Pacific. Low diversity of threat made it easier to identify strategic priorities around which to focus R&D efforts and experimentation. With respect to carrier air power, "the American ability to point at the Japanese as a clear potential opponent was an asset in many ways; it provided a criterion against which they could judge their tactics and equipment."[136] A consensus existed that U.S. strategic priorities lay in the Pacific, and even the army planned operations against Japan. The army came to appreciate the importance of mobilization planning and more broadly the need to understand the requirements for a future great power war.

A long-term orientation helped prepare the United States for novel contingencies in the future. For example, planning for Red and Red-Orange "provided valuable experience from which the services drew when they confronted really dangerous enemies in two oceans on the eve of World War II."[137] The Color Plans formed the foundation for the Rainbow Plans—a new set of plans based on coalition war situations against Japan and the Axis powers with Great Britain figuring as an ally of the United States. In 1939, Chief of Naval Operations Admiral Harold R. Stark observed that "the Red Plan had provided the basis for District Mobilization Plans on the Atlantic coast even though it 'was never realistic.'"[138] Red-Orange prepared the army to make tough political-strategic choices by establishing the principle that "should the United States fight in both oceans, it must first deal with its more dangerous enemies in the Atlantic before moving offensively against Orange in the Pacific."[139]

To a more limited extent, U.S. financial and economic engagement shaped the political environment in Europe. American capital was needed for the commercialization of German reparation bonds. And "since French policy in the Ruhr and especially in the Rhineland was linked to the commercialization of German reparation obligations, the availability of American capital affected the entire climate of European politics."[140] American bankers and officials used inducements of additional credits and loans to encourage Franco–German security negotiations, which ultimately produced the Locarno Treaty. By the early 1930s, the Depression sapped the nation's economic and financial power that had been relied on to help stabilize Europe.

From the 1920s to the mid-1930s, the United States was preeminent by all indicators of power, unhampered by imperial commitments, and burdened with few peacetime demands on strategic resources. Yet U.S. planners seriously thought about long-term threats to the nation's security, despite the nation's invulnerability, geographic remoteness, and lack of overseas commitments. The United States planned for several different conflict environments and potential enemies. The navy and marine corps anticipated waging war in the Pacific under new sets of constraints, which required the development of new and innovative strategies, tactics, doctrines, and technologies. The army made important strides in mobilization planning, preparing in peacetime for the demands of great power war.

U.S. strategy reflected the nation's overwhelming economic potential relative to the near total economic devastation of its traditional European enemies and its delimited regional rather than global geopolitical horizon. Low diversity of threat allowed U.S. planners to focus on the Pacific. Resources for defense were cut, though never to prewar levels. Planning assumed a long-term horizon, in sharp contrast to the incremental adaptive response to current circumstances that characterized British strategy. The United States adopted a shaping strategy that it had the industrial capacity to back up.

EVALUATION OF HYPOTHESES ON SOURCES OF STRATEGY

Britain was a declining power with dwindling economic resources. British leaders banked on a fast-follower strategy and their ability to reconstitute. Britain was also a global power with vast imperial interests. Lesser strategic contingencies emerged on the heels of the armistice, so the British opted to deal with the near term rather than minimize risk over the long term or across both time frames. Lesser strategic contingencies associated with imperial security were less technologically demanding, weakening Britain's defense industrial base and undermining its ability to reconstitute when more serious threats emerged. Despite the windows of opportunity created by a hiatus in great power competition and rapid changes in technology, the British failed to exploit those opportunities. This was not because of functional organizational imperatives; the services had quite ambitious armaments programs in the early 1920s. Nor was it the result of cognitive planning shortcuts. Rather, it was the product of high diversity of threat facing a declining power. Domestic pressure did shrink the size of the defense pie, but the key issue was how scarce resources were allocated. Treasury policy was important but hardly the sole culprit.

The United States was a rising power with a less diverse threat environment. The United States had the opportunity and seized it to shape the future competitive environment in the Pacific, through naval arms control as well as technological, tactical, and doctrinal innovation. As a defensively advantaged state, the United States displayed the diplomatic flexibility and long-horizon investment strategies predicted by Hypothesis B1 but did not neglect innovation, as Hypothesis B3 predicts. Instead, the United States innovated by focusing on a relatively narrow set of contingencies in the western Pacific.

In both Great Britain and the United States, defense spending was cut after World War I, as predicted by Hypothesis D1, but there were observable differences. In a declining Britain, postdemobilization defense effort dropped below prewar levels. In a rising United States, it stabilized above prewar levels. This is evident both in defense expenditures and manpower levels.

With respect to hypothesis on organizational tendencies, there is evidence of organizations responding in service-specific ways. However, what emerges in the British case is how high diversity of threat complicated strategic assessment, and this fed parochial organizational imperatives. Moreover, the services did take cues from politicians once a consensus developed around planning for small wars, peacekeeping operations, and policing duties rather than a great power war against a technologically sophisticated adversary. This general guideline left room for the services to respond in service-specific ways. So the RAF, as a new organization intent on establishing its legitimacy, focused on substituting its technology for army manpower in imperial policing, thus demonstrating the RAF's superior capabilities in performing the peacetime duty of most concern to civilian leaders.[141] When it became politically expedient, Chief of Air Staff Hugh Trenchard championed strategic bombing. And once strategic bombing became its core mission, RAF leaders vigorously objected to using air power to support mechanized warfare and withheld resources from the navy to defend convoys from submarine attack.[142]

On the other hand, the British army dramatically revised its orientation and did so in a way that undermined the organization's power and resources. The War Office followed the explicit instructions issued to it by the Cabinet in 1922 to focus on home security, imperial defense, defending garrisons and strategic ports, and supplying the British component of the garrison of India. Any remaining troops at home should be organized into an expeditionary force for a minor extra-European war.[143] It eschewed preparing for the only type of war that would permit it to modernize. Imperial policing did not require a modern army with mechanized units, and mechanization could come only at the expense of units essential for policing duties. The result was an army "equipped for imperial operations in the late 1930s and prepared neither intellectually nor in terms of its table of organization to meet the German Army on the Continent."[144] The army's fate was closely tied to Britain's geopolitical imperatives—those of an island nation with no continental competitors but a scattered empire to manage. Military institutions are often chastised for preparing to fight the last war. The British did no such thing, and Brian Bond and Williamson Murray surmise that they "would have performed far *better* on the battlefields of the Second World War had they ruthlessly prepared to fight the last war."[145]

The stunted development of British naval air power is often attributed to the long period of RAF control over the Naval Air Arm.[146] The RAF controlled research, experimentation, development, and supply of aircraft, leaving few opportunities for carrier proponents to prove their case. The RAF depleted naval aviation of its top leaders and trained personnel and prevented the establishment of a solid career path for naval aviators. Yet when one analyzes the source of this dual control and how it interacted with systemic dynamics to shape British strategic choices, an interesting pattern emerges. Countries like Britain, Italy, and Germany with independent air forces were also the nations most vulnerable to land-based aerial attack. Naval aviation suffered in each due to acute rivalry between navies and air forces for control over air assets.[147] By contrast, the Americans and Japanese lacked an independent air force, which was no bureaucratic accident.[148] Geostrategic considerations were the key drivers behind decisions to create independent air forces.

In the U.S. case, support for the dominance of functional organizational imperatives driving strategic decisions under uncertainty is also weak. The navy was anything but incrementally adaptive. U.S. leaders had made extensive political commitments in the Far East. Should they decide to make good on those promises, the navy would have to execute a strategic offensive against Japan. Revisionists maintain the Philippines were really not important and that naval leaders called for their defense because it justified a large battle fleet and the Mahanian-type engagement they hoped to fight.[149] But it was civilians who defined the national interest as defense of the Philippines and the Open Door in China. The fact remained that Japan could not menace the continental United States nor the Western Hemisphere. It could, however, close the Open Door.

The U.S. navy had fewer carriers and aircraft than it wanted, to be sure, but this was not because naval leaders were unaware of the potential of carrier air power. The low proportion of investment in carriers (10 percent from 1919 to 1941) was the result of treaty limits on carrier tonnage. A movement of resources toward naval aviation was evidenced by growth in the percentage of the naval budget expended on carriers and their aircraft; however, most modernization money went for battleships. Thomas Hone argues that the pace of technological change for battleships supported continued modernization.[150] Advances in design introduced the possibility that the battleship could retain its armor and endurance levels while increasing its speed. Treaty limits on individual displacement meant the only way to build faster warships was to increase the efficiency of engineering designs, which was costly. With battle ship costs rising, fewer dollars were left to buy other ship types.

Constraints on carrier development were not due to bureaucratic rivalry in an era of scarce resources nor to organizational inertia. Leaders of the battleship-dominated U.S. navy appreciated the need for naval air power. As early as 1919, there was support among the senior leadership to develop aviation to its fullest.[151] The moving force behind carrier aviation—Admiral William Moffett—was a battleship admiral, and his biggest allies were other battleship admirals like Joseph Reeves and William Sims. There was significant gun club opposition, but many battleship commanders supported carrier development.

In the area of mobilization planning, army thinking advanced significantly between the wars and in ways that cannot be explained as an incremental adjustment to prewar practices. The army pursued industrial mobilization planning, fundamentally rethinking how it should wage war despite public hostility and the dearth of resources provided by Congress until the point where war was just over the horizon.

Armored warfare was incrementally adaptive, but this was not the result of bureaucratic inertia. Rather, Congress would not support mechanization for financial reasons and because of General Pershing's testimony that mechanization was not relevant for continental defense. That decision made it easier for the infantry to pursue its parochial interests by ensuring tanks conformed to infantry tactics. Once the infantry was designated as the using arm, all design work on heavy tank models was cancelled.[152] The performance of obsolete equipment reinforced the opinions of the tank skeptics over the tank enthusiasts. Although the parochial interests of the infantry were served, these were not the sole or dominant factors behind the Army's adaptive approach to tank warfare.

The course of American armor development was affected by domestic political decisions, but the lessons of the war provided the initial set of experiences that framed decisions about armor.[153] This lends support to cognitive theories, particularly hypothesis C1a, which predicts that recent conflicts will shape future projections. The World War I experience created the interpretive frame through which subsequent tank experience was viewed. Most army officers saw the role of the tank through a static warfare frame, rather than a mobile warfare frame. World War I experience informed Pershing's 1919 testimony to Congress, and that testimony was instrumental in Congress's decision to disband the tank corps. Hypotheses on organizational imperatives underestimate leadership support for mechanization and elevate a secondary level factor (infantry parochialism) to a primary level cause by overlooking the process by which wartime experience shaped Pershing's views on the tank and his subsequent testimony, which in turn influenced congressional decisions that only then resulted in increased infantry control over mechanization.

With respect to the role that cognitive limitations played in shaping strategic choice more broadly, the experience of World War I should have had a decisive impact on how British political and military leaders set priorities among threats, risks, and national security goals. Direct involvement in combat would have provided a dramatic and vivid experience, but even being politically aware would have made the war a highly salient event in the minds of leaders. Yet there developed a strong reaction to even thinking about, let alone preparing for, another continental war. Arguably, the lesser contingencies that erupted after the armistice commanded attention at the expense of the Great War. However, given the toll that World War I extracted in life and materiel, it is difficult to imagine it being extinguished by pressures for imperial defense and policing. Yet extinguished it was. Britain's officer corps, military institutions, political leadership, and society were so determined to escape the horrors of the last war that they avoided thinking about it.[154] The chief lesson of the First World War—to avoid ever repeating the experience—proved to be so highly salient and unambiguous that it seemed unnecessary to study the Great War, let alone prepare for another one. This type of avoidance looks very much like a motivational effect, but it paints an incomplete picture of British behavior, particularly in the services where waging war and thinking about the unthinkable should be priorities. Motivational effects explain the desire to avoid war at almost any price, but the desire "never again" to fight a major war does not dictate strategy. One could prepare to fight, or one could prepare to deter. When the British government began to rearm in 1935, increased military strength was still not conceived of as practical preparation for Continental war.[155] The whole of British society simply refused to think about future great power war. The evidence shows how the smaller conflicts that erupted immediately after the war provided a postwar context for strategic reorientation. Short-term contingency response trumped long-term strategic planning, and small war contingencies of the present were extrapolated into the future based on the dangerous assumption that current threats were representative of future threats.

Although there was a role for domestic politics, cognitive limitations, and organizational imperatives, the broad contours of strategy are best understood as strategic responses to an external environment by states with relative differences in power operating under uncertainty. Evidence from interwar Britain and the United States supports the causal impact of relative power and complexity on strategic choice. As a rising power, the United States logically pursued a shaping strategy. As a declining power, Britain adapted to preserve as long as possible the power it still possessed.

Hypotheses on complexity include the effects of proximity of threats, their number and diversity, and the extent of interdependence. The evidence suggests that the number and diversity of threats are more consequential for strategic choice than are proximity or interdependence. For the British, low threat produced serious budget cutbacks, which weakened the defense sector, hindered research and development, and stunted innovation. These undermined responsiveness to rising threats later on and the quality of weapon systems the British could muster once war broke out. A highly diverse threat environment exacerbated Britain's situation further by complicating strategic assessment.

Inability to predict with any degree of confidence whom they would be fighting and when exacerbated the resource problem and compromised the scope and nature of innovation. Having more specific incentives, the Americans knew who the most likely enemy would be, the type of war they needed to fight, and what they needed to produce. This created an environment conducive to innovation.

5 UNITED STATES, 1990–2010

TWENTY YEARS HAVE PASSED since the Cold War ended. We have now experienced an interwar period equal in length to the one between the two world wars. Unlike the prior interwar period, the uncertainty engendered by the end of the Cold War shows few signs of abating. U.S. planners continue to face an extremely complex security environment, one characterized by a large number of threats, a diverse set of consequential security actors, and a globalized and interdependent world in which ideas and technologies are diffusing at an accelerating pace.

Like the other interwar periods examined in this volume, the post–Cold War era has coincided with a period of strategic pause. Discussion about a "decades-long 'strategic pause' during which the United States could ready itself for the rise of China or some other great power or coalition of great powers" has ceased but the balance of power has been remarkably stable since 1989. China is rising but far from a near-peer competitor. "The new century is still a moment of unprecedented great-power peace. [And] . . . by any historical standard, the danger of global conflict among wealthy nations is at an all-time low."[1]

A hiatus in great power rivalry presents new uncertainties and new opportunities. Periods of transition offer strategic opportunities because, during fluid times, "one can affect the shape of the world to come."[2] The model developed in Chapter 2 attributes uncertainty to structural conditions in the security environment and incomplete information about that environment. Logically, when new "types" of threats emerge, the burden of incomplete information increases because knowledge about, experience with, and operational concepts to deal with emerging threats do not exist. Systems designed to monitor past threats may be ill suited for new types of adversaries. National technical means that were honed against a conventional threat, for example, help little with monitoring and assessing violent extremist groups. The same critique applies to current human collection efforts where well-developed human intelligence capabilities that can differentiate among multiple strands of Islam, tribal groups, and intra- and intersectarian tension are desperately needed. Compounding the uncertainty today is the fact that, for the first time in history, some of the greatest threats come from the *least* rather than the *most* capable states in the system—from weak and failed states and ungoverned and undergoverned areas that have become sanctuaries for violent nonstate actors. Philip Bobbitt writes,

> For five centuries it has taken the resources of a state to destroy another state. ... In the past every state knew that its enemy would be drawn from a small class of nearby potential adversaries with local interests. But because of globalization and new methods of mass destruction, this is no longer true.[3]

The historical cases in this volume examine how leaders respond to challenges during uncertain times, how they allocate defense effort between present threats and future contingencies, and how they strike a balance across military and civilian departments. The most powerful states face the most complexity because they have broader interests, more commitments, and greater ambitions. Like their historic counterparts, U.S. leaders have not escaped these difficult choices. Current operations suggest one set of futures: transforming the Middle East; prevailing in small wars, counterinsurgencies, and irregular warfare; and countering violent extremist groups with special operations forces and soft power. Yet it is not self-evident that fighting Islamist terrorism will be the preeminent security challenge of coming decades. It has become commonplace to criticize the transformation efforts of the past twenty years for their failure to meet the requirements of counterinsurgency warfare, which is the current focus of most of the U.S. military's resources and operational effort.[4] Transformation, according to Frederick Kagan, should focus on solving immediate, clearly identified problems.[5] The smaller, lighter, more mobile military forces emphasized by Secretary Rumsfeld proved to be ill suited for restoring civil order. But investing resources and developing capabilities for the types of operations now underway risks leaving the nation ill prepared for different types of threats that will certainly arise in the future and that may be far more consequential for American power, position, and influence. The decline of Britain was hastened far more by the Germans, Japanese, and Americans than by insurgents.

A world of peer strategic competition would drive resources toward nuclear forces, satellites, long-range warning systems, tactical ballistic missile defense, space attack, and information warfare. Major regional conflict against an Iran or North Korea would require heavy maneuver forces, air power, and combat naval groups. If the primary threat were identified as terrorism, resources would shift to crime prevention, soft power nonmilitary forces, information operations, Special Forces, and surgical strike capabilities. If the chaos posed by failed states is the primary threat, the U.S. military would need to expend resources on capabilities to conduct peace and relief operations.[6] Colin Gray observes,

> We cannot know whether great-power wars are passé. But if we get it wrong, and in doing so act with confidence to express such a view in military posture, the negative consequences could be dire.... The future does not belong to small wars of an irregular kind; alas, it belongs to both regular and irregular warfare. Both interstate wars and insurgencies assuredly will scar the new century.[7]

Management scholars have shown how leading companies typically fail to stay on top when technologies or markets change. Leading states risk a similar fate. Clearly no condition of unipolarity will ever be permanent, but, as Stephen Biddle argues, "An important responsibility of grand strategists and the American political elite is to delay, if we can, this condition of the rise of a rival power." The "war on terror" may be the top priority, but this cannot crowd out entirely considerations of a longer-term nature, be it China or Russia or "some other rising power [that] comes to challenge our current position in the world in ways that could create a risk of much more serious military conflict at much higher levels of intensity with much higher levels of loss of life." Biddle concludes that decline may be inevitable, but "it can be later rather than sooner," and we must do what we can to postpone that day, to leverage superiority to position the nation to deter rising states from becoming threats in the future and to confront tomorrow's unknowns.[8]

U.S. strategists have been more aware of this than hegemons in earlier times. By the turn of this century, the United States embarked upon a set of policies geared toward "staying on top—that is, maintaining the strategic advantage, having more influence than others, and setting the agenda for global affairs—*for as long as necessary*—to avert truly bad events and generally move the world in a direction favorable to freedom, democracy, peace, and prosperity."[9] America responded to a similar impulse at the end of World War II—exploiting preponderant power to shape and guide the international system toward conditions more favorable to it and maintaining the military capability to preserve those conditions.[10]

RELATIVE POWER AND STRATEGIC PREFERENCES

This chapter examines how the United States has responded in an uncertain world and the forces that have shaped strategic choice. The argument advanced here is that relative power and the complexity of the state's external strategic environment set the key parameters for strategic choice. There is little debate that the United States is the preponderant power in the world today, particularly in the military realm, even given the strains caused by wars in Iraq and Afghanistan. The United States possesses "command of the commons"—air, oceans, and space.[11] Economically, the United States still far outstrips its next major competitor in gross national income, total gross domestic product, and purchasing power parity.[12]

There is less of a consensus on whether the United States is a hegemon and how significant has been its decline. The United States had been the predominant world power since the early part of the twentieth century. America's share of world GDP rose from 8.9 percent in 1870 to 19 percent in 1913, peaked at 28 percent in 1951 and declined to about 21 percent in 1975. It remained stable at 21 to 22 percent from 1975 to 1990. The peak in the 1950s owed much to the "World War II effect"—the devastation of Europe's economies made the U.S. economy seem disproportionately large. The 1975 numbers are a more accurate reflection of U.S. relative preponderance. On the other hand, the dollar has been eroding as the world's lead currency since the 1970s. The United States has run a trade deficit in goods since 1971 and turned into a debtor nation in 1986. More telling are indicators of high-tech competitiveness. The United States was long the leader in scientific excellence and technological innovation, and these qualities have been critical to America's competitive edge in the military and economic arenas. The United States still leads the world in research and discovery, but its "advantage is eroding rapidly as other countries commit significant resources to enhance their own innovative capabilities."[13]

America still possesses military supremacy and is currently preeminent by many economic indicators but is undeniably experiencing relative decline. That decline is relative chiefly to China, however, whose rise is still some time off. China is not yet a credible near-peer competitor because materially it cannot spend enough to overtake the United States. Other great powers pose less of a challenge to America's position. Russia is a greatly dissatisfied power. As Vladimir Putin lamented in 2005, "The collapse of the Soviet Union was [the] major geopolitical disaster of the century."[14] It intends on recovering as much of the Soviet Union's status, territory, and influence as possible. Yet despite the Kremlin's determination to regain its great power status and its recent assertiveness in foreign policy, a result of renewed self-confidence due to oil and gas wealth and a perception that the United States is overextended abroad and weakened, Russia has yet to arrest its military, economic, and social decline.[15] Europe faces serious economic, scientific, and demographic challenges and no longer aspires to be a great military power.[16] So America's power position is likely to linger.

Faced with uncertainty about its strategic environment, a preeminent power like the United States might adapt to preserve the system it dominates as predicted by Hypothesis P4. Adapting is a logical response for leading powers trying to hold on to their position. It characterized Britain's strategic response in the inter–world war period. On the other hand, a preeminent power may try to perpetuate its dominant position by shaping in line with Hypothesis P5, using its preponderant power to create a more favorable strategic environment and shift the terms of future competition to its advantage, even if this undermines the current terms of competition from which it benefits. Relative power alone does not provide a clear prediction for leaders. The nature of complexity is important. Leaders have global interests and commitments and so face a large number and wide variety of threats. According to Hypothesis E1, this creates pressure to adapt to a diverse range of missions and markets and to a wide array of near-term contingencies. Being defensively disadvantaged also creates pressures to adapt as described by Hypothesis B2. Although by some indictors the United States is defensively advantaged by virtue of its geographic distance from hostile powers, as a global power its "borders" no longer coincide with its continental landmass. Commitments to allies and the global nature of U.S. interests mean that, even in a physical sense, the United States no longer is defensively advantaged. In today's globalized world where ideas, information, and illicit goods move freely and rapidly, the notion of insularity—which, by delivering defensible borders, traditionally allowed states to privilege long-term economic growth at the expense of near-term military preparations—has virtually lost all meaning. Again, we would expect the United States to adapt. In sum, high diversity of threats and low defensive advantage favor a strategy of adapting.

Evidence indicates that America's strategic response to the post–Cold War world was one of adapting in the 1990s. For the leading power, adapting is logical—preserving a scaled-down version of a Cold War force structure and the relationships that had served America so well. Organizational inertia reinforced adapting; but, by the late 1990s, evidence of shaping began to emerge. The attacks of September 11 brought home the novelty and complexity of the new security environment. The Bush administration's response was to embark on a strategy of muscular shaping that included policies of military transformation, preventive war, and regime change with the intent of dissuading future adversaries, getting ahead of threats before they develop, preventing more dangerous futures, and shaping a world more hospitable to American interests and values. As events in Iraq and Afghanistan dragged on, they diverted U.S. attention from the broader strategic goal of preserving the Pax Americana. U.S. strategy began to migrate back toward adapting. Evidence for this has been most pronounced in the military domain. Military transformation has come to be viewed as a way to respond to the current challenges of stability and reconstruction operations. Readiness needs are trumping procurement and modernization. Force structure, doctrine, and training are being driven by the requirements of waging counterinsurgency (COIN) operations in response to conflicts currently underway.

The case study that follows describes America's security environment since the end of the Cold War. It examines U.S. strategic choices and evaluates the sources of those choices and the competing hypotheses advanced to explain them.

Security Environment

The defining characteristic of the post–Cold War security environment and what distinguishes it from the preceding four decades is the absence of a specific enemy and more precisely any conceivable great power strategic competitor. As a result, how U.S. leaders have thought about their security environment has been shaped as much by what the current environment is *not* as by what it is. So, for example, talk of global conflict and a global challenger gave way to talk of regional aggression and regional hegemons, the arms race took back seat to nuclear proliferation, and interstate conflict was downplayed relative to transnational threats. The certainty of the Cold War security environment was replaced by recognition of unprecedented complexity and a search for organizing constructs to impose order on that complexity.

The 1991 *National Security Strategy*, released within a month of Iraq's invasion of Kuwait, focused on containing regional conflict and countering regional aggression. Regional challenges were originally conceived in terms of an Iraq-style threat to vital U.S. interests, but Secretary of Defense Dick Cheney's *Defense Strategy for the 1990s: The Regional Defense Strategy* had evolved to include a broader set of regional problems.[17] The focus on regional contingencies remained the cornerstone of U.S. strategy throughout the 1990s, and "regional security" became the new organizing principle. This reflected three factors: the reality of small regional conflicts throughout the decade; uncertainty and lack of consensus on future threats, which placed a premium on maintaining regional stability; and the influence of the first Gulf War, although few other conflicts during the decade could be considered regional aggression of a similar nature. Long-standing commitment to bilateral arms control was replaced by nonproliferation as the prime nuclear worry, driven in part by the newly independent states that came into being with the Soviet collapse.

The effort to adjust to the new environment by focusing on regional geopolitical realities lost steam when the Clinton administration began to focus on broader "security" problems, including food, the environment, and the economy. The 1994 *National Security Strategy of Engagement and Enlargement* noted "no military threats to the nation's physical security." To the extent that military threats were identified, they continued to be seen as regional cross-border aggression. The next highest military priority was maintaining a credible overseas presence. Transnational threats increasingly crowded the security agenda along with the spread of weapons of mass destruction, terrorists, drugs, international crime, environmental degradation, and massive population flows. National security was subordinated to domestic economic issues and revitalizing the U.S. economy. The liberalization of high-performance computer (HPC) export controls in 1993 and 1995 exemplified how commercial interests trumped national security concerns.[18]

The *Bottom Up Review (BUR)* of U.S. defense forces in 1993 acknowledged the increasing complexity of the post–Cold War world in describing new dangers such as WMD proliferation, ethnic and religious strife, and threats to democratic reform. For the first time, economic strength was identified as a core national security priority. A Clinton Doctrine eventually emerged, which called for greater participation in multilateral peace and humanitarian operations to support engagement. The United States increasingly became involved in "operations other than war," peace operations, and small-scale contingencies in places like Panama, Haiti, Somalia, Bosnia, and Kosovo, which were more frequent, larger, and of longer duration than initially anticipated.

The 1997 *National Security Strategy* was released before the 1998 U.S. Embassy bombings in the East African capital cities of Dar es Salaam, Tanzania, and Nairobi, Kenya. It maintained the same priorities as previous years but for the first time made mention of the need to protect America's information infrastructure. China was viewed as a potential threat; but, as with the NIS states, engagement was the way to manage the problem. Over the next several years, the strategic outlook remained stable but with increasing concerns expressed about terrorism, failed states, and humanitarian disasters. By the end of his second term Clinton had retreated from "engagement and enlargement" and settled on a more restricted definition of vital national interests: protection of territory, citizenry, allies, economy, and infrastructure.

The George W. Bush administration came into office determined to reverse what it perceived as the previous administration's inability to separate the important from the trivial.[19] It refocused U.S. attention on areas of strategic concern, which meant power relationships and great power politics, particularly Russia and China. Only these big powers could radically upset international peace, stability, and prosperity. Rogue regimes like North Korea and Iran were a concern as supporters of terrorism and possessors of WMD. How the threat from al Qaeda and Osama Bin Laden fit into the conventional wisdom is discussed in the *9/11 Commission Report*.[20] Evidence suggests that, despite intelligence reports, there remained skepticism among senior decision makers about Bin Laden's role as a terrorist leader, doubt that terrorism would produce catastrophic results, and no consensus that we were on the verge of confronting a new type of threat. Nor "was the Department of Defense fully engaged in the mission of countering al Qaeda" before 9/11 "although this was perhaps the most dangerous foreign enemy then threatening the United States." The 9/11 Commission writes,

> Beneath the acknowledgment that Bin Laden and al Qaeda presented serious dangers, there was uncertainty among senior officials about whether this was

just a new and especially venomous version of the ordinary terrorist threat America had lived with for decades, or was radically new, posing a threat beyond any yet experienced. Such differences affect calculations about whether or how to go to war.[21]

The Bush national security team began to talk explicitly about uncertainty, which had been a cornerstone of the regional defense strategy crafted by Dick Cheney and Paul Wolfowitz in the early 1990s. Both men assumed top positions in the new Bush administration. Ryan Henry, principal deputy undersecretary of defense for policy, reported that when Donald Rumsfeld arrived at the Pentagon in 2001, he understood that the planning assumptions in place assumed a single predictable strategic adversary. By contrast, "Uncertainty defines the strategic and operational environment today. We can't tell where the next threats will come from or when they will materialize."[22]

"Uncertainty" remained a popular catchphrase in defense circles to describe the strategic landscape, even after the attacks of September 11. The 2005 *National Defense Strategy of the United States of America* asserted,

> Uncertainty is the defining characteristic of today's strategic environment. ... We contend with uncertainty by adapting to circumstances and influencing events. It is not enough to react to change. This strategy focuses on safeguarding U.S. freedoms and interests while working actively to forestall the emergence of new challenges.[23]

In late 2005 Henry explained that "the shock of 9/11 demonstrated how uncertain the world had become, and that day profoundly changed our perception of the immediacy and gravity of the risks we face."[24] In spring 2006, Henry reiterated, "The security environment at the start of the twenty-first century is perhaps the most uncertain it has been in our nation's history"[25] and said that America's global defense posture had to adapt to contend with that uncertainty. National security leaders were fully aware that America's security environment had become more complex than at any other time in recent history: There were more threats, more novel and diverse threats, and a far more interdependent world.

Defense planners continued to search for a framework that captured this complexity. The Department of Defense developed a taxonomy of threats to guide its 2005 *Quadrennial Defense Review* of military forces. The taxonomy proposed four categories of threat: traditional, irregular, catastrophic, and disruptive. "Traditional" threats come from states that employ military force in a conventional conflict to challenge U.S. power. "Irregular" threats come from weak states and nonstate actors that employ unconventional methods, like terrorism or insurgency warfare, to erode U.S. power. "Catastrophic" threats aim to paralyze U.S. power through WMD attacks or catastrophic acts of terror. "Disruptive" threats are those that upset a critical strategic balance and typically come from breakthrough technological advances that, when exploited by others, counter or cancel the leader's current military advantage. These are not discrete categories, but that is a reflection of the nature of the threat environment more than thinking about it. As Mackubin Owens points out, war is always multidimensional, and future adversaries are likely to be "hybrids," both at the lower and upper ends of the conflict spectrum. China, for example, is unlikely to confine its actions to traditional types of competition but should be expected to exploit asymmetric modes of confrontation. At the low end of the spectrum as well, groups like Hezbollah have and will continue to exhibit statelike capabilities, as demonstrated in its 2006 war with Israel.[26]

Irregular threats currently receive the lion's share of attention as the U.S. government and its international partners try to disrupt and defeat al Qaeda and the global militant Islamist movement. Al Qaeda has proven to be a novel adversary and an adaptable one. Since 9/11 it has evolved from a unified organization dominated by a powerful leadership core into a loose network of associated groupings spanning the globe with various financial, logistical, and operational ties. It has aligned itself with struggles across Asia, North Africa, Europe, and the Middle East in an attempt to co-opt local groups into a broader global struggle. It possesses a sophisticated propaganda machine that exploits the Internet to disseminate and amplify its messages and to recruit adherents. It also exploits the virtual safe haven of the Internet for fundraising and operational planning. Whereas strong states have traditionally been perceived to be greater threats than weak states, al Qaeda has reversed that assessment. It benefits from the semipermissive environment afforded by ungoverned or undergoverned areas that provide physical safe havens for illicit actors to operate freely and from the indirect support provided by corrupt regimes. Combating violent extremism remains a pressing challenge for the United States and one that has increasing potential to threaten the homeland as homegrown terrorist cells and plots continue to be discovered and as religious extremists succeed in finding opportunities to pursue their cause in the United States.[27]

Al Qaeda is currently under pressure in Pakistan and Afghanistan. Its operational leadership has been degraded. The U.S troop increase in Afghanistan will escalate the pressure on al Qaeda's capabilities and ability to operate. Pakistan's military is eliminating militant strongholds in the Northwest Frontier Province and Federally Administered Tribal Areas. Indiscriminate targeting of Muslim civilians in Iraq and Pakistan has alienated many sympathizers and undermined the group's legitimacy.[28] However, al Qaeda's use of the Internet as a virtual safe haven still remains a key battlefield in the "hearts and minds" struggle, and its exploitation of tribal conflicts in safe havens like Yemen, the Sahel, and Somalia provide fertile ground for training, recruitment, and operational planning.

How the United States has responded to greater diversity in threat types also has been shaped by a rapidly evolving technological landscape. Advances in range, strike, stealth, sensors, precision-guided munitions, microelectronics, computers, information processing, and biotechnology, many of which had their origins in the 1980s, are diffusing at an accelerating pace because of the Internet and globalization with often unanticipated consequences. Modern communications technology is being exploited by nonstate actors, most successfully by al Qaeda, in unprecedented and unanticipated ways to amplify their message and conduct globally dispersed operations. The information domain has become a critical battleground for twenty-first-century conflicts and may prove decisive in conflicts with nonstate adversaries. Large states have proven to be far less agile in operating in the information domain. There has also been an explosion of nongovernmental organizations, private security firms, criminal groups, and diaspora communities that are connected through information technology. The synergy among these developments has produced a proliferation of more diverse and consequential security actors and a world that is in many ways more unpredictable and more dangerous than previous periods of strategic pause.

Strategic Responses

Two indicators of strategic posture are the proportion of the nation's resources devoted to defense and how those defense resources are allocated. Defense spending as a proportion of total U.S. government spending (Table 5.1, Column C) peaked in 1987 at the height of the Reagan military buildup, bottomed out in 1998, and gradually rose after 9/11. Defense spending as a percentage of GDP (Table 5.1, Column E) reflects the same trend. It declined after the Vietnam War to a low point of 4.7 percent of GDP in 1979. The defense buildup of the 1980s boosted it to 6.2 percent by 1986, after which it gradually fell. By 2000, defense discretionary spending was 3 percent of GDP, reflecting the end

Table 5.1. U.S. national defense, federal spending, and gross domestic product, fiscal year 1980 through fiscal year 2007 (outlays in billions of current dollars).

Fiscal year	A Defense outlay	B Federal outlay	C Defense as a percentage of federal spending	D GDP	E Defense as a percentage of GDP
1980	134	590.9	22.7	2,726.7	4.9
1981	157.5	678.2	23.2	3,054.7	5.2
1982	185.3	745.7	24.8	3,227.6	5.7
1983	209.9	808.4	26	3,440.7	6.1
1984	227.4	851.9	26.7	3,840.2	5.9
1985	252.7	946.4	26.7	4,141.5	6.1
1986	273.4	990.4	27.6	4,412.4	6.2
1987	282	1,004.1	28.1	4,647.1	6.1
1988	290.4	1,064.5	27.3	5,008.6	5.8
1989	303.6	1,143.8	26.5	5,400.5	5.6
1990	299.3	1,253.1	23.9	5,735.4	5.2
1991	273.3	1,324.3	20.6	5,935.1	4.6
1992	298.4	1,381.6	21.6	6,239.9	4.8
1993	291.1	1,409.5	20.7	6,575.5	4.4
1994	281.6	1,462	19.3	6,961.3	4
1995	272.1	1,515.8	18	7,325.8	3.7
1996	265.8	1,560.6	17	7,694.1	3.5
1997	270.5	1,601.3	16.9	8,182.4	3.3
1998	268.5	1,652.7	16.2	8,627.9	3.1
1999	274.9	1,702	16.2	9,125.3	3
2000	294.5	1,789.2	16.5	9,709.8	3
2001	304.9	1,863.2	16.4	10,057.9	3
2002	348.6	2,011.2	17.3	10,377.4	3.4
2003	404.9	2,160.1	18.7	10,808.6	3.7
2004	455.9	2,293	19.9	11,499.9	4
2005	495.3	2,472.2	20	12,237.9	4
2006	521.8	2,655.4	19.7	13,015.5	4
2007	552.6	2,730.2	20.2	13,667.5	4

SOURCE: *The Budget for Fiscal Year 2009, Historical Tables* (Washington, DC: Office of Management and Budget, 2010).

Table 5.2. U.S. active duty military personnel, 1985–2009.

Year	Army	Navy	Marines	Air Force	Tot Active
1985	780,787	570,705	198,025	601,515	2,151,032
1986	780,980	581,119	198,814	608,199	2,169,112
1987	780,815	586,842	199,525	607,035	2,174,217
1988	771,847	592,570	197,350	576,446	2,138,213
1989	767,741	592,652	196,956	570,880	2,130,229
1990	732,403	581,856	196,652	535,233	2,046,144
1991	710,821	570,966	194,040	510,432	1,986,259
1992	610,450	541,883	184,529	470,315	1,807,177
1993	572,423	509,950	178,379	444,351	1,705,103
1994	541,343	468,662	174,158	426,327	1,610,490
1995	508,559	434,617	174,639	400,409	1,518,224
1996	491,103	416,735	174,883	389,001	1,471,722
1997	491,707	395,564	173,906	377,385	1,438,562
1998	483,880	382,338	173,142	367,470	1,406,830
1999	479,426	373,046	172,641	360,590	1,385,703
2000	482,170	373,193	173,321	355,654	1,384,338
2001	480,801	377,810	172,934	353,571	1,385,116
2002	486,542	385,051	173,733	368,251	1,413,577
2003	499,301	382,235	177,779	375,062	1,434,377
2004	499,543	373,197	177,480	376,616	1,426,836
2005	492,728	362,941	180,029	353,696	1,389,394
2006	505,402	350,197	180,416	348,953	1,384,968
2007	522,017	337,547	186,492	333,495	1,379,551
2008	543,645	332,228	198,505	327,379	1,401,757
2009	553,044	329,304	202,786	333,408	1,418,542

SOURCE: Department of Defense, Defense Manpower Data Center, Statistical Information and Analysis Division; available at http://siadapp.dmdc.osd.mil/index.html

of the Cold War and the economic growth of the 1990s. As of 2005, defense discretionary spending had climbed back to 4 percent of GDP. These patterns in defense allocation are consistent with a posture of adapting by the Clinton administration and shaping by the Bush administration.

Military personnel levels declined from 2.1 million in 1989 to 1.4 million by 1998 (Table 5.2). A steady decline is consistent with a post–Cold War demobilization and gradual adaptation to diminished military requirements. However, requirements quickly climbed as U.S. forces took on new missions in the Persian Gulf, Somalia, Haiti, and the Balkans. Concurrently, a vision of military transformation being promulgated, that of an information revolution in military affairs, called for a lean, quickly deployable and highly lethal armed force, integrated with information technologies and capable of projecting power rapidly and globally. Steady-state numbers in active duty military personnel since 2000 are not inconsistent with defense transformation, a hallmark of shaping.

To understand how defense resources are allocated, two indicators of military strategy are particularly instructive: the allocation of defense resources between the near term and long term, varying from readiness to modernization; and the related dimension of innovation-adaptation. The allocation of

Table 5.3. U.S. Department of Defense outlays by subfunction, fiscal year 1980 through fiscal year 2007 (in billions of current dollars).

Fiscal year	A Personnel	B Percentage of total	C Operations and modernization	D Percentage of total	E (B+D) Percentage of operations	F Procurement	G Percentage of total
1980	40.9	31	44.8	34	65	29	22
1985	67.8	28	72.3	29	57	70.4	29
1990	75.6	26	88.3	30	57	81	28
1991	83.4	32	101.7	39	71	82	31
1992	81.2	28	91.9	32	60	74.9	26
1993	75.9	27	94	34	61	69.9	25
1994	73.1	27	87.9	33	60	61.8	23
1995	70.8	27	91	35	62	55	21
1996	66.7	26	88.7	35	61	48.9	19
1997	69.7	27	92.4	36	63	47.7	18
1998	69	27	93.4	36	63	48.2	19
1999	70	27	96.3	37	64	48.8	19
2000	76	27	105.8	38	65	51.7	18
2001	74	25	112	39	64	55	19
2002	86.8	26	130	39	65	62.5	19
2003	106.7	28	151.4	39	67	67.9	18
2004	113.6	26	174	40	66	76.2	17
2005	127.5	27	188.1	40	67	82.3	17
2006	116.3	23	192.6	38	60	88.8	17
2007	109.9	22	161.5	32	54	89.7	18

resources between operations and modernization is one indicator of the proportion of defense effort devoted to the near term versus the long term. Operations and support activities include totals for the operations and maintenance account and military personnel account. Aside from the sharp peak associated with the 1991–1992 Persian Gulf War, operations and support gradually rose as a percentage of the overall share of the Department of Defense (DOD) budget throughout the 1990s (Table 5.3, Column E). Spending on modernization includes the sum of the research and development account and the procurement account. Modernization spending steadily fell over the 1990s (Table 5.3, Column J). Both trends are consistent with a posture of adapting in the 1990s with its emphasis on near-term demands over investment for the future.

Table 5.3. U.S. Department of Defense outlays by subfunction, fiscal year 1980 through fiscal year 2007 (in billions of current dollars). *(Continued)*

H Research development test and evaluation	I Percentage of total	J (G+I) Percentage of modernization	K Military construction	L Percentage of total	M Family housing	N % Total	O Other	P DoD Total
13	10	32	2.5	2	1.7	1	-1	130.9
27	11	40	4.3	2	2.6	1	0.5	245.1
38	13	41	5.1	2	3.5	1	-1.2	289.7
35	13	44	3.5	1	3.3	1	-46	262.3
35	12	38	4.3	1	3.3	1	-3.3	286.8
37	13	38	4.8	2	3.3	1	-6.4	278.5
35	13	36	5	2	3.3	1	2.7	268.6
35	13	35	6.8	3	3.6	1	-2.4	259.4
37	14	34	6.7	3	3.8	2	1.8	253.1
37	14	33	6.2	2	4	2	1.2	258.3
37	15	33	6	2	3.9	2	-1.9	256.1
37	14	33	5.5	2	3.7	1	0.06	261.3
38	13	32	5.1	2	3.4	1	1.6	281.2
41	14	33	5	2	3.5	1	0.5	290.3
44	13	32	5.1	2	3.7	1	-0.5	332
53	14	31	5.9	2	3.8	1	-1.5	387.3
61	14	31	6.3	1	3.9	1	1.7	436.5
66	14	31	5.3	1	3.7	1	1.5	474.2
71	14	31	7.3	1	3.8	1	2.4	512.1
72	14	32	8.3	2	3.9	1	3.5	504.9

SOURCE: *The Budget for Fiscal Year 2009, Historical Tables* (Washington, DC: Office of Management and Budget).

The relative share of each to the other shows that in the 1980s, modernization approached nearly two-thirds of operations and support. In 1997, modernization dropped to half of operations and support. Operations and support activities absorbed approximately 60 percent of DOD budget authority while modernization activities consumed half that proportion, near 30 percent. Those numbers have remained relatively stable up to the present. Part of the trend toward the increasing share of operations and maintenance has been the rising costs for military personnel (a major portion of which is health care costs) and a high operational tempo (OPTEMPO). The smaller shares devoted to modernization during the Clinton years are a direct legacy of the procurement holiday of the 1990s, which was possible because the military had so much modern weaponry from the Reagan buildup (Table 5.3, Column G). Part of the explanation for the rise in the defense budgets under George W. Bush was the need to replace and refurbish aging equipment deferred during the Clinton years. However, budget allocation to specific systems during the George W. Bush administration shows an emphasis on funding systems deemed to be transformational. Secretary of Defense Donald Rumsfeld reported in May 2006 that the U.S. military had more than 3,000 unmanned aerial vehicles (UAVs) as compared to 132 in 2001 and that Special Operations Forces had grown to 6,000 troops with its own separate command and a budget twice as large as in 2001.[29] The George W. Bush administration also doubled spending on missile defense from $5 billion per year in previous administrations to $9 billion per year.[30]

Another indicator of adapting in the 1990s was the effort to preserve the existing balance of forces in the face of pressures to downsize the military. The regional security strategy of the George H. W. Bush administration called for a military that could fight two simultaneous major regional conflicts and a "Base Force" that would provide that capability. The Base Force review was initiated in 1989 on the eve of the Soviet collapse by Chairman of the Joint Chiefs of Staff Colin Powell as a way to preempt a large peace dividend that might shift resources from defense to social programs. The Base Force is instructive for several reasons. It would reduce the U.S. military by approximately 25 percent but not alter its structure fundamentally. The force would be smaller but organized in the same way, to fight less demanding but similar types of conventional wars. It was never the intent or expectation that the U.S. military would focus on peacekeeping or nation building; in other words, nonmilitary tasks that have occupied peacetime militaries in the past. Primary worries centered on Iraq, North Korea, and to some degree Iran. Bush senior sent no forces to Bosnia and had only limited involvement in Somalia. Hypothetical enemies were rogue states and regional powers with sizable military forces that might force the United States into conventional confrontations. The Base Force was designed to maintain a slightly downsized but still preponderant military, consistent with a strategy of adapting. The Base Force also gave high priority to readiness.

The Clinton administration's *Bottom Up Review* of U.S. defense forces in 1993 continued the emphasis on adapting, consistent with Base Force assumptions and the experience of the Gulf War. It endorsed the two-war strategy, maintained Cold War readiness levels, and preserved service budget shares, as well as existing force structure and modernization strategies. As the U.S. military increasingly became involved in "operations other than war" and small-scale contingencies, readiness needs crowded out modernization priorities and funds routinely migrated from investment accounts to operations and support accounts. The ability to respond to two simultaneous Desert Storm–like regional conflicts remained the guidepost for military planning with a focus on Iraq and North Korea. The 1997 *Quadrennial Defense Review* (QDR) anticipated continued participation in peace operations but reaffirmed the emphasis on two simultaneous major regional contingencies, treating peace operations and other smaller-scale contingencies as "lesser-included cases." The 200,000 forward deployed troops in Europe and Asia remained in place while resource constraints permitted only selective modernization.

The 1997 QDR had diverged little from the *BUR* or its predecessor, the Base Force. The upshot was maintenance of a force structure that was essentially Cold War "light." Funds for long-range modernization continued to migrate to operations accounts as U.S. participation in peace operations grew more than initially anticipated. Subsequent *National Security Strategies* until 2001 adopted the same strategic outlook, although they expressed increasing concerns about terrorism, failed states, and humanitarian disasters.

The 1990s had produced several efforts to adapt American military strategy in light of the implosion of the Soviet Union and end of the Cold War. Although the military of 2000 looked remarkably similar to that of a decade earlier, defense leaders had begun to grapple with a more complex security environment. Explicit discussions of shaping had already emerged. The 1993 *BUR* called on the United States to prevent conflict by promoting democracy and, on the military, to begin engaging in shaping activities like military-to-military contacts with the former Soviet Union. The 1997 QDR advanced a strategy of "shape, respond, prepare," with the military shaping the environment through deterrence and engagement, responding to a spectrum of conflicts from small-scale contingencies to major theater war, and preparing for an uncertain future. The military was also seen as the tool of choice for dealing with other problems: WMD proliferation, the drug trade, organized crime, uncontrolled immigration, and threats to the homeland. Nonproliferation, essentially a shaping strategy, had replaced the adaptive notion of arms control and would subsequently be superseded by the more aggressive shaping strategy of counterproliferation.

It was then-Governor Bush's September 1999 Citadel speech that explicitly called for "creating the military of the next century." Bush reiterated his commitment to transformation early on in his administration: "We are witnessing a revolution in the technology [of] war. Power is increasingly defined not by size, but by mobility and swiftness. Advantage increasingly comes from information. . . . Our goal is to move beyond marginal improvements to harness new technologies that will support a new strategy. . . . " An Office of Force Transformation, led by Vice Admiral Arthur Cebrowski, USN (Ret), a leading advocate of transformation in the U.S. navy, was established, and the services were directed to develop transformation roadmaps. The Bush administration's commitment to transformation was formalized in the September 2001 *Quadrennial Defense Review Report* published by the Department of Defense.

Transformation became one of the George W. Bush administration's highest defense priorities and the heart of a strategic approach committed to preventing any nation from surpassing or equaling the United States militarily. Deputy Secretary of Defense Paul Wolfowitz had quietly advocated for a robust shaping strategy in 1992 as under secretary of defense for policy in Bush senior's administration. The 1992 draft Defense Planning Guidance (DPG) had called for containing emerging regional powers and actively blocking the rise of any potential competitor to the United States to ensure that America remained the sole superpower. It specifically identified allies—Germany, Japan, India—as potential threats to be suppressed.[31] The DPG enraged U.S. allies and was retracted and replaced with calls for military cooperation based on multilateral organizations.[32]

Wolfowitz resurrected this shaping strategy nearly a decade later in the 2002 *National Security Strategy*: "Our forces will be strong enough to dissuade potential adversaries from pursuing a military build-up in hopes of surpassing, or equaling, the power of the United States." The doctrine of military preponderance emphasized the need to prevent wars by dissuading adversaries from building dangerous new capabilities in the first place.[33] This shaping strategy greatly relied on the military. Transformation was defined both broadly as a sweeping set of reforms designed to prepare the U.S. military for a new era and sustain America's strategic position and narrowly as a revolution in how the U.S. military fights. Initially geared toward major combat operations, transformation is now discussed in terms of stability and reconstruction operations. This is an interesting development given that no state has ever modernized for a stability and reconstruction force; modernization is usually pursued for major combat operations against a chief competitor. An underlying assumption of the defense community was that the United States depends, and will continue for the next century to depend, on technological superiority for its military security and, by extension, its national security.

Even as the events of September 11 signaled the onset of the global war on terror, the president and his senior leadership continued to emphasize the importance of transforming U.S. forces, capabilities, and institutions. A renewed sense of urgency was conveyed: "Transformation is not a goal for tomorrow, but an endeavor that must be embraced in earnest *today*."[34] The war on terror was cited as evidence of the need for transformation. In January 2002 at National Defense University, Secretary of Defense Rumsfeld made the case for aggressive pursuit of transformation goals and their continued relevance even after the terrorist attacks of 9/11.[35] The United States still needed to protect the U.S. homeland and bases overseas, project and sustain power in distant theaters, deny enemies sanctuary even in the most remote corners of the world, protect our information networks from attack, use information technology to link up different kinds of U.S. forces so that they can fight jointly, and maintain unhindered access to space and protect our space capabilities from enemy attack. The Afghan campaign reinforced the importance of these goals, in particular the ability to project force over long distances to fight distant adversaries. Secretary Rumsfeld continued,

> We need rapidly deployable, fully integrated joint forces capable of reaching distant theaters quickly and working with our air and sea forces to strike adversaries swiftly, successfully, and with devastating effect. We need improved intelligence, long-range precision strikes, sea-based platforms to help counter the access denial capabilities of adversaries.[36]

Secretary Rumsfeld argued that the United States must continue to transform, precisely to meet the threat of terrorism and terrorist WMD in particular. Transformation became the heart of a strategic approach to ensure the United

States would remain competitive in the face of a diverse array of unpredictable threats being fed by the information revolution and globalization, that no nation would surpass or equal it militarily, and that no competitor would even try.[37]

Transformation leveraged developments that well predated 9/11 and that were anchored in pursuit of an information revolution in military affairs (IT-RMA). *Joint Vision 2020*, issued in May 2000, had called on the United States to "work to shape the international security environment in ways favorable to American interests, be willing and able to respond to the full spectrum of crises as needed, and prepare now for an uncertain future." Transformation was a keyword in the 2001 QDR, and the document's explicit emphasis on change reflected the view that an RMA was transforming the nature of military engagements such that large, centralized groupings of soldiers had become a liability rather than an asset. It also reflected the accelerating trend toward multiple, small missions and the expectation that the United States had to be able to respond to simultaneous overlapping crises in all parts of the world while also transforming to prevail against a larger number of more diverse threats from terrorists and insurgents to North Korean rockets and Serbian strongmen. QDR 2001 is significant because it codified the uncertainty facing the United States by advancing a doctrine of contingency-based training and experimentation. Acknowledging the ultimate strategic unknown—the identity of the threat—the review did not anticipate whom the United States would be fighting but concentrated on *how* it would fight or on a "capabilities-based" approach, altering a fundamental tenet of military planning.

Consistent with the flexibility that underwrites shaping strategies, QDR 2001 called for more flexible basing and moving forces out of Western Europe to respond to a broader range of global contingencies. The United States began to realign its global defense posture—updating the types, locations, numbers, and capabilities of U.S. military forces—with the expressed intent of positioning forces for the decades ahead. The numbers of U.S. forward stationed forces had been dramatically reduced in the mid-1990s, but they had remained concentrated in Western Europe and Northeast Asia. In 2004, a new global defense posture strategy was adopted that, among other things, gradually shifted U.S. forces in Western Europe south and eastward and replaced legacy maneuver divisions in Europe with a lighter more easily deployable Stryker capability. Both posture changes were designed for more rapid deployment to the Middle East, Africa, and other hot spots. Additional expeditionary maritime capabilities and long-range strike assets were deployed forward in Alaska, Hawaii, and Guam. Under Secretary of Defense for Policy Douglas Feith described the logic: "President Bush and Secretary Rumsfeld likewise are thinking about the relatively distant future. In developing plans to realign our forces abroad, they are not focused on the diplomatic issues of the moment, but on the strategic requirements and opportunities of the coming decades," much in the way Dean Acheson was conscious of creating institutions that would long endure after World War II.[38]

Assessing innovation-adaptation by focusing on specific technologies and organizational structures is possible retrospectively but difficult to do contemporaneously for a few reasons. First, we cannot know *ex ante* which systems will prove to be truly transformational; hence we cannot know which systems to focus on in our assessment. Some technologies, like UAVs, real-time battlefield information networks, and precision munitions, appear to be transforming the way the military fights, so the emphasis on these types of systems could be used as a rough indicator of innovation. To the extent that transformation requires investment in future systems, an emphasis on research, development, and experimentation would suggest innovation.

Second, transformation is a process that occurs over time. It involves long-term efforts to change institutions and career paths, reallocate financial resources, transform the technological and industrial bases, and sustain political will for change. It is possible, however to assess the first steps in the process, which typically involve conceptual innovation and realistic experimentation and testing of new ideas. Evidence shows that the U.S. military has developed a vision of future warfare and conducted field experiments to test transformational concepts.

The 1990s have been described as "a lost decade" for transformation.[39] The services mouthed transformation but did not terminate any major acquisition programs. Transformation became a means to justify existing systems.[40] Well aware that they would see budget cuts in the 1990s, each of the services sought to reinvent itself to justify its budget. It is significant how they reshaped their images—in ways consistent with ideas about transformation that were circulating in the 1990s and subsequently championed by the George W. Bush administration. A perceptual revolution was underway with important consequences for how the U.S. military planned to organize and operate. Changes in force structure, force posture, and equipment have followed to include a more digitized, mobile, expeditionary, and networked army, a navy more able to deliver precise attacks, and a shrinking of traditional garrisons in Europe and Korea.

In 1996 the joint chiefs of staff published *Joint Vision 2010 (JV2010)*, a conceptual template that argued that information technology and precision strike had brought about a basic change in how wars would be fought on land, at sea, and in the air. Army transformation was governed by *Army Vision 2010*, the blueprint for the army's response to *JV 2010*. *Army Vision 2010* called for leveraging technology, lightening up heavy forces, and heavying up light forces. Heavy forces had the necessary firepower but required extensive support and too much time to deploy. Light forces could deploy rapidly but lacked firepower. The conceptual lynchpins of *Army Vision 2010* were dominant maneuver (application of information and mobility to employ widely dispersed joint operations), precision engagement (systems to locate the target and engage with precision), full dimensional protection (control of the battle space), focused logistics (fusion of information, logistics, and transportation technologies to provide rapid crisis response and sustain operations), and information superiority (capability to collect, process, and disseminate information while denying an adversary's ability to do the same).

Force XXI was the focus of force design activities in the 1990s that would supersede the 1980s Army of Excellence. Force XXI was revolutionary in two ways. A full panoply of newly emergent, computer-driven constructive and virtual simulation methods, equipment, and software was joined to actual live field simulation to test and analyze new military unit designs. Force XXI was the first design activity to embody "digitization"—a linked, instantaneous, and common picture of the unfolding battle. The key development vehicle to test future force designs was a division-sized Experimental Force (EXFOR). The EXFOR explored future doctrinal and organizational concepts for a digitized brigade in a series of advanced warfighting experiments. More radical operational and organizational changes were explored in the follow-on "Army after Next" project. Although the army responded well to technological changes, planning still assumed a strategic environment in 2020 much like that of 1997. Nation-states would be the most important political units with warfare chiefly a struggle between nation-states protecting national interests. The army was capitalizing on information technology to improve its effectiveness, but war was still seen as political, episodic, violent, state-centric, and distinct from peace.

In October 1999, Army Chief of Staff General Eric Shinseki launched a new vision to make the army more strategically relevant—mobile and lethal. The Kosovo war showed that the army lacked units that could both strike hard and move quickly. Originally called the Objective Force, the Future Force would be a medium force that would be strategically responsive, agile, rapidly deployable, versatile, lethal, survivable, and sustainable across the entire spectrum of military operations. Army transformation centered on creating a new generation of unmanned ground vehicles, air vehicles, sensors, and munitions linked by an information network. The Future Combat System (FCS) would enable a new organization roughly equivalent to the size of a current brigade to fight with the combat power and lethality of a current division.

There were questions about the wisdom of a homogenous force with one uniform type and about the large investment requirements of the FCS. Spurred by 9/11, the army accelerated its transformation into a power projection force by migrating its division-centric force of large, mostly armored divisions of around 15,000 soldiers designed to fight major theater wars toward a brigade-centric force composed of 3,000 to 4,000 soldier combat brigade units designed for expeditionary demands across the globe.

Army transformation succumbed to pressures to adapt to current challenges. The pre-9/11 army had adopted the guiding principle that a technology-enabled force would be able to see first, understand first, act first, and finish decisively. But the wisdom of focusing on technological enablers and a narrow range of weapons platform was challenged in both Iraq and Afghanistan by enemies who were difficult to locate, who did not wear uniforms or use military vehicles, and who had years to observe and develop weapon systems that created an asymmetric advantage. More generally, technology in and of itself could not account for cultural and social factors. Resources were shifted to the counterterror fight. A strategic decision was made to optimize for the current threat, accepting risk in the ability to synchronize and mass effects for conflict with a more formidable foe.

A discernible shift in focus occurred in December 2006 with the publication of the Army/Marine *Counterinsurgency Field Manual*, FM 3-24 and Marine Corps *Warfighting Publication* 3-33.5. These put into place a doctrine for asymmetric warfare and codified counterinsurgency (COIN) lessons like the importance of nonlethal operations and interagency participation. Characterized as a new doctrine that channels military culture toward the skill sets demanded by COIN—protecting the population, building local institutions, and encouraging economic development—rather than those demanded by swift decisive operations against a conventional enemy, the publications coincided with the departure of Secretary of Defense Rumsfeld from the Pentagon in 2006. A growing consensus emerged that Iraq and Afghanistan discredited network-centric warfare concepts like information supremacy and the ability of precision strikes to hit enemy centers of gravity, particularly in a war where the center of gravity is the population. For a conventionally minded military, it is significant that official doctrine for counterinsurgency now exists. Counterinsurgency puts a premium on leader continuity and area expertise. Field training has incorporated huge changes, but manning policies, revision of institutional training, functional specialties, and recruiting guidelines have not changed significantly after eight years of protracted conflict.

The U.S. navy of the 1990s faced neither a peer nor a superior naval adversary. Active duty personnel fell from 570,966 in 1991 to 373,193 in 2000 (Table 5.3), and warships declined from 529 in 1991 to 341 in 2000. The navy knew it had to adapt to the new strategic environment and develop a vision to replace the Cold War–era Maritime Strategy. Marginalized in Operation Desert Storm, the navy responded by reinventing itself to support the land battle rather than to conduct war at sea. Power projection from sea to land superseded the traditional mission of sea control. The new navy concept went hand-in-hand with the marines' focus on expeditionary units (MEUs). The navy kept its structural and physical building blocks—carrier battle groups, naval tactical aviation, amphibious ready groups, and MEUs—but billed itself as an integral part of regional land operations such as those in Somalia, Haiti, and Bosnia.

In 1992, the navy published . . . *From the Sea*, which talked about naval expeditionary forces moving into littoral areas, conducting joint operations, and enabling other services to execute their missions. The navy created N-85, the Expeditionary Warfare Division commanded by a marine and using all of the navy's available resources for land operations. *Forward . . . From the Sea* was published in 1994, building on . . . *from the Sea*. The navy continued to focus on power projection and a combat-credible forward presence and proposed mobile sea bases to increase flexibility. Reflecting a balance between efforts to counter regional aggression and the reality of U.S. roles in peacekeeping in the 1990s, *Forward . . . from the Sea* asserted the utility of naval power projection in peacekeeping and other situations short of war.

Navy force structure remained remarkably stable despite a new focus on power projection and forward operations. Nonetheless, the navy had developed a vision of future warfare, articulated in *Forward . . . from the Sea* and in the chief of naval operations' 1997 essay, "Anytime, Anywhere: A Navy for the

21st Century." The navy's dominant concept for future warfare was "network-centric warfare." The Naval War College was designated as the focal point for innovation within the service, and it began conducting fleet battle experiments to explore new concepts and organizations to carry out network-centric warfare. With the disintegration of the Soviet Union, naval forces made the shift away from operations on the sea to projection of power from the sea to shape events in the littorals. An open ocean, blue water naval strategy designed to fight a high-volume, high-speed Soviet threat was supplanted by a regional, littoral, expeditionary focus.

In 2005, the concept of the "1,000-ship Navy" emerged, providing an interesting parallel to the Fisher era's fleet unit concept. Like its predecessor, the 1,000-ship navy represented a vision of coordinated effort to safeguard global maritime interests. The United States recognized it did not possess the capability to ensure the security of the maritime domain on its own, just as Britain had realized a century earlier. The 1,000-ship Navy envisions cooperative partnerships and alliances with other nations and private stakeholders to establish a global network of maritime nations to improve maritime awareness, enable crisis response, and enhance maritime security. Like the fleet unit concept, increased interoperability among participating navies is critical. The U.S. navy would lead the integration effort and identify technology availability and requirements for navies to participate in the network. Like its predecessor, however, the concept risks being seen as an initiative aimed at bending international maritime forces to the naval hegemon's agenda.

The navy's white papers provided the foundation for the marine corps' *Operational Maneuver from the Sea* (OMFTS) concept published in January 1996 by Commandant General Charles C. Krulak. OMFTS exploited significant enhancements in information management, battlefield mobility, and the lethality of conventional weapons to respond to a new series of threats that had produced chaos in the littorals. An important assumption of OMFTS was the need to operate in urban or suburban environments. The Commandant's Warfighting Laboratory, established in October 1995, served as a catalyst for experimentation. The corps embarked on a five-year experimentation plan and a series of exercises to examine future warfighting concepts. It also took the lead in exploring military operations in urban terrain and with nonlethal weaponry.[41]

The air force was successful early on in demonstrating its relevance to the post–Cold War challenges in the air war over Serbia. The 1990 air force White

Paper *Global Reach—Global Power* made the case for the service's strategic importance in shaping the international environment. Put to the test in the Balkans, Afghanistan, and Iraq, the air force emerged tired but successful. The air force articulated its vision of future warfare in *Global Engagement: A Vision for the 21st Century Air Force*. The 1996 paper argued that the air force should evolve from an air and space force to a space and air force and finally to a space force. It also recommended that the service more fully exploit unmanned vehicles. The air force established six battle labs to explore emerging areas and formed operational squadrons devoted to information warfare and UAVs. In 2000, *Global Vigilance, Reach, and Power* scaled back the goal of a space force, emphasizing the usefulness and complementarity of space to terrestrial operations. Air power was attractive because it offered the possibility of light engagement overseas (for humanitarian purposes) and made the limited use of force more palatable.

Evidence shows that all the services accepted the need to transform. Each promoted a vision built on an advanced common C^4I backbone. Each conducted war games, advanced concept technology demonstrations, and advanced war-fighting experiments aimed at developing new operational concepts and organizational configurations. Resource allocation under George W. Bush emphasized research and development. The administration proposed new funding for satellite communications, space-based radar, UAVs, a wideband secured global communications network, and upgraded data links to combat platforms and troops.[42] The Bush administration believed that the wars in Iraq and Afghanistan would demonstrate how these capabilities had provided the United States with military dominance and strategic influence. But the wars did not validate that vision. Rather, they accelerated a retreat from shaping and a return to adapting with an emphasis on the near-term and counterinsurgency warfare.

Operation Enduring Freedom (OEF), the U.S. effort to eliminate Afghanistan as a base for terrorist operations, validated many aspects of transformation including the importance of UAVs, global positioning system, real-time battlefield information networks, precision munitions, and the innovative use of special forces. The technologies designed for a peer competitor with large technically advanced forces demonstrated value against lesser military actors.[43] The combination of special operations forces, precision air power, and indigenous forces was labeled the "Afghan model,"[44] an airpower-dominant way of war with ground forces used as target spotters that could deliver strategic effects with few casualties.⁴⁵ Initial success in Afghanistan gave transformation a boost, but the operation also displayed much continuity with the past.⁴⁶ Afghanistan involved substantial close combat and demonstrated the continued value of traditional ground forces. Operation Iraqi Freedom (OIF) ultimately dampened enthusiasm for the Afghan model. Although OIF relied on expanded information networks, troops at the brigade level and below had far less situational awareness than did higher headquarters.⁴⁷ As the conflicts in Iraq and Afghanistan became more protracted, dominance through technology was put to the test and came up short.⁴⁸ Transformation concepts proved their worth in decisive combat operations but were marginal to post-conflict or Phase IV operations that involve establishing security, stability, and reconstruction, all critical to counterinsurgency operations.⁴⁹

In mid-2008, just as the Bush administration was ending its tenure in office, Defense Secretary Robert Gates approved a new *National Defense Strategy*. Gates identified the fight against al Qaeda and other terrorist organizations as the nation's top national security priority. He embraced the term *the Long War* to describe the fight against Islamist extremism and equated the current struggle with those against Nazi Germany and Soviet Russia. The military should focus on "irregular" rather than conventional warfare to defeat a complex transnational foe in a "long-term, episodic, multi-front, and multi-dimensional" fight that requires marshalling of soft power as well as hard power.⁵⁰

The first war of the information age pitted the United States against the type of enemy never envisioned in the 1990s. An enemy weak by conventional standards adopted an asymmetric strategy that relies on the information domain to amplify its power. Using military force to kill and capture terrorists and to disrupt their physical networks could buy time but not be a long-term solution. The center of gravity—the primary source of the terrorists' moral and physical strength, power, and resistance—is the population, more specifically the hearts and minds of politically uncommitted Muslims. The challenge has become one of denying terrorists new recruits and passive community support, while discrediting their ideology and undermining their legitimacy.

It is well understood that the military cannot sustain a generation's long war against extremism.⁵¹ Even if it could, the solution does not lie in military operations alone. A coordinated whole of government approach must leverage civilian departments to address the underlying conditions that breed terrorists and sustain their ideas. The United States has invested in the military, law enforcement, and intelligence tools for the counterterrorism fight. But to shape the environment and get out ahead of terrorism before it takes hold requires diplomacy, information operations, economic and social development, civil society, and rule of law.

In November 2007, Secretary Gates gave what was described as "groundbreaking" speech by a senior Defense Department official:

> One of the most important lessons of the wars in Iraq and Afghanistan is that military success is not sufficient to win.... Economic development, institution-building, and the rule of law, promoting internal reconciliation, good governance, providing basic services to the people, training and equipping indigenous military and police forces, strategic communications, and more—these, along with security, are essential ingredients for long-term success.[52]

Gates acknowledged that "funding for non-military foreign-affairs programs has increased since 2001, but it remains disproportionately small relative to what we spend on the military and to the importance of such capabilities." The 2007 budget for the "Department of Defense—not counting operations in Iraq and Afghanistan—is nearly half a trillion dollars. The total foreign affairs budget request for the State Department is $36 billion—less than what the Pentagon spends on health care alone. There were only about 6,600 professional Foreign Service officers—less than the manning for one aircraft carrier strike group." Gates called for "a dramatic increase in spending on the civilian instruments of national security—diplomacy, strategic communications, foreign assistance, civic action, and economic reconstruction and development."

Enhancing the resources and capacity of civilian agencies, particularly the Department of State, is still in its infancy. Gates recently proposed a major overhaul of the way the Pentagon and State Department conduct nation building by establishing three long-term funds totaling $2 billion to stabilize strife-ridden countries and address failing states like Yemen and Somalia that are becoming havens for terrorists. The proposal aims to end disputes that escalated over Iraq and Afghanistan about whether civilians or the better-funded military should be in charge of stabilization and put to rest accusations that U.S. foreign policy has become overly militarized. It "sets forth a new approach that could transcend these debates. It argues for a new model of shared responsibility and pooled resources for cross-cutting security challenges."[53]

Gates announced a reordering of U.S. defense programs in April 2009—terminating the F-22 raptor program at 187 aircraft, shrinking the size of the U.S. fleet below 313 ships, cutting space and missile defense programs, and cancelling the FCS.⁵⁴ These types of cuts indicate a decision to accept a greater level of risk with respect to U.S. supremacy in air and space. They also reflect a reordering of spending priorities to support an ambitious domestic agenda. Massive expenditures on energy, health care, and education necessarily require cuts in defense spending. Thomas Donnelly writes, "The budget cuts Mr. Gates is recommending are not a temporary measure to get us over a fiscal bump in the road. Rather, they are the opening bid in what, if the Obama administration has its way, will be a future U.S. military that is smaller and packs less wallop."⁵⁵

The Obama administration's newly released *National Security Strategy* in May 2010 repeatedly calls for America to shape the international system and renew its leadership for the long term. But the language of shaping has not been reflected in actions to preserve and extend the Pax Americana. Frederick Kagan captured the rationale for strategic readjustment. Fueled by the conflicts in Iraq and Afghanistan, "We should shorten our gaze and focus on immediate operational challenges and problems first, on visible near- and mid-term threats second, and only then on long term threats and opportunities."⁵⁶ Integrating a rising China into the existing international order while containing its military power may be the most significant long-term challenge, particularly as China spreads its influence across the Middle East and Africa. But those forces that breed terrorism and extremism are the proximate danger. A severe economic downturn has further undermined efforts to shape and position the nation for a future world of new competitors and new types of competition.

Shaping is a risky strategy that invites backlash. This is evident in the strategic retreat currently underway. Transforming societies in the Middle East has been rejected. U.S. objectives in Afghanistan, as described by President Obama in his West Point speech on December 8, 2009, no longer include establishing a Western-style democracy. Nor does Obama talk about advancing "opportunity and justice," which had been included in his administration's March 2009 strategy review.⁵⁷ Victory is now defined as denying al Qaeda sanctuary in Afghanistan and Pakistan, defeating the terrorist group and dismantling it.

The decision to augment U.S. forces in Afghanistan by 30,000 troops followed a lengthy strategy review that revealed deep fissures within the Obama administration about how to defeat al Qaeda—from a narrower counterterrorism (CT) strategy to a broader counterinsurgency strategy. While the narrow

CT strategy championed by Vice President Joe Biden was rejected, the current effort will focus on the more discrete objectives of disrupting and defeating al Qaeda, reversing the Taliban's momentum, and strengthening the capacity of Afghanistan's security forces and government. President Obama made it clear to his generals that the U.S. goal is to diminish the Taliban enough so that the Afghan government can contain it and proceed with reconciliation.

Arguably, the "new approach" does not mean commanders on the ground will wage war in a fundamentally different way from what General Stanley McChrystal outlined in his initial assessment in August 2009.[58] Obama's plan resembles the surge strategy in Iraq—standing up indigenous military forces so U.S. troops can "stand down" and providing "breathing space" for local governance and infrastructure to develop. U.S. reinforcements will focus on securing population centers where the Taliban hold greatest sway to reverse enemy momentum. They will support more responsive local government and develop community-defense militias. They will target development in key population centers and if possible persuade the Taliban to lay down arms and reconcile. However, McChrystal's characterization of his mission as "defeating the insurgency" defined as "a condition where the insurgency no longer threatens the viability of the state" was rejected by the Obama administration as too expansive and too much like an Iraq-style counterinsurgency operation. The desired end state is "more informal local security arrangements than in Iraq, a less-capable national government and a greater tolerance of insurgent violence."[59] The narrower mission of degrading the Taliban rejects full-scale nation building. General McChrystal and now General Petraeus use the term *counterinsurgency* but the White House has not since the president's West Point speech. Administration officials have denied that the July 2011 exit date they set would be the end of a U.S. commitment but rather stated that it would be the beginning of a gradual withdrawal. The narrower explicit objectives, rejection of an Afghanistan-wide counterinsurgency effort, and a short timeline for achieving those objectives represent a clear retreat from a robust shaping strategy.

America's post–Cold War diplomatic strategy mirrors trends in the military domain—adapting under Clinton and shaping under Bush. Clinton's foreign policy was tied to domestic renewal. It looked to collective and multilateral institutions to meet international challenges and crises. *A National Security Strategy of Engagement and Enlargement* spells out,

> No matter how powerful we are as a nation, we cannot secure these basic goals unilaterally . . . The threats and challenges we face demand cooperative,

multinational solutions. Therefore, the only responsible U.S. strategy is one that seeks to ensure U.S. influence over and participation in collective decisionmaking in a wide and growing range of circumstances.[60]

Clinton championed assertive multilateralism and multinational military cooperation with the United Nations as a global peacekeeper. The United States adopted a posture of followership abroad—what has been described as "going along as the biggest member of a vague consensus."[61] Foreign policy was risk averse, reactionary, and crisis driven whether with respect to Haiti, Somalia, or Bosnia. The deaths of U.S. Army Rangers in Somalia in 1993 led the administration to eschew arduous peacemaking operations for lower-risk peacekeeping activities.

Clinton showed little interest in bolstering NATO early on, and rifts developed over policy in Bosnia. Midterm elections ushered in a Republican Congress eager to expand NATO into Eastern Europe and to displace the Clinton strategy of "going along" with severe restrictions on U.S. military commitments to U.N. missions. Richard Haass reflected, "It speaks volumes about [the Clinton] administration that, in his second term, the first post–Cold War president has focused most of his foreign policy efforts on NATO, a child of the Cold War."[62] He appropriately pointed out that NATO expansion is not "the modern-day equivalent of NATO's creation" and predicted that dynamics in the Asia-Pacific region and the Middle East would be far more consequential for the post–Cold War world.

There has been no shortage of explanations offered for the strategic void in foreign policy that characterized the Clinton administration[63]—financial constraints, a public economically insecure and uninterested in foreign affairs, personal presidential style characterized by "indecisiveness and sporadic engagement,"[64] obsession with public opinion polls, inattention to foreign policy, and a focus on domestic politics and economics. But Clinton's approach is not surprising given the absence of clarity and predictability of the post–Cold War era. Typically, preeminent powers adapt to preserve the status quo. Moreover, like Britain between the world wars, post–Cold War America has extensive global interests and commitments and faces a large number and wide variety of security challenges as well as many near-term security demands. In a resource-constrained environment, resourcing for near-term demands invariably comes at the expense of shaping for the future.

Clinton's diplomacy was characterized by multilateralism, incremental change, and preservation and expansion of existing institutions like NATO and the United Nations. George W. Bush's diplomacy was characterized by flexibility and greater unilateralism. The Bush administration came into office calling for "pragmatic multilateralism" and "coalitions of the willing." Long-standing arrangements like the antiballistic missile (ABM) treaty were abandoned. Military operations were undertaken that relied on short-term, ad hoc, or "tactical" coalitions and partnerships. The Bush team argued more agility was needed to deal with diverse transnational threats. Fixed alliances gave way to flexible coalitions of the willing. When traditional allies like Germany and France bridled at joining a U.S.-led coalition to overthrow Iraqi dictator Saddam Hussein, Secretary Rumsfeld remarked, "The mission or objective should determine the alliance or coalition, not vice versa." "Old Europe" and post–World War II institutions were devalued in favor of any and all countries and partners willing to support specific goals related to the struggle against global terror.

Volumes have been written on the decision by the Bush administration to invade Iraq and overthrow Saddam Hussein.[65] Debates have raged on whether or not preventive war has a long history in U.S. foreign policy.[66] The relevant point here is that preventive war designed to overthrow a regime to prevent its future action and promote regime change, versus preempting in response to preparations for aggressive action, is a quintessential shaping strategy. Bush's second inaugural speech enshrined the strategy of promoting democracy, tying America's future security to democratic reforms across the world.

The administration's more activist approach could also be seen in less obvious ways, such as the December 2002 *National Strategy to Combat Weapons of Mass Destruction Proliferation*. The strategy acknowledged the value of traditional nonproliferation measures such as diplomacy, arms control, threat reduction assistance, and export controls but placed increased emphasis on countering proliferation once it has occurred and interdicting the movement of WMD materials, technology, and expertise to hostile states and terrorist organizations. The strategy gave "preemptive interdiction" preeminence over more traditional nonproliferation efforts. In May 2003, following the failed interception of a North Korean shipment of Scud missiles to Yemen, President Bush unveiled the Proliferation Security Initiative (PSI), a new channel for interdiction cooperation outside of treaties and multilateral export control regimes. Detractors have gone so far as to argue that the PSI represents the broadest application of international power projection by the United States in the post–Cold War era, entailing the ability to conduct naval surveillance, interdiction, and eventually unbridled military action in all the world's oceans.

At a minimum, the PSI is another example of diplomatic flexibility, essentially an American-led "coalition of convenience," in this case for the purpose of strengthening nonproliferation cooperation. Traditional antiproliferation cooperation was displaced with à la carte or selective multilateralism. It also reflected an emerging consensus in the United States after the attacks of September 11 that the United States did not need the collective legitimacy of the United Nations. The Bush administration applied the same principle of flexibility to law as it did to intergovernmental cooperation.

Finally, diplomatic relationships were reexamined by Bush with a particular eye toward strengthening alliances in Asia. Believing that great power competition was likely to shift from Europe to Asia, Bush renegotiated U.S. military presence in northeast Asia and reentry into Southeast Asia and upgraded its "strategic partnerships" with Japan and India. All these moves indicated a shift in strategic focus toward Asia, undeniably with the intent of containing the growing military power of China.[67] The United States pursued an initiative to share civilian nuclear technology with India, signifying de facto recognition of India as a legitimate nuclear power. It encouraged Japan to abandon postwar restraints on its military and embrace more ambitious regional security goals. Military cooperation with Vietnam and Indonesia also deepened.[68] It can be argued that

> ... far from maintaining a unilateralist approach to American security, the Bush administration [was] cementing a globe-spanning structure of strategic partnerships that has the potential not only to "contain" China, but also to sustain and enhance the liberal international order of the post-Soviet era.[69]

A retreat from shaping is evident in the Obama administration's strategic posture in Asia, where America's greatest long-term strategic challenge is managing relations with a rising China. Since the late 1990s, the Department of Defense has acknowledged China's great power aspirations. The Pentagon's 1999 *Annual Report on the Military Power of the People's Republic of China* declared that "China's primary goal is to become a strong, modernized, unified and wealthy nation. It views its nation's standing in relation to the position of other 'great powers.' Beijing clearly wants to be recognized as a full-fledged great power."[70] When the Joint Chiefs of Staff released their core planning document, *Joint Vision 2020*, in mid-2000, it assumed that the major arena of competition would be Asia and that America's most likely competitor would be China. The focus on China as a major great power competitor was accepted by the Bush administration, whose strategy was a "long-term effort to shape the choices the leadership in Beijing makes about how to use China's increasing regional and global influence" by using a "combination of a strong U.S. regional presence and a series of creative diplomatic initiatives to encourage Beijing to seek increased influence through diplomatic and economic interactions rather than coercion..."[71]

The Obama administration adopted a policy of "strategic reassurance" to convince the Chinese that the United States has no intention of containing its rising power but will accommodate its rising ambitions. In his July 2009 speech at the first meeting of the Strategic Economic Dialogue between the United States and China, Obama declared that

> Some in China think that America will try to contain China's ambitions; some in America think that there is something to fear in a rising China. I take a different view.... I believe in a future where China is a strong, prosperous and successful member of the community of nations; a future when our nations are partners out of necessity, but also out of opportunity.[72]

Robert Kagan and Dan Blumenthal argue that "for decades, U.S. strategy toward China has had two complementary elements. The first was to bring China into the 'family of nations' through engagement. The second was to make sure China did not become too dominant, through balancing." The Clinton administration normalized trade and pushed for China's entry into the World Trade Organization (WTO) but at the same time strengthened the U.S. military alliance with Japan. The Bush administration developed close economic ties with China but forged a strategic partnership with India and deepened relations with Japan, Singapore, and Vietnam.[73]

The Obama administration abandoned containment and endorsed engagement. Strategic reassurance, grounded in a belief that America is facing inevitable decline, reflects the policy of a declining hegemon accommodating a rising challenger. Paradoxically, this policy is likely to hasten decline. Cuts in key military systems will invariably undermine the ability to contain the growing military power of China.

Conclusion

With the end of the Cold War, a single overarching threat was replaced by distinct strategic arenas in Eurasia, the Middle East, and Far East. This regionalization of security reflected important changes in the post–Cold War security environment but not all of the complexity. That emerged more fully with the attacks of September 11, 2001, and the decision to launch a "global war on terror."

In the first decade after the Cold War, America's response to uncertainty was to adapt by making incremental adjustments in the military's force posture, preserving and extending the alliance structure of the Cold War, and privileging readiness in an effort to respond to unanticipated contingencies across the globe. As a global power, the United States potentially faced a wide range of security challenges and thus professed a desire to prevail across the spectrum of conflict, which implied high mission diversity. However, in practice, the obsession with large conventional wars remained, and other smaller-scale contingencies were treated as lesser included problems. If the United States could prevail in a major theater war, it could prevail across the spectrum of conflict. The Clinton administration viewed multilateral operations as a relatively risk-averse way to engage with the international community. However, the interventions and peace operations of the 1990s forced the United States increasingly to respond to near-term developments and the rising demands of a range of smaller-scale contingencies. Small-scale problems and threats from medium powers prevented the husbanding of resources for larger threats in the more distant future. Peace operations that dragged on reinforced the strategy of adapting as resources migrated from modernization to operations and maintenance accounts. That which was once seen as a means to shape—peace operations—ultimately sapped resources and capabilities for the longer term. In the 1990s, adapting was the dominant strategy in practice, although official documents, like the 1997 QDR, prominently spoke of shaping the strategic environment to discourage military competition, maintain U.S. superiority over current and potential opponents, and exert global leadership.

The George W. Bush administration came into office determined to reorder U.S. strategic priorities. Not content to simply react to the tectonic shifts occurring in the global strategic environment, the Bush administration sought to exploit the nation's preponderant power to shape and guide the international system toward conditions more favorable to the United States. The world had changed from one with predictable threats to one of great complexity with threats arising from multiple and unknowable sources. To be in a position to master this new environment, the United States must curtail multilateral endeavors in favor of coalitions that fit the mission, privilege flexibility over long-standing alliance relationships, transform the U.S. military as the spearhead of a shaping strategy to dissuade others from even trying to challenge U.S. preponderance, reorient the global posture of U.S. forces to increase flexibility and adaptability, and prepare the United States for future competitors most likely to arise in Asia.

The attacks of September 11 had many consequences, but two are particularly relevant here. First, they reinforced pressures to shape that had been present since the early 1990s and seemed to confirm the direction in which Rumsfeld was pushing U.S. defense policy. Military operations in Afghanistan that relied on the unprecedented integration of ground–air communications to link special operations forces with strike aircraft portended a victory of sorts in the short term, although they could provide no long-term solution to an absence of effective governance. Second, the war in Iraq that was launched to politically transform the Middle East and a surge of forces in Afghanistan to spearhead an equally ambitious political transformation there have so increased short-term requirements that organizational planning energy has been consumed at the expense of innovating and preparing for a complex future. A grand strategy of shaping through military power has collapsed under its own weight.

EVALUATION OF HYPOTHESES
ON THE SOURCES OF STRATEGY

Like the historical cases examined in this study, strategic choices made by U.S. leaders in a complex post–Cold War environment have been influenced by structural and nonstructural pressures and circumstances. Leaders responded to domestic pressures to reduce defense spending, produce a peace dividend and deemphasize the nonmilitary dimensions of security in favor of greater focus on domestic economic and social issues. With threats receding, resources shifted from defense to social and economic programs. Domestic coalitions influenced the implementation of strategy in predictable ways. Internationalists in the Clinton administration favored cooperative or institutional shaping strategies while nationalists in the Bush administration preferred muscular shaping.

With the intentions of other actors more ambiguous, technological threats become a focus of military planning, and predictable cognitive shortcuts were adopted. A romance with capability-based planning, the two Major Regional Contingency (MRC) planning guidelines, and a technological approach to military transformation provide support for technological and cognitive hypotheses about planning in uncertain times. Collectively, these tendencies reinforced inclinations to rely on recent experience as a harbinger of the future. Throughout the 1990s, the first Gulf War cast a shadow over planning and thinking about future wars. With Iraq's invasion of Kuwait came the rise of planning for regional conflict. Regional conflict was stated as the organizing principle of national security strategies as early as 1991 and continued to hold sway with primary worries centered on Iraq, North Korea, and Iran.

Organizational dynamics also influenced strategic responses. In the 1990s, organizational resistance to change preserved a scaled-down Cold War force structure and the existing budget shares of the military services. All the services assumed they would lose personnel, and the Base Force was proposed to allow the military to drive how cuts would be made. Transformation was often an exercise in recasting existing programs and systems as revolutionary when they were not. Organizational change was incremental as the military services sought to reinvent themselves to justify their programs in a lean resource environment.

The overarching contours of U.S. strategy, however, are most consistent with the interpretation that strategic responses to a complex security and technological environment reflect concerns with relative international position. Adapting, which characterized the 1990s, was logical for the leading power, reinforced by the global nature of U.S. interests and obligations and organizational biases toward incremental change. But a campaign for a "revolution in military affairs" was underway, championed by defense intellectuals and by the Office of Net Assessment (ONA) in the Department of Defense, who had identified large significant changes in warfare that could be traced back to the 1960s with the emergence of the first generation of long-range precision strike systems. Analogies were made to a previous period of major change in warfare, the 1920s and 1930s, which seemed analogous to the current period given its political and technological complexity. The result was a very self-conscious attempt, which reached fruition during the George W. Bush administration, to leverage technological and social changes that were underway and shape a future that would extend America's relative power advantage. A period of large-scale, rapid technological and social change reinforced a belief in the importance of strategic management and of exploiting opportunities that past hegemons had squandered.

A structural argument receives additional confirmation if it can be shown that decision makers acted for reasons associated with their relative power position. Deprived of a Soviet threat as a result of a geopolitical revolution, defense intellectuals and practitioners made the case that the United States should be preparing for the emergence of a future peer or near-peer competitor because this was the only significant threat to American power and position.

6 CONSEQUENCES OF STRATEGIC CHOICES

WHEN THREATS ARE UNCLEAR, traditional planning procedures are of limited utility because the underlying assumption—the identity of the enemy—has been overturned. Faced with a foggy environment, it may seem wise to hedge—to prepare for multiple possible futures, to develop a portfolio of capabilities to get the best expected outcome across a range of contingencies. This is a particularly attractive course of action for global powers that need to operate against different types of adversaries with different capabilities in different types of operational environments. Hedging, however, turns out to be very expensive, even for the wealthiest states. Hedging is often politically untenable because politicians need to make big bets and convey complete confidence in their policies to fend off political attack. Pursuing a niche strategy is one alternative. It builds on existing competencies and invests in specialized capabilities. The risk of a niche strategy is that it increases dependence on partners and a division of labor to operate across the full spectrum of conflict.

The argument advanced in this book is that the strategies adopted when threats are low have important consequences for power, position, and future preparedness. Political and military leaders today can make more informed decisions if they study the strategic choices made by past leaders in uncertain times and the consequences of those choices. Every strategy has risks. G. John Ikenberry writes,

> In a world of multiple threats and uncertainty about their relative significance in the decades to come, it is useful to think of grand strategy as an "investment" problem. Where do you invest your resources, build capacities, and take

actions so as to maximize your ability to be positioned to confront tomorrow's unknowns? Grand strategy is about setting priorities, but it is also about diversifying risks and avoiding surprises.[1]

In the international relations scholarship, two central arguments have been made about how to preserve and augment power and position. Offensive realists counsel states to focus on internal resource aggregation. Institutionalists advise states to bind themselves to multilateral institutions. In periods of strategic pause, states should take advantage of windows of opportunity to rebuild, reposition, and if possible lengthen the lead they already enjoy over competitors. Uncertain times should not simple be managed; they should be leveraged for the purposes of preserving and augmenting power, position, and influence.

REFORMING AND RECONSTITUTING

The historical record shows that the investment choices states make are greatly influenced by their relative power. Weakened states have fewer choices than do rising, declining, and preeminent states. Reforming and reconstituting is a strategy for seriously weakened powers like post-Crimea Russia. In the aftermath of the Crimean War, Russia's technological and military backwardness was undeniable. So was the fact that they resulted from the poor state of the economy and the relative decline in the empire's economic position. Russian leaders accurately perceived their country's backwardness and were committed to enacting policies to recover, catch up, and make the empire a great power again.

Russia opted, as predicted, to pursue a strategy of reform and reconstitute. The autocracy began a program of reforms from above combined with a policy of international restraint to provide breathing room for their ambitious domestic efforts. To safeguard the state's fiscal integrity, military spending was reduced and capital investment in private industry, commerce and agriculture increased.[2] Significant military changes were enacted, but equally important were nonmilitary improvements, including the abolition of serfdom and adoption of free labor and private enterprise. These reforms went a long way toward reconstituting Russia's power despite difficulty keeping up with economic and military changes underway elsewhere in Europe.

The Russian case highlights some of the risks of a reform and reconstitute strategy. First, economic and social changes take time to pay off, so reforming and reconstituting creates vulnerabilities to near-term challenges. Military reforms in education, conscription, and reorganization into military districts provided benefits,[3] but Russia's military establishment also needed financial investment to manage near and mid-term challenges. Instead, military budgets were capped. So, for example, establishment of universal military conscription eventually allowed for the expansion of the army up to 1,067,000 troops, 41,000 officers, and three million reservists, but Russia was unable to fit its troops with an effective modern rifle until 1904.[4] Backward states often face no-win choices when trying to resource for near-term contingencies and prepare for the future. As predicted in Chapter 2, cuts deemed necessary to shore up the economy can undermine military capacity in the near term. They may also jeopardize long-term reforms. Fuller documents how fiscal crisis in the 1880s led to the indefinite postponement of railway construction producing a deadly transportation gap.[5]

Second, scarcity of resources encourages planners to focus on threats that are likely to have the gravest consequences, slighting preparation and planning for other perhaps lesser although not "lesser included" contingencies. By the 1870s, Russian strategy had become Eurocentric because the Central European threat had the most potentially significant consequences for Russia's great power position. Worst-case planning with respect to a German attack drove strategic planning, and professional strategists failed to plan for other contingencies or prepare and resource for other theaters.[6] By 1900, Russian strategists predicted that war with Japan would come in the near future, but the Ministry of War did not seriously consider this contingency because it would have diverted resources from the European theater. A Ministry of War report to the tsar in 1900 argued that preoccupation in the Far East detracted from security in the west; diversion of funds to Siberian railroads compromised rail construction in the west; and the entire forward policy in East Asia was a huge drain on resources better spent elsewhere.[7] Yet war against Turkey and Japan occurred long before Russia ever took up arms against Germany.

Third, reforming and reconstituting is particularly challenging in a period of rapid technological change. Russia was running quickly, but the rest of the field was also running—and running faster. Post-Crimea reforms were on a scale not seen since Peter I. The problem was that, by the latter half of the nineteenth century, the rest of Europe was moving ahead at an even more rapid pace. This was also the case in economic growth. The years 1888 to 1904 were a period of unprecedented economic boom in the Russian Empire. The economic stimulus strategy of the Ministry of Finance was paying off, and

Russia was attracting more foreign capital than ever. But Russia's military potential did not significantly improve and in key ways actually deteriorated because an economic boom kept Germany well in the lead.[8] The Ministry of Finance remained tightfisted, forcing the military to invest what resources it had in just trying to keep up with its competitors. Russia tried to stay abreast of developments in Europe by emulating technological innovations, but the rapid pace of improvements abroad made Russian systems virtually obsolete by the time they came on line.

Finally, reforming and reconstituting is a strategy of necessity, not choice. By definition, it requires significant changes in how the state provides for its security with all the attendant implications for strategy, organization, doctrine, and finances. Unsurprisingly, this often invites backlash that unravels aspects of the reform enterprise. Such was the case in Russia with the counterreforms of Alexander III.[9] A similar fate befell the Ottoman Empire when reforms introduced during the Tanzimat period (1839–1876) were diluted by backlash and counterreforms during the Hamidian era that followed.[10]

ADAPTING

Adapting is a strategy adopted by declining and overextended powers that are trying to hang onto "market share," stave off decline, or at minimum slow the rate of decline. Declining hegemons face tough choices trying to sustain their power during a period of strategic pause because they have a diverse set of strategic requirements. The exemplar of this is Britain in the inter–world war period.[11]

As a declining power facing a complex strategic environment and pressing near-term demands, Britain's strategic posture of adapting with a focus on near-term challenges and a fast-follower strategy was logical, but it carried risks. Adapters are more likely to cling to preexisting assumptions about the environment because they have a motivated bias toward stability, incremental change, and defense of the status quo. The Ten Year Rule is a case in point. In 1928 it was made annually self-perpetuating, and it was not abandoned until 1932. Adapters risk falling behind when technology is rapidly changing, and this occurred in mechanized warfare and carrier aviation. The preference for preserving the diplomatic status quo also carried risks, and these materialized too. The desire to retain flexibility in their European alliance strategy prevented the British from influencing the French early on, when their diplomatic leverage was greatest. This left the French to rely on an eastern alliance system and the Belgians to rely on the French.[12] In the Pacific, Britain's reluctance to align with any power to secure their interests did not reduce the diversity of missions for which they had to prepare. And the capital ship programs Germany and Italy launched in the 1930s drastically reduced the number of capital ships the British could send to the Far East. Britain simply had too many diverse commitments to meet.

Revisionist historians have marshaled evidence to challenge the contention that Britain's defense capacity—in the armed forces and the industrial base—was allowed to fall to dangerously low levels. They have dispelled claims that the aircraft industry was on the verge of bankruptcy or that the RAF was using World War I aircraft in the 1930s.[13] Retrenchment between 1928 and 1933 produced deficiencies in the aircraft industry, but policies like the creation of a shadow industry for aircraft production—factories that could rapidly convert to aircraft production[14]—helped to compensate. Britain remained the largest exporter of military aircraft in the 1920s to mid-1930s, so industry did not have to rely only on domestic demand.[15] Naval expenditures declined, but this was because funds were shifted to procurement for the RAF, although defense expenditures for the RAF were by far the smallest of all the services until 1937.[16] Britain also retained the world's leading naval-industrial complex, even as it conceded parity to the U.S. Navy. By the early 1930s, defense expenditures had fallen below those of most other great powers, but revisionists attribute this to expenditure increases in other countries, not to British cuts.[17]

In critically important ways, however, military capacity was compromised. Naval air power suffered. The inferior quality and low numbers of carrier aircraft compromised the potential of British carriers and the ability of naval aviation to make the leap from ancillary weapon to backbone of the fleet.[18] Nor, despite the experience of the First World War, was much emphasis placed on the development of aircraft for commerce protection. In the early years of the war, much of Britain's bomber striking force had to be diverted for escort and antisubmarine duties. Revisionists agree most with conventional historical interpretations on the consequences for the army and for mechanized warfare.[19] Budget cuts hit the army hardest of all the services. The British General Staff remained interested in mechanized warfare, but Britain lost its technical lead in, and industrial capacity and manufacturing expertise for, tank production.[20]

The government proved to be very shortsighted when it came to maintaining the industrial base requirements for mechanized warfare and Britain fell behind in the design, development, and production of tanks.[21] Between 1923 and 1933, the annual allocation for the purchase and maintenance of all army weapons averaged less than those allocated to the other services. Between 1927 and 1936, the sum available annually for tank experimentation averaged between £22,500 and £93,750, while the cost of a single experimental medium tank could be £29,000.[22] Financial restrictions on tank orders led to the loss of designers, draughtsmen, and mechanical engineers and confined research and development to two contractors, which the War Office could barely keep alive.[23] When rearmament began, Britain possessed no good multipurpose medium tank ready for production, and the General Staff was forced to turn to a railway company to develop prototypes for a medium tank with a purpose-built engine in 1937.[24] Nor did the army possess light automatic infantry weapons, modern field guns, or antiaircraft weapons. During the first two years of World War II, British ground forces were condemned "to fight with thoroughly inadequate equipment such as the 2-pound anti-tank gun—a gun which the army fully recognized as inadequate for use against a Continental opponent."[25]

The army also lost emergency strength and the capacity to expand. In 1922, the War Office could dispatch an expeditionary force of only one cavalry and two infantry divisions immediately and another infantry division only six weeks after mobilization. Combat support elements were unable to meet mobilization requirements, and the Territorial Army remained a weak cadre for expansion.[26] By 1935, the army possessed less than one division capable of active service against a European enemy. In early 1938, the army could field only two infantry divisions, both deficient in modern equipment.[27]

The strategic decision to retool for the imperial security mission undermined innovation in conventional war-making capabilities and crippled Britain's capacity for mechanized warfare. By August 1939 Britain's monthly tank production exceeded Germany's, but the British were far behind in how to employ tanks on the modern battlefield because planning was focused on providing reinforcements for India.[28] Michael Howard summarizes,

> These [imperial policing] activities, together with protective duties in that Alsatia of the international capitalist system, China, occupied the British Army quite as fully as had its comparable imperial policing duties before the General Staff had begun to play its European War Games in 1905.... The vast corpus of experience fighting in Europe was allowed to melt away: not until 1932 was a Committee set up to study the lessons of the First World War. Experiments with armoured warfare were taken up half-heartedly and abandoned with little reluctance.[29]

Innovation in the Royal Navy also lagged, but this can be attributed to the diverse strategic and operational environments facing a resource-constrained power.[30] To operate in Europe's narrow waters in close proximity to enemy land-based air, the British pioneered development of armored aircraft carriers that could absorb heavy damage.[31] Given treaty limits on carrier displacement, armoring decreased ship size and hangar volume. It was British practice to store aircraft in the hangar, so armoring carriers limited airplane capacity and thus offensive capability.[32] The British entered World War II with obsolete carriers, an inadequate number of nearly obsolete aircraft, and inexperienced in offensive carrier warfare. They were far surpassed by their American and Japanese counterparts.

Britain lacked the resources to deal with the multiplicity of risks inherent in a very diverse threat environment. For the Royal Navy,

> fundamental uncertainty about what they needed to produce exacerbated [the resource] problem. The ability to predict who they would be fighting and when was especially uncertain, and this shortcoming had a direct bearing on the capabilities the Royal Navy needed to produce. Having more specific incentives, the Americans and Japanese were better placed, at least to know what they wanted. Knowing what they needed to do helped create a more conducive climate to innovation.[33]

A similar assessment could be made of the army and RAF. Both faced competing operational demands; and, to the extent that their fates were tied to the imperial security mission, this undercut their ability to prepare to engage a true strategic competitor.

A low level of threat accounts for some reduction in armed forces; but, between 1919 and 1932, cuts made exceeded the normal demobilization to be expected as soldiers return home after hostilities cease. British planners judged that smaller armed forces were sufficient and could be expanded when necessary. The army was given lowest priority, and so army deficiencies were severest. Britain's dominant strategic preference was to adapt, but the nation had too many diverse requirements to adequately meet them all given cuts in defense spending to shore up the economy. Economic strengthening was viewed as both desirable as an end in itself and as a means to deter future aggression.[34] Reducing defense spending to strengthen the economy is more consistent with a strategy of reform and reconstitute and may ultimately be necessary for any declining power. But, for global powers with extensive near-term demands, this widens the gap between defense effort and strategic requirements and ultimately accelerates decline. British choices ultimately compromised future power and position. The problem for Great Britain was not simply one of too few resources; it was that combined with too many diverse strategic requirements. This historical case offers many cautionary lessons for the United States today.

SHAPING

Shaping is a strategy for rising powers. The United States in the interwar period shows how rising powers can leverage a shaping strategy to strategically position themselves for the future, particularly because they are not burdened with the global demands that occupy a hegemon. Between the wars, U.S. strategists and planners had the luxury to focus on positioning the nation for attaining regional dominance in the Pacific region. A range of scenarios was studied, rigorous simulations were conducted, and lessons of the First World War were closely scrutinized. U.S. leaders recognized the nation was emerging as a Pacific power that needed the capacity to project power across a vast ocean expanse to protect vulnerable interests in the Far East. But shaping carries risks. Shapers are more likely to overprepare for particular futures and underprepare for others, producing large payoffs in some scenarios but large losses in others. This proved to be less of a problem for the United States because it was not yet a global power with global interests and commitments. To the extent that it had regional aspirations, it prepared itself to operate in the Pacific. Shaping through technological innovation may also prompt others to respond, thereby undermining the shaper's existing technological lead. In the arena most relevant for the United States—naval air power—the entry costs were exceedingly high.

Gearing one's strategic posture to the future can undermine near-term capabilities and responsiveness, but the United States had few existing commitments. The most persistent near-term demands were in Latin America. Once the European powers lost their influence there following World War I, the United States had become the dominant force and was using military intervention to arbitrate its interests. The marines occupied Nicaragua (1912–1933), Haiti (1914–1934), the Dominican Republic (1916–1924), and Cuba (1917–1933). But the corps still managed to transform itself into an amphibious force. By 1928, President Hoover renounced Woodrow Wilson's policies of shaping through democracy promotion, and all occupying forces withdrew by 1934.

The Good Neighbor Policy (1932–1954) put an end to military intervention and diplomatic interference in Latin America. With termination of the Platt Amendment, the United States renounced the right to intervene in Cuba. Peacetime duties and lesser contingencies did not exist to distract from preparation for future challenges of far greater import to the nation's relative power and strategic position.

Finally, shapers are more likely to face diplomatic backlashes because shaping, which seeks to alter the status quo, is an inherently offensive grand strategy. Yet the United States had retreated from it most the controversial policies in Latin America, while following a cooperative approach to shaping in the Pacific.

Shaping is also a strategy that can benefit preeminent powers, although the risks of shaping are greater for leading powers than they are for rising powers. Two cases of leading powers that launched shaping strategies—early twentieth-century Britain and early twenty-first-century America—shed light on the potential and risks of shaping.

Britain at the beginning of the twentieth century sought a unilateral capability to protect all its imperial interests from any hostile combination of rival great powers. Naval power was critical to achieving this objective. Although the Royal Navy was in no near-term danger of losing its superiority, by 1904 the possibility was on the horizon. Several options were available to the British. They could ignore the problem, continue business as usual, and defend the two-power standard. Any expansion of a rival's navy would have to be surpassed by British building in greater numbers. In a period of rapid technological change, this meant "even units of recent vintage had to be replaced by new model types. . . . the need to keep pace with and even anticipate technological change through state sponsored research or cooperative development efforts with private industry posed novel problems of management and was terribly expensive."[35]

A second option was to contract Britain's strategic vision and shed imperial commitments. But rarely does a leading state willingly retreat from empire unless it has no choice. A third option was to augment capabilities diplomatically, drawing on the model of the Anglo–Japanese alliance. Relying on allies entails risks, and the British viewed alliance diplomacy as an unreliable foundation for grand strategy.[36] The Anglo–Japanese alliance had provided little payoff and nearly drew Britain into war with Russia.

A final option, which the British pursued, was to launch a transformation in warfare that would allow Britain to do more with less. Lambert opines,

Depending upon one's perspective the move was either: a rational attempt to maintain relative status through adoption of an alternative approach to warfare—or a desperate gamble that mortgaged Britain's remaining maritime assets on the successful exploitation of new technologies.[37]

There were risks associated with a strategy of leveraging emerging technologies. It continually undermined the present fleet on which Britain's security rested. Britain enjoyed a near-monopoly on the supply of steam coal around the world, which it abandoned when it shifted to oil-powered ship engines. When it introduced the dreadnought, all naval powers began to build dreadnoughts, and "German naval ambitions seemed to take on a new breath of life."[38] Fisher's opponents argued Britain should wait for other nations to innovate, and Britain would follow with an improved model, taking advantage of her superior speed in shipbuilding. At the time, neither proponents nor opponents of "transformation" realized that

> Britain's reputation for superior shipbuilding speed rested on shaky ground. Considering what was known in 1905, the Dreadnought was a grave mistake for Britain; yet hindsight has shown that technological lead time was the critical issue. As a British admiral wrote recently "Fisher gained for us time—priceless time—the equivalent of, say, five years." On the dreadnought issue, Fisher was utterly right but for the wrong reason.

Britain gained a long technological lead on her competitors, "especially since Germany needed £11,000,000 and eight years to broaden the Kiel Canal before her dreadnoughts were useful."[39]

Fisher believed revolutionary developments would keep Britain prepared, competitors—particularly Germany—off balance and prove advantageous in the long-term:[40]

> His actions were controversial and inconsistent when viewed in the murky light of contemporary politics, power and panic: today they appear to have been guided by a single-minded and unshakable awareness of danger. He recognized the danger from an aggressor and, even more, the danger from those who did not recognize it.[41]

While there were some deficiencies in British armaments—navy mines and army heavy artillery—and more could have been done with industrial capacity to produce munitions, overall there was no evidence of general technological backwardness, which positioned the British well for World War I.[42]

An unintended consequence of British policy was to stimulate the diffusion of innovations to potential rivals. In the economic domain, Britain did little to stem the transfer of innovations, and Fisher's industrial policy actually promoted it:

> The transmission overseas of high quality engineering practice which naturally resulted was of great importance for European technology and could well bear comparison with the effect produced in the 1850s and 1860s by the general diffusion of another British engineering novelty—the railway.[43]

British firms operated in Russia from 1903 to 1914 building battleships, gun foundries, shipyards, artillery shells, and torpedoes. A contract was signed in 1905 by which "British firms would make available to the Russian constructors their designs, their guarantee of quality and of expert supervision, and any patents relevant to the work in hand. The most modern shipbuilding knowledge was thus made available to Russian industry."[44]

Another unintended consequence resulted from the diplomatic flexibility that is a hallmark of shaping. Britain's preference for flexibility produced uncertainty due to the noncommittal nature of the ententes with France and Russia.[45] Peden goes so far as to conclude that "Britain's lack of clear alliance with France and Russia gave Germany cause to hope that Britain might stay out of a European war."[46]

Amidst much controversy, the United States launched a shaping strategy at the turn of the twenty-first century that was based on military transformation, preventive war, and regime change.[47] We are still in the midst of a strategic pause; thus we must be careful about lessons drawn from this case. Critics of shaping have been quick to reject its potential. Defense transformation, they argue, "never considered conflicts such as those in Afghanistan and Iraq in which our troops are now engaged" and these experiences "provide strong warnings that we should abandon the orthodoxy of defense transformation."[48] But the path they chart—constructing a grand strategy around a generational long war against extremism—has potentially serious risks as interwar Britain shows.

Defense transformation—"technological advances that 'lock out' potential adversaries from the 'market' of future conflict"[49]—is a quintessential shaping strategy. Like Britain nearly a century earlier, a period of strategic pause was viewed by U.S. planners as a window of opportunity to solve the paradox of newly emerging threats, growing operational demands, and limited resources and to prepare for an uncertain future. Proponents argued it was the only way to preserve U.S. military superiority and sustain and extend U.S. leadership. Transformation would increase U.S. military strength while cutting costs in weapon systems and overseas deployments. It would reduce risks to American troops. Integration of information technology and achievement of dominant battle space awareness were force multipliers that would overwhelm the capacity of any opponent to act.[50] Transformation did bear some fruit in the conventional combat phase of operations, although it was not tested against a peer or near-peer competitor. It has proven to be virtually irrelevant to postconflict reconstruction, which is critical to counterinsurgency warfare.

Shaping has risks, and many have materialized. First, shaping can undermine political influence because the strategy is not viewed as a benign policy, particularly when it leads to a drive for military superiority to prevent any challenger from emerging or when it results in preventive war. Second, technological superiority makes coordination with allies and other friendly nations difficult. Operations in Kosovo revealed a significant gap between U.S. and European allied military capabilities that led to political friction over sharing defense burdens and created problems on the battlefield. In Bosnia, the United States was perceived as advising and even pressuring allies to take certain risks with their forces that it was not prepared to take with its own. Third, transformation sacrifices mass and diversity of forces that provide an insurance policy against the unforeseen—such as simultaneous wars in Iraq and Afghanistan. Fourth, overreliance on information systems creates new vulnerabilities to attack and disruption. A force dependent on network and network centric warfare proved to be vulnerable when it lost communications and information superiority.[51] Finally, as in previous times, a unilateralist diplomatic strategy produces uncertainty among partners who doubt the commitment of the shaper to common causes. On the other hand, emphasizing coalitions of the willing over more rigid alliances realistically recognizes that even close allies will not always agree on all objectives and all contingencies and that coalitions may be stronger if states can decide when it is in their interest to support a cause.

TOWARD WHICH FUTURE?

Today the United States faces competing strategic imperatives and great uncertainty about which adversaries and contingencies will prove to be the most consequential in the future. Prosecuting the war on terror and delaying the rise of a superpower challenger present competing operational requirements. Problems of terrorism and violent extremism are spreading with globalization and threatening the U.S. homeland. A robust strategy to roll back terrorists and reengineer the failed states that host them is enormously expensive and extremely risky. Biddle argues that such an ambitious undertaking "tends, other things being equal, to run down your economic condition in ways that make it easier for a rising challenger elsewhere to eventually equal your economic power" and pose a formidable threat.[52]

Arguably, the only type of actor that can challenge America's preeminent position and ability to operate globally is a near-peer or peer competitor. Multiple open-ended commitments to combat terrorism and rebuild failed states risks diffusing U.S. power and producing an unbalanced force poorly suited to respond to provocations by an adversary with formidable conventional capabilities.[53] On the other hand, too great a focus on peer competition will produce a balance of capabilities ill suited for counterinsurgency. Moreover, husbanding resources to delay decline makes it nearly impossible to energetically prosecute a global strategy against al Qaeda and its associated movements.[54] Undeniably, America's preoccupation with the "war on terror" represents a strategic opportunity for rising powers like China.

Is it possible for the United States to husband resources to meet distant strategic challenges while also rebuilding failed states and combating terrorism? The conundrum facing the United States today resembles that which we now know in retrospect faced interwar Britain—with one important caveat, namely that Britain was further along the trajectory of economic and military decline. Now, as then, several different warfare futures exist, each championed by a particular service, each compelling, and each likely to be part of America's strategic future. Systemic warfare will require missiles, precision guided munitions, and space-based assets. Cyberwar will be waged from computer terminals by civilian infowarriors trying to disrupt conventional operations and shape the information environment to compensate for weaknesses in conventional capabilities. Peacewar will embroil the military in low-intensity constabulary duties. Dirty war will be waged against nonstate actors and terrorists in a world of failed states and acute ethnic and religious violence.[55] The inescapable reality, as the 9/11report soberly concluded, is that "Insight for the future is . . . not easy to apply in practice. It is hardest to mount a major effort while a problem still seems minor. Once the danger has fully materialized, evident to all, mobilizing action is easier—but it then may be too late."[56]

History shows that others can catch up quickly and unpredictably. It would be a mistake to project the past onto the present . . . or the present into the future. The United States, at least, given its global interests, is likely to face multiple security and warfare futures. Planning for inevitable conflict with a rising China, assuming that great power war is a thing of the past, and prematurely locking into any one vision of the future are all dangerous courses of action. Throughout the 1990s, the United States followed a strategic posture of adapting to an evolving security landscape. It then shifted course and tried to shape the international system. The challenge for the United States is to attend both to systemic developments, like the rise of a strategic competitor that could destabilize the military balance in areas of vital interest, and to the asymmetric challenges of weaker states and violent nonstate actors. At a minimum, in uncertain times U.S. leaders should not shy away from trying to create the type of world it would like to live in when it is a much weakened power. Decline is not yet a condition but is still a choice.[57]

Like the British in the post-Crimea era, the leading state strived to redefine the terms of military power and competition by launching a revolution in military affairs to cement its preponderance into the future. The logic for the most powerful state, as for dominant firms, is to seize the window of opportunity afforded by a strategic pause to reshape the contours of competition to one's advantage. Shaping in the post–Cold War period has relied mostly on military power. The United States, like its predecessors, must appreciate the connection between its national security and its economy. Elements of reform and reconstitute—educational and economic reform—are critical to sustaining and extending U.S. power and position. Military and technological superiority alone are not sufficient to secure the United States and promote the nation's interests and values. The challenges posed by al Qaeda and associated movements (AQAM), the challenges of postconflict stabilization and reconstruction, and the requirements of counterinsurgency warfare all demonstrate that there is no purely military solution for many contemporary or future security challenges. This does not mean that military capability is not relevant. Rather, all of the tools of national power—hard and soft—must be coordinated if we are to shape the environment to prevent the emergence of hostile actors and diminish the conditions that breed them. For global powers that face demanding near-term obligations and competing operational priorities, sustaining a shaping strategy requires political commitment, recognition that future conditions may create an even more inhospitable and challenging operating environment for a weakened United States, and a belief that the country still has an opportunity to extend its status.

Shaping is a strategy for the strong... and some would say the arrogant. Adapting is a strategy for the weakening and the overwhelmed. Reforming and reconstituting is a strategy for the unoccupied... and arguably the clever. In uncertain times, states should strive continually to create competitive advantage rather than simply nurture the sources of power that have sustained them up to that point. Underestimating uncertainty can be extremely dangerous if it results in overreliance on past trends and overlooking alternative futures. It can lead to missed opportunities if one defensively reacts to current events, failing to take advantage of the opportunities uncertainty provides to move the system in a particular direction, increasing the possibility that a more desirable future will materialize.

REFERENCE MATTER

NOTES

Chapter 1: The Fog of Peace

1. The condition of increased interdependence is at the crux of the both the security problems and security solutions that Thomas P. M. Barnett focuses on in *The Pentagon's New Map: War and Peace in the Twenty-First Century* (New York: Putnam, 2004).

2. Williamson Murray, "Innovation: Past and Future," in Williamson Murray and Allan Millett, eds., *Military Innovation in the Interwar Period* (Cambridge, UK: Cambridge University Press, 1996), 301.

3. See, for example, Randall L. Schweller, *Unanswered Threats: Political Constraints on the Balance of Power* (Princeton, NJ: Princeton University Press, 2006).

4. Arnold Wolfers, *Discord and Collaboration: Essays on International Politics* (Baltimore: The Johns Hopkins University Press, 1962).

5. Talbot C. Imlay and Monica Duffy Toft, eds., *The Fog of Peace and War Planning: Military and Strategic Planning under Uncertainty* (London and New York: Routledge, 2006) note similar deficiencies in the literature and present a series of case studies focused on military planning.

6. Robert Kagan, "Power and Weakness," *Policy Review* 113 (June 2002).

7. John Gerring, "What Is a Case Study and What Is It Good for?" *American Political Science Review* 98:2 (May 2004), 349.

8. *Report of the Defense Science Board Task Force on Strategic Communication* (Washington, DC: Office of the Under Secretary of Defense for Acquisition, Technology, and Logistics, September 2004), 11.

9. I am not alone in drawing on a body of theory originating from a different discipline; nor am I the first to draw on the literature from managerial studies. See Alexander Cooley, *Logics of Hierarchy: The Organization of Empires, States and Military Occupations* (Ithaca, NY: Cornell University Press, 2005). The field of international

relations has made extensive use of methods and theories borrowed from economics. The market metaphor—that "self-interest drives the behavior of firms and states alike; a selection mechanism ensures the disappearance of states and firms that stray too far from accurate self-interested decision-making; and the properties of both international systems and markets vary according to the number of actors in the system" (Richard Sherman and M. Scott Solomon, "IR Theory's Evolving Economic Metaphor," paper presented at the International Studies Association Hong Kong Conference [July 2001], p. 2)—is a central assumption of Waltzian neorealism and is also key to neoliberalism. See Kenneth Waltz, *Theory of International Politics* (Reading, MA: Addison-Wesley, 1979). Several classics, such as Barry Posen, *The Sources of Military Doctrine: France, Britain, and Germany between the World Wars* (Ithaca, NY: Cornell University Press, 1984), have imported concepts and ideas from the corporate organizational literature. What I am doing is firmly in the tradition of a fertile research strategy, namely leveraging a well-developed and unused resource to gain new insights.

10. I thank Chris Demchak for pointing these similarities out to me.

11. Robert Jervis, "The Remaking of a Unipolar World," *The Washington Quarterly* (Summer 2006), 7–8.

12. Jervis, "The Remaking of a Unipolar World"; Condoleezza Rice, "Transformational Diplomacy," Washington, DC, January 18, 2006.

13. Jervis, in "The Remaking of a Unipolar World," attributes America's revolutionary impulse to its preponderant power, political culture, and President George W. Bush's religious convictions.

14. On disruptive innovations, see Clayton M. Christensen, *The Innovator's Dilemma* (New York: HarperCollins, 2003); Terry C. Pierce, *Warfighting and Disruptive Technologies: Disguising Innovation* (Frank Cass, 2004).

15. Julio Casillas, Percy Crocker Jr., Frank Fehrenbach, Kevin Haug, and Ben Straley, "Disruptive Technologies: Strategic Advantage and Thriving in Uncertainty," in Mohanbir S. Sawhney and Ranjay Gulati (eds.), *Kellogg TechVenture 2000 Anthology*, pp. 203–29 (Evanston, IL: Nminds Publications, 2000).

16. Michele Zanini and Sean J. A. Edwards, "The Networking of Terror in the Information Age," in John Arquilla and David Ronfeldt, eds., *Networks and Netwars: The Future of Terror, Crime, and Militancy* (Santa Monica, CA: RAND, 2001), pp. 29–60.

17. Andrew F. Krepinevich, *The Quadrennial Defense Review: Rethinking the US Military Posture* (Washington, DC: Center for Strategic and Budgetary Assessments, 2005), pp. 44–45.

Chapter 2: Strategic Choice in Uncertain Times

1. Peter Paret asserts that all actions in war find their initiation and development in peacetime (Foreword by Peter Paret in Harold R. Winton, *To Change an Army* [Lawrence: University Press of Kansas, 1988]). Bruce Menning argues that "wartime

performance (the province of battle and operations analysis) could be fully understood only with reference to prewar preparation (the province of concept and infrastructure)" (Bruce W. Menning, *Bayonets Before Bullets: The Imperial Russian Army, 1861–1914* [Bloomington: Indiana University Press, 1992], 2).

2. Frank Knight, *Risk, Uncertainty, and Profit* (Chicago: University of Chicago Press, 1971; originally published 1921), xiv.

3. J. M. Keynes, "The General Theory of Employment," *Quarterly Journal of Economics* 51 (1937), 209–223.

4. For an analysis of uncertainty as a variation on risk, see Hugh G. Courtney, Jane Kirkland, and S. Patrick Viguerie, "Strategy under Uncertainty," *Harvard Business Review* (November–December 1997).

5. Ernest May, ed. *Knowing One's Enemies: Intelligence Assessment before the Two World Wars* (Princeton, NJ: Princeton University Press, 1984).

6. Kenneth N. Waltz, *Theory of International Politics* (Reading, MA: Addison-Wesley, 1979), 170.

7. Stephen Van Evera, "Offense, Defense, and the Causes of War," *International Security* 22 (Spring 1998): 5–43; Stephen Van Evera, *Causes of War: Power and the Roots of Conflict* (Ithaca, NY: Cornell University Press, 1999).

8. John J. Mearsheimer, *The Tragedy of Great Power Politics* (New York: Norton, 2001).

9. Charles Glaser, "The Security Dilemma Revisited," *World Politics* 50 (October 1997), 171–201; Randall L. Schweller, *Unanswered Threats: Political Constraints on the Balance of Power* (Princeton, NJ: Princeton University Press, 2006).

10. Andrew Kydd, "Why Security Seekers Do Not Fight Each Other," *Security Studies* 7 (Autumn 1997), 114–154. Costly signaling theory proposes that expensive and often seemingly arbitrary or wasteful behavior is designed to convey honest information benefiting both signalers and observers. Costly signals reveal information about the underlying qualities of the signalers, qualities that are important to the observers and will affect social interaction, but that are not directly observable (for example, political intent, dedication to cooperation) (Amotz Zahavi, "Mate Selection: A Selection for Handicap," *Journal of Theoretical Biology*, No. 53 [1975], 205–214; Herbert Gintis, Eric Alden Smith, and Samuel Bowles, "Cooperation and Costly Signaling," *Journal of Theoretical Biology*, No. 213 [2001], 103–119; Kenneth A. Schultz, *Democracy and Coercive Diplomacy* [Cambridge, UK: Cambridge University Press, 2001]).

11. Balance-of-threat theory characterizes threat in terms of properties of the external environment, but it is not a systemic theory. The variables that drive Walt's theory are not systemwide, like the offense–defense balance or distribution of power, but rather specific to some states: high aggregate resources; proximity; large offensive capabilities; and aggressive intentions (Stephen M. Walt, *The Origins of Alliances* [Ithaca, NY: Cornell University Press, 1987], 21–26).

12. Chris C. Demchak, *Complex Machines: Modernization in the U.S. Armed Services* (Ithaca, NY: Cornell University Press, 1991).

13. Frank G. Hoffman, "Small Wars Revisited: The United States and Nontraditional Wars," *Journal of Strategic Studies* 28 (December 2005), 913–940.

14. P. W. Singer, *Corporate Warriors: The Rise of the Privatized Military Industry* (Ithaca, NY: Cornell University Press, 2003), 174–175.

15. The literature on revolutions in military affairs, both historical and contemporary, is a broad one. See Clifford J. Rogers, ed., *The Military Revolution Debate: Readings on the Military Transformation of Early Modern Europe* (Boulder, CO: Westview, 1995); Andrew Krepinevich, "Cavalry to Computer: The Pattern of Military Revolutions," *The National Interest* (Fall 1994), 10–42; Eliot A. Cohen, "A Revolution in Warfare," *Foreign Affairs* 75:2 (March/April 1996), 37–54; John Arquilla and David Ronfeldt, "Cyberwar Is Coming!" *Comparative Strategy* 12:2 (April–June 1993), 141–165; Alvin and Heidi Toffler, *War and Anti-War* (New York: Warner, 1993).

16. Technological change has been characterized as gradual and incremental, as well as rapid and discontinuous. The punctuated equilibrium framework of evolutionary biology reconciles these views, and it has been applied to the subject of revolutions in military affairs to show how short bursts of rapid change are interspersed with longer periods of slower, incremental change. These transformations may result from a technological innovation, or they may result from macrosocial changes that influence how a state mobilizes resources to provide security. Or a military transformation may be the result of existing technologies linked together in a new application (Rogers, *The Military Revolution Debate*, 77; Major Steven M. Leonard, *Inevitable Evolutions: Punctuated Equilibrium and the Revolution in Military Affairs* [Fort Leavenworth, KS: School of Advanced Military Studies, US Army Command and General Staff College, 2001]).

17. See Emily O. Goldman and Leslie C. Eliason, eds., *The Diffusion of Military Technology and Ideas* (Stanford, CA: Stanford University Press, 2003).

18. Walt, *Origins of Alliances*.

19. Jennifer Mitzen, "Ontological Security in World Politics: State Identity and the Security Dilemma," *European Journal of International Relations* 12 (2006), 341–370.

20. J. L. Bower and C. M. Christensen, "Disruptive Technologies: Catching the Wave," *Harvard Business Review* (January–February 1995), 43–53; Casillas et al., "Disruptive Technologies"; C. M. Christensen and M. Overdorf, "Meeting the Challenge of Disruptive Change," *Harvard Business Review* (March–April 2000), 67–76.

21. Richard K. Betts, "Systems for Peace or Causes of War? Collective Security, Arms Control, and the New Europe," *International Security* 17/1 (Summer 1992), 14–15.

22. "The Forgotten Dimension of Strategy," in Michael Howard, ed., *The Causes of War and Other Essays* (Cambridge, MA: Harvard University Press, 1983), 101–115.

23. For an overview of prospect theory, see Jack S. Levy, "Introduction to Prospect Theory," *Political Psychology* 13/2 (1992), 171–186; Robert Jervis, "Political Implications

of Loss Aversion," *Political Psychology* 13/2 (1992), 187–204; and Jack S. Levy, "Prospect Theory and International Relations: Theoretical Applications and Analytical Problems," *Political Psychology* 13/2 (1992), 283–310. For an application of prospect theory to U.S. post–Cold War strategy and foreign policy, see Emily O. Goldman and Larry Berman, "Engaging the World: First Impressions of the Clinton Foreign Policy Legacy," in Colin Campbell and Bert A. Rockman, eds., *The Clinton Legacy* (New York: Chatham House Publishers, 2000), 238–242.

24. Peter Smith Ring, "The Environment and Strategic Management," in Jack Rabin et al., eds., *Handbook of Strategic Management*. New York: Marcel Dekker, 1989.

25. Christopher J. Lamb, *Transforming Defense* (Washington, DC: National Defense University Press, 2005).

26. They can also improve their understanding about the incentives of new types of security actors through theoretical development.

27. Acquiring sufficient military capabilities to withstand any threat that could be posed, Glaser argues, trumps the need for information about the intentions of the adversary (Charles L. Glaser, *Rational Theory of International Politics: The Logic of Competition and Cooperation* [Princeton, NJ: Princeton University Press, 2010]).

28. Courtney et al., "Strategy under Uncertainty."

29. The terms *shaping* and more specifically *environment shaping* have been used in different ways in the national security field to refer to very broad efforts to promote regional stability to more specific military assistance programs. These uses of the terms should not be confused with the way *shaping* is being employed here.

30. These are ideal types. States usually pursue mixed strategies, although it is possible to identify a state's dominant strategy.

31. See Posen, *The Sources of Military Doctrine*, on incremental responses to uncertainty.

32. Victoria Tin-bor Hui, "Toward a Dynamic Theory of International Politics: Insights from Comparing Ancient China and Early Modern Europe," *International Organization* 58 (Winter 2004), 181–183.

33. Ian Roxborough and Dana Eyre, in "Which Way to the Future?" *Joint Forces Quarterly* (Summer 1999), 28–34, propose four images of future war: systemic war, cyberwar, peacewar, and dirty war.

34. Jack Snyder, *Myths of Empire: Domestic Politics and International Ambition* (Ithaca, NY: Cornell University Press, 1991); Charles A. Kupchan, *The Vulnerability of Empire* (Ithaca, NY: Cornell University Press, 1994).

35. One should not assume that the ability of leaders to assess their relative power and position is straightforward and uncontested. Aaron L. Friedberg, in *The Weary Titan: Britain and the Experience of Relative Decline, 1895–1905* (Princeton, NJ: Princeton University Press, 1988), describes the complexity involved in governments' assessment of relative power and the reluctance in particular to accept relative decline. When I

use terms like *hegemon, rising power, declining power,* and *states in the trough of the power curve,* I am referring to post hoc analytic categories to make predictions about state behavior. At the same time, I examine how leaders at the time viewed their relative power. If there is a large gap between my assessment and perceptions at the time, I would expect that my predictions would be incorrect (William C. Wohlforth, "The Perception of Power: Russia in the Pre-1914 Balance," *World Politics* 39 [April 1987], 353–381).

36. The term *blitzkrieg* is often used to describe these German doctrinal innovations, but historians agree the term is a misnomer. See Robert Citino, "Beyond Fire and Movement: Command, Control and Information in German *Blitzkrieg*," in Emily O. Goldman, *Information and Revolutions in Military Affairs* (London: Routledge, 2005), 135.

37. Friedberg, *The Weary Titan*; Schweller, *Unanswered Threats*; Robert Jervis, *Perception and Misperception in International Politics* (Princeton: Princeton University Press, 1976).

38. Emily O. Goldman and Leo J. Blanken, "The Economic Foundations of Military Power," in Peter Dombrowski, ed., *Guns and Butter: The Political Economy of International Security* (Boulder, CO: Lynne Rienner, 2005), 35–38; Dale C. Copeland, *The Origins of Major War* (Ithaca, NY: Cornell University Press, 2000).

39. Arvind Virmani, "Global Power from the 18th to 21st Century: Power Potential, Strategic Assets and Actual Power," Working Paper No. 175 (New Delhi: Indian Council for Research on International Economic Relations, November 2005).

40. Paul Kennedy, *The Rise and Fall of the Great Powers: Economic Change and Military Conflict from 1500–2000* (New York: Random House, 1987), xvi.

41. Goldman and Blanken, "The Economic Foundations of Military Power."

42. Josef Joffe, in "'Bismarck' or 'Britain'? Toward an American Grand Strategy after Bipolarity," *International Security* 19 (Spring 1995), 101–102, traces the different approaches to sustaining power by Britain and Germany to their geographic positions.

43. Over time, technological innovations have reduced the advantages of geographic distance. Air power, nuclear weapons, and the information age have reduced the geographic space between states, slowly negating the benefits traditionally derived from insularity. Still, not even nuclear weapons have entirely reduced geography's relevance. Fighting in Bosnia could spread more readily to neighboring European states than to the United States.

44. Robert Jervis, "The Remaking of a Unipolar World," *The Washington Quarterly* (Summer 2006), 14.

45. Ring, "The Environment and Strategic Management."

46. Joao Resende-Santos, "Anarchy and Emulation of Military Systems: Military Organizations and Technology in South America, 1870–1930," *Security Studies* 5 (Spring 1996), 218.

47. Jeffrey W. Taliaferro, "Security Seeking under Anarchy," *International Security* 25, 3 (Winter 2000/01), 141.

48. Miroslav Nincic, Roger Rose, and Gerard Gorski, "The Social Foundations of Strategic Adjustment," in Peter Trubowitz, Emily O. Goldman, and Edward Rhodes, eds., *The Politics of Strategic Adjustment: Ideas, Institutions, and Interests* (New York: Columbia University Press, 1999), 179.

49. Peter Trubowitz, "Geography and Strategy: The Politics of American Naval Expansion," in Peter Trubowitz, Emily O. Goldman, and Edward Rhodes, eds., *The Politics of Strategic Adjustment: Ideas, Institutions, and Interests*. New York: Columbia University Press.

50. Carl Conetta, "We Can See Clearly Now: The Limits of Foresight in the pre–World War II Revolution in Military Affairs (RMA)," Project of Defense Alternatives Research Monograph #12 (March 2, 2006), 4.

51. Steven E. Lobell, "War Is Politics: Offensive Realism, Domestic Politics, and Security Strategies," *Security Studies* 12 (Winter 2002/3), 165–195, examines free traders and economic nationalists in Britain. Etel Solingen, in *Regional Orders at Century's Dawn: Global and Domestic Influences on Grand Strategy* (Princeton, NJ: Princeton University Press, 1998), examines internationalists (who favor economic liberalization) and statist-nationalists (who oppose economic liberalization and support more militant policies). Peter Trubowitz's *Defining the National Interest* (Chicago: University of Chicago Press, 1998) focuses on regional coalitions.

52. Kevin Narizny, "Both Guns and Butter, or Neither: Class Interests in the Political Economy of Rearmament," *American Political Science Review* 97: 2 (May 2003), 203–220.

53. Jan S. Breemer, "Technological Change and the New Calculus of War: The United States Builds a New Navy," in Peter Trubowitz, Emily O. Goldman, and Edward Rhodes, eds., *The Politics of Strategic Adjustment: Ideas, Institutions, and Interests*. New York: Columbia University Press.

54. Ibid.

55. Posen, *Sources of Military Doctrine*.

56. Jack Snyder, *The Ideology of the Offensive* (Ithaca, NY: Cornell University Press, 1984).

57. See Posen, *Sources of Military Doctrine*; Richard Betts, *Soldiers, Statesmen, and Cold War Crises* (Cambridge, MA: Harvard University Press, 1977); Timothy David Moy, *Hitting the Beaches and Bombing the Cities: Doctrine and Technology for Two New Militaries, 1920-1940*, PhD Dissertation, University of California at Berkeley, 1987; Graham T. Allison, *Essence of Decision* (Boston: Little, Brown and Company, 1971); Edward L. Katzenbach Jr., "The Horse Cavalry in the Twentieth Century: A Study in Policy Response," *Public Policy* 7 (1958), 120–149; and Herbert Kaufman, *The Limits of Organizational Change* (Tuscaloosa: University of Alabama Press, 1971).

58. Shelley Taylor, "The Availability Bias in Social Perception and Interaction," in Daniel Kahneman, Paul Slovic, and Amos Tversky, eds., *Judgment under Uncertainty: Heuristics and Biases* (Cambridge, UK: Cambridge University Press, 1982), pp. 190-200; Amos Tversky and Daniel Kahneman, "Availability: A Heuristic for Judging Frequency and Probability," *Cognitive Psychology* 5 (1973), 207-232; and Amos Tversky and Daniel Kahneman "Judgment under Uncertainty," *Science* 185 (1974), 1124-1131.

59. Paul J. DiMaggio and Walter W. Powell, "The Iron Cage Revisited: Institutional Isomorphism and Collective Rationality in Organizational Fields," *American Sociological Review* 48 (April 1983), 151.

60. Resende-Santos, "Anarchy and Emulation of Military Systems," p. 196; Waltz, *Theory of International Politics*, p. 127.

61. On relevancy, see James Mahoney and Gary Goertz, "The Possibility Principle: Choosing Negative Cases in Comparative Research," *American Political Science Review* 98:4 (November 2004), 653-669.

62. On formal versus informal units, see John Gerring, "What Is a Case Study and What Is It Good for?" *American Political Science Review* 98: 2 (May 2004), 341-154.

63. Posen, in *The Sources of Military Doctrine*, operationalizes this variable in terms of innovation-adaptation-stagnation. While states have stagnated as an outcome, this is never a policy choice.

64. Offensive realists posit a short time horizon. Uncertainty is unavoidable, so states should favor military preparedness over long-term economic prosperity. Defensive realists predict states will prefer long-term economic growth over short-term military preparedness when geography provides defense against invasion or when a state is surrounded by weak neighbors (Taliaferro, "Security Seeking under Anarchy," 140; Stephen G. Brooks, "Dueling Realisms," *International Organization* 51, 3 [Summer 1997], 452).

65. Patricia A. Weitsman, "Intimate Enemies: The Politics of Peacetime Alliances," *Security Studies* 7, 1 (August 1997), 156-192; Patricia A. Weitsman, *Dangerous Alliances: Proponents of Peace, Weapons of War* (Stanford, CA: Stanford University Press, 2004).

66. See Joseph Chamberlain's calls for imperial federation in the free trade-tariff debate of 1901-1902, to halt Britain's exports of coal and machinery, which were assisting others to industrialize.

67. Stephen E. Lobell, *The Challenge of Hegemony: Grand Strategy, Trade and Domestic Politics* (Ann Arbor: University of Michigan Press, 2003), refers to this as a choice between cooperation and punishment toward potential challengers. See also Claus Hofhansel, *Commercial Competition and National Security: Comparing U.S. and German Export Control Policies* (Westport, CT: Praeger, 1996).

68. For offensive realists who see acute uncertainty in the international environment, potential adversaries and/or problematic allies should be contained. For

defensive realists, status quo states can be engaged. Revisionist states may have to be contained, but engagement is one means to transform a revisionist state into a status quo power.

69. Lobell argues that one's attitude toward potential challengers depends on whether the challenger is a liberal contender or an imperial contender. Liberal contenders should be engaged; imperial contenders should be punished or contained (Lobell, *Challenge of Hegemony*).

70. William C. Wohlforth, "Realism and the End of the Cold War," *International Security* 19 (Winter 1994/95), 98, hypothesizes that declining challengers are more likely to retrench and reform than declining hegemons.

71. Donald T. Campbell, "'Degrees of Freedom' and the Case Study," in E. Samuel Overman, ed., *Methodology and Epistemology for Social Science* (Chicago: University of Chicago Press, [1975] 1988), 380.

72. Enlargement of the North Atlantic Treaty Organization (NATO), which reoriented NATO for new order, represented a move to break out of the old order and reshape a new order.

73. This was clearly the preference of post-Crimea Russia and post–Cold War China.

74. Gerring, "What Is a Case and What Is It Good for?" 348.

75. For example, declining powers that try to adapt instead of reform and reconstitute, like Ottoman Turkey, are likely to hasten rather than forestall their decline (Emily O. Goldman, "Cultural Foundations of Military Transformation," *Review of International Studies* 32:1 (January 2006), 69–91).

Chapter 3: Post-Crimean War Period, 1856–1910

1. F. R. Bridge and Roger Bullen, *The Great Powers and the European State System: 1815–1914*. (New York: Longman, 1980), 82–83.

2. Krepinevich, "Cavalry to Computer," 34–36.

3. David Schimmelpenninck Van Der Oye, "Reforming Military Intelligence," in David Schimmelpenninck Van Der Oye and Bruce W. Menning, eds., *Reforming the Tsar's Army: Military Innovation in Imperial Russia from Peter the Great to the Revolution* (Cambridge, UK: Cambridge University Press 2004), 140.

4. G. C. Peden, *Arms, Economics and British Strategy: From Dreadnoughts to Hydrogen Bombs* (Cambridge, UK: Cambridge University Press, 2007), 33–34.

5. James Sturgis, "Britain and the New Imperialism," in C. C. Eldridge, ed., *British Imperialism in the Nineteenth Century* (London: Macmillan, 1984), 85.

6. Nicholas A. Lambert, *Sir John Fisher's Naval Revolution* (Columbia: University of South Carolina Press, 1999), 17.

7. Jon Sumida, "The Admiralty and British Imperial Grand Strategy, 1889–1918," draft paper, June 28, 2001.

8. Jacob W. Kipp, "The Russian Navy and the Problem of Technological Transfer: Technological Backwardness and Military-Industrial Development, 1853–1876," in Ben Eklof, John Bushnell, and Larissa Zakharova, eds., *Russia's Great Reforms, 1855–1881* (Bloomington: Indiana University Press, 1994), 118.

9. William C. Fuller, *Strategy and Power in Russia, 1600–1914* (New York: Macmillan, 1992), 263.

10. Ibid., 269.

11. Ben Eklof, John Bushnell, and Larissa Zakharova, eds. *Russia's Great Reforms, 1855–1881* (Bloomington: Indiana University Press, 1994).

12. Fuller, *Strategy and Power in Russia*, 273.

13. John S. Bushnell, "Miliutin and the Balkan War: Military Reform vs. Military Performance," in Ben Eklof, John Bushnell, and Larissa Zakharova, eds., *Russia's Great Reforms: 1855–1881* (Bloomington: Indiana University Press, 1994), 155.

14. Fuller, *Strategy and Power in Russia*, 307–308.

15. Kipp, "The Russian Navy and the Problem of Technological Transfer," 117.

16. Walter M. Pintner, "The Burden of Defense in Imperial Russia, 1725–1914," *The Russian Review* 43 (1984), 248.

17. Ibid., 248–250.

18. Fuller, *Strategy and Power in Russia*, 300–301.

19. Jacob W. Kipp, "Strategic Railroads and the Dilemmas of Modernization," in Schimmelpenninck Van Der Oye and Menning, eds., *Reforming the Tsar's Army: Military Innovation in Imperial Russia from Peter the Great to the Revolution* (Cambridge, UK: Cambridge University Press), 88.

20. Kipp, "The Russian Navy and the Problem of Technological Transfer," 117.

21. Kipp, "Strategic Railroads and the Dilemmas of Modernization," 88.

22. Ibid.

23. G. K. Kruger, "Russia's 'Disadvantaged Position' after the Crimean War: An Examination of the Root Causes and the Relevance of Military Material Technology," Draft (August 15, 1994).

24. Fuller, *Strategy and Power in Russia*, 363.

25. Kipp, "The Russian Navy and the Problem of Technological Transfer," 118.

26. Ibid.

27. Bushnell, "Miliutin and the Balkan War," 147–150; Bruce W. Menning, *Bayonets before Bullets*.

28. Bushnell, "Miliutin and the Balkan War," 145–147.

29. Ibid., 152–156.

30. Kipp, "The Russian Navy and the Problem of Technological Transfer," 120–121.

31. Ibid., 126.

32. Ibid., 127.

33. Ibid., 120.

34. Ibid.
35. Ibid.
36. Ibid., 123.
37. Ibid.
38. Ibid., 130–133.
39. Fuller, *Strategy and Power in Russia*, 287.
40. Ibid., 295.
41. Ibid., 297.
42. Ibid., 298.
43. Ibid., 342, 344–346.
44. Menning, *Bayonets before Bullets*, 11.
45. Fuller, *Strategy and Power in Russia*, 270.
46. Quoted in Kipp, "The Russian Navy and the Problem of Technological Transfer," 117.
47. Fuller, *Strategy and Power in Russia*, 332.
48. Ibid.
49. Ibid., 290.
50. Ibid., 372–373.
51. Ibid., 281.
52. Ibid., 289.
53. Andrew D. Lambert, "The Royal Navy, 1856–1914: Deterrence and the Strategy of World Power," in Keith Neilson and Elizabeth Jane Errington, eds., *Navies and Global Defense: Theories and Strategy* (Westport, CT: Praeger, 1995), 73–74.
54. Jon Sumida, "The Admiralty and British Imperial Grand Strategy, 1889–1918," 1.
55. Suzanne Y. Frederick, "The Anglo-German Rivalry, 1890–1914," in W. R. Thompson, ed., *Great Power Rivalries* (Columbia: University of South Carolina Press, 1999).
56. Ibid.
57. Nicholas A. Lambert, "Transformation and Technology in the Fisher Era: The Impact of the Communications Revolution," *The Journal of Strategic Studies* 27 (June 2004), 272–297.
58. Jon T. Sumida, *In Defense of Naval Supremacy: Finance, Technology and British Naval Policy, 1889–1914* (Boston: Unwin Hyman, 1989).
59. Frederick, "The Anglo-German Rivalry."
60. Dan Van der Vat, *Standard of Power: The Royal Navy in the Twentieth Century* (London: Hutchinson, 2000).
61. Paul Kennedy, *Strategy and Diplomacy, 1870–1945* (London: George Allen & Unwin, 1983), 141.
62. Van der Vat, *Standard of Power*.
63. Ibid.

64. Ibid; J. McDermott, "The Revolution in British Military Thinking from the Boer War to the Moroccan Crisis," in Paul M. Kennedy, ed., *The War Plans of the Great Powers, 1880–1914* (London: George Allen & Unwin, 1979).

65. Lambert, *Sir John Fisher's Naval Revolution*.

66. Jon Sumida, "Geography, Technology, and British Naval Strategy before the First World War: Mahanian Theory versus Fisherian Practice in the Dreadnought Era," draft paper (March 7, 2001), 5.

67. Arthur Marder, *The Anatomy of British Sea Power: A History of British Naval Policy in the Pre-Dreadnought Era, 1880–1905* (New York: Octagon Books, 1976), 4.

68. Peden, *Arms, Economics and British Strategy*, 22.

69. Herbert Wrigley Wilson, *Battleships in Action* (Boston: Little, Brown and Company, 1969), 3–4.

70. John Beeler, *British Naval Policy in the Gladstone-Disraeli Era, 1866–1880* (Stanford, CA: Stanford University Press, 1997), 42.

71. Eugene L. Rasor, "The Manning Question in the Royal Navy in the Early Ironclad Era," in Robert William Love Jr., ed., *Changing Interpretations and New Sources in Naval History* (New York: Garland Publishing, 1980), 210.

72. Jon Tetsuro Sumida, "British Naval Administration in the Age of Fisher," *Journal of Military History* 54 (1990), 8-9; Rasor, "The Manning Question in the Royal Navy," 212.

73. Marder, *Anatomy of British Sea Power*, 265 n.39.

74. Sumida, "British Naval Administration," 3.

75. Beeler, *British Naval Policy*, 43.

76. Marder, *Anatomy of British Sea Power*, 121.

77. Sumida, "Admiralty and British Imperial Grand Strategy," 2.

78. Ibid., 3.

79. Sumida, *In Defense of Naval Supremacy*.

80. Michael Howard, *The Continental Commitment* (London: Temple Smith, 1972).

81. Sumida, "Admiralty and British Imperial Grand Strategy," 2.

82. Sumida, "Geography, Technology, and British Naval Strategy," 5.

83. Sumida, "Admiralty and British Imperial Grand Strategy," 8–9.

84. Lambert, "Transformation and Technology in the Fisher Era," 273.

85. Ibid., 275–276.

86. Ibid.

87. Ibid.

88. Ibid., 276–277.

89. Nicholas A. Lambert, "Admiral Sir John Fisher and the Concept of Flotilla Defense," *Journal of Military History* 59 (1995) 639–660; Nicholas A. Lambert, "Dreadnought—The Revolution That Never Was," draft manuscript.

90. Lambert, "Transformation and Technology in the Fisher Era," 277–278.

91. Sumida, *In Defense of Naval Supremacy*.
92. Lambert, *Sir John Fisher's Naval Revolution*.
93. Lambert, "Transformation and Technology in the Fisher Era," 282.
94. Ibid.
95. Ibid., 283.
96. Ibid.
97. Ibid., 285.
98. Ibid., 292–293.
99. Ibid., 285; Sumida, "The Admiralty and British Imperial Grand Strategy," 8–9.
100. Lambert, "Transformation and Technology in the Fisher Era," 278–279.
101. Lambert, "Dreadnought—The Revolution That Never Was," 8.
102. Arthur J. Marder, *Fear God and Dread Nought: The Correspondence of Admiral of the Fleet Lord Fisher of Kilverstone*, Vol. 1 (London: Jonathan Cape, 1952), 174.
103. Lambert, "Transformation and Technology in the Fisher Era," 280.
104. Sumida, "British Naval Administration," 4.
105. Paul L. Robertson, "Technical Education in the British Shipbuilding and Marine Engineering Industries, 1863–1914," *Economic History Review* 27 (1974), 222.
106. Clive Trebilcock, "British Armaments and European Industrialization, 1890–1914," *Economic History Review* 26 (1973), 264.
107. Peden, *Arms, Economics and British Strategy*, 24; Arthur J. Marder, *Fear God and Dread Nought: The Correspondence of Admiral of the Fleet Lord Fisher of Kilverstone*, Vol. II (London: Jonathon Cape, 1956), 29–30.
108. Peden, *Arms, Economics and British Strategy*, 24.
109. Lambert, "Transformation and Technology in the Fisher Era," 280–281.
110. Nicholas Lambert, "Economy of Empire? The Fleet Unit Concept and the Quest for Collective Security in the Pacific, 1909–1914," in Keith Neilson and Greg Kennedy, eds., *Far Flung Lines: Studies in Imperial Defense in Honour of Donald Mackenzie Schurman* (London: Frank Cass, 1996), 61.
111. Ibid., 63.
112. Ibid.
113. Marder, *Fear God and Dread Nought, Vol II.*, 22.
114. Lambert, "Admiral Sir John Fisher and the Concept of Flotilla Defense," 641; Nicholas A. Lambert, "British Naval Policy, 1913–1914: Financial Limitation and Strategic Revolution," *Journal of Modern History* 67 (1995), 595–626.
115. Lambert, *Sir John Fisher's Naval Revolution*, 101–109; Lambert, "Dreadnought—The Revolution That Never Was," 5.
116. Sumida, "British Naval Administration," 17.
117. Samuel R. Williamson, *The Politics of Grand Strategy: Britain and France Prepare for War, 1904–1914* (Cambridge, MA: Harvard University Press, 1969).
118. McDermott, "Revolution in British Military Thinking," 111.

119. Peden, *Arms, Economics and British Strategy*, 17.
120. Williamson, *Politics of Grand Strategy*.
121. Ibid., 15.
122. McDermott, "Revolution in British Military Thinking."
123. Peden, *Arms, Economics and British Strategy*, 17–18.
124. Williamson, *Politics of Grand Strategy*.
125. Edward Ingram, "Great Britain and Russia," in W. R. Thompson, ed., *Great Power Rivalries* (Columbia: University of South Carolina Press, 1999), 286.
126. McDermott, "Revolution in British Military Thinking."
127. Ibid.
128. Williamson, *Politics of Grand Strategy*.
129. Ingram, "Great Britain and Russia."
130. Sumida, "Admiralty and British Imperial Grand Strategy," 9.
131. Sumida, "British Naval Administration," 3.
132. Fuller, *Strategy and Power in Russia*, 459–461.
133. Paul Dukes, *A History of Russia: Medieval, Modern, Contemporary*. 2nd edition (Houndmills, Basingstoke, Hampshire: Macmillan, 1990), 167.
134. Fuller, *Strategy and Power in Russia*.
135. Menning, *Bayonets before Bullets*.
136. Bruce W. Menning, "Mukden to Tannenberg: Defeat to Defeat, 1905–1914," in F. W. Kagan and R. Higham, eds., *The Military History of Tsarist Russia* (New York: St. Martin's Press, 2002), 203.
137. Lambert, "Admiral Sir John Fisher and the Concept of Flotilla Defense," 644.
138. Ibid., 648.
139. Fuller, *Strategy and Power in Russia*, 268.
140. Dietrich Geyer, *Russian Imperialism: The Interaction of Domestic and Foreign Policy, 1860–1914*, translated by B. Little (Oxford: Berg, 1987), 20.
141. Menning, *Bayonets before Bullets*.

Chapter 4: Inter-World War Period, 1918–1939

1. Krepinevich, "Cavalry to Computer," 36.
2. Conetta, "We Can See Clearly Now," 2–3.
3. See Richard English and Michael Kenny, eds., *Rethinking British Decline* (New York: St. Martin's Press, 2000); Friedberg, *The Weary Titan*; Alan Sked, *Britain's Decline. Problems and Perspectives* (Oxford, UK: Basil Blackwell, 1987); Sidney Pollard, *Britain's Prime and Britain's Decline: The British Economy 1870–1914* (London: Edward Arnold, 1989).
4. Friedberg, *The Weary Titan*, 86–87.
5. John Robert Ferris, *Men, Money, and Diplomacy* (Ithaca, NY: Cornell University Press, 1989), 37.

6. Mark R. Brawley, *Afterglow or Adjustment? Domestic Institutions and Responses to Overstretch* (New York: Columbia University Press, 1999).

7. Friedberg, *The Weary Titan*, 24.

8. English and Kenny, "Conclusion: Decline or Declinism?" 280.

9. "The central idea in the convergence literature is that there is a negative correlation between the productivity growth rate and the initial level of productivity. This can be explained most intuitively by the fact that it is easier for a lagging economy to imitate via adoption of technology or organization from abroad than to innovate at the frontier" (Stephen Broadberry and Mary O'Mahony, "Britain's Twentieth Century Productivity Performance in International Perspective," in Nicholas Crafts, Ian Gazeley, and Andrew Newell, eds., *Work and Pay in 20th Century Britain* [Oxford, UK: Oxford University Press, 2007]).

10. Ibid.

11. Quoted in Paul Kennedy, *The Rise and Fall of the Great Powers*, 229–230.

12. Ibid., 231.

13. Quoted in Charles Kupchan, *The End of the American Era* (New York: Knopf, 2002), chapter 1.

14. Malcolm Chalmers, *Paying for Defence: Military Spending and British Decline* (London: Pluto Press, 1985), 8.

15. Arguably, a declining power would have to be much weakened to adopt reform and reconstitute.

16. Conversation with Nicholas A. Lambert. In the 1920s, there were more ships out in the empire on police actions than in 1910, so much so that there were mutinies because sailors did not want to be deployed overseas. In 1935, the British could not reinforce the Japanese squadron because they needed enough personnel at home to rotate overseas. Retention problems were also serious, all constraining the ability to exercise power.

17. Ferris, *Men, Money, and Diplomacy*, 92–93.

18. Ibid., 154–155; K. Jeffrey, *The British Army and the Crisis of Empire, 1918–1922* (Manchester, UK: Manchester University Press, 1984).

19. Ferris, *Men, Money, and Diplomacy*, 154–155.

20. Stephen Roskill, *Naval Policy between the Wars* (New York: Walker, 1968), 181–203.

21. The group included Foreign Secretary George Curzon, Colonial Secretary (1919–1921) Alfred Milner, South African Prime Minister Jan Smuts, Colonial Secretary (1924–1929) Leopold Amery, and diplomat Sir Mark Sykes.

22. Brian Bond, *British Military Policy between the Two World Wars* (London and New York: The Clarendon Press and Oxford University Press, 1980), 12–13.

23. Quoted in Ferris, *Men, Money, and Diplomacy*, 116.

24. T. R. Moreman, in "'Small Wars' and 'Imperial Policing': The British Army and the Theory and Practice of Colonial Warfare in the British Empire, 1919–1939,"

The Journal of Strategic Studies 19 (1996), 105–131, argues that the British even failed to prepare systematically for these contingencies.

25. Ferris, *Men, Money, and Diplomacy*, 54.
26. Brawley, *Afterglow or Adjustment?* 211.
27. It makes most sense to compare figures three years prior to World War I, working backward from 1911, and after the war from 1922 onward. Higher figures between 1919 and 1922 reflect demobilization and British intervention in the Russian civil war.
28. Statistics available in Lambert, *Sir John Fisher's Naval Revolution*, 305.
29. Quoted in Ferris, *Men, Money, and Diplomacy*, 176.
30. Ibid., 180.
31. Ibid., 117–118.
32. Brian Bond and Williamson Murray, "The British Armed Forces, 1918–39," in Allan R. Millett and Williamson Murray, eds., *Military Effectiveness, Volume II: The Interwar Period* (Winchester, MA: Allen and Unwin, 1988), 115–116.
33. G. A. H. Gordon, *British Seapower and Procurement between the Wars: A Reappraisal of Rearmament* (Basingstoke, UK: Macmillan, 1988).
34. Bond and Murray, "British Armed Forces," 108, 125.
35. David Edgerton, *Warfare State: Britain 1920–1970* (Cambridge, UK: Cambridge University Press, 2006), 15–58.
36. Ferris, *Men, Money, and Diplomacy*, 29.
37. Quoted in Michael Howard, *The Continental Commitment*, 98.
38. Quoted in Bond, *British Military Policy*, 24–25.
39. Moreman, "'Small Wars' and 'Imperial Policing,'" 106.
40. Ferris, *Men, Money, and Diplomacy*, 71.
41. Bond, *British Military Policy*, 75
42. Quoted in Moreman, "Small Wars and Imperial Policing," 107.
43. Bond, *British Military Policy*, 101.
44. Ibid., 124–125.
45. Ibid., 114–115; Bond and Murray, "British Armed Forces," 107.
46. Ferris, *Men, Money, and Diplomacy*, 66.
47. Moreman, "'Small Wars' and 'Imperial Policing,'" 108.
48. J. P. Harris, "British Armour and Rearmament in the 1930s," *The Journal of Strategic Studies* 11 (1988), 233.
49. Ferris, *Men, Money, and Diplomacy*, 82.
50. Edgerton, *Warfare State*, 29–30.
51. Geoffrey Till, "Adopting the Aircraft Carrier: The British, American, and Japanese Case Studies," in Williamson Murray and Allan R. Millett, eds., *Military Innovation in the Interwar Period* (Cambridge, UK: Cambridge University Press, 1996), 198.
52. Nicholas Lambert, correspondence with author.

53. Edgerton, *Warfare State*, 43.
54. Ferris, *Men, Money, and Diplomacy*, 48.
55. Kennedy, *Rise and Fall of the Great Powers*, 315.
56. Bond, *British Military Policy*, 78.
57. Ferris, *Men, Money, and Diplomacy*, 152.
58. Ibid., 147–154.
59. Howard, *Continental Commitment*, 94–95.
60. Ferris, *Men, Money, and Diplomacy*, 154.
61. Ibid.
62. Quoted in Bond, *British Military Policy*, 80.
63. Quoted in ibid., 93.
64. Nicholas Lambert, correspondence with author.
65. Ian Nish, *Alliance in Decline* (London: Athlone Press, 1972).
66. Ferris, *Men, Money, and Diplomacy*, 146–147.
67. Ibid., 200.
68. Moreman, "'Small Wars' and 'Imperial Policing,'" 107.
69. Ibid., 125.
70. Edgerton, *Warfare State*, 23, 43.
71. Peden, *Arms, Economics and British Strategy*, 125–126.
72. Ibid., 161.
73. John Braeman, "Power and Diplomacy: The 1920s Reappraised," *Review of Politics* 44 (July 1982), 345.
74. Ibid., 358.
75. Robert K. Murray, *The Harding Era: Warren G. Harding and His Administration* (Minneapolis: University of Minnesota Press, 1969); Michael J. Hogan, *Informal Entente: The Private Structure of Cooperation in Anglo-American Economic Diplomacy, 1918–1929* (Columbia: University Press of Missouri, 1977).
76. Emily O. Goldman, *Sunken Treaties: Naval Arms Control between the Wars* (University Park, PA: Pennsylvania State University Press, 1994); Russell F. Weigley, "The Role of the War Department and the Army," in Dorothy Borg and Shumpei Okamoto, eds., *Pearl Harbor as History: Japanese–American Relations, 1931–1941* (New York: Columbia University Press, 1973), 170; Louis Morton, "War Plan *ORANGE*: Evolution of a Strategy," *World Politics* (January 1959), 221–250.
77. Dorothy Borg argues, "The theory that during the first four decades of the twentieth century the policy of the United States was dictated by a firm determination to defend the Open Door and the integrity of China proved tenuous.... the United States, as an emerging world power still uncertain of its role in the international community, was not likely to adhere steadfastly to any course" (Dorothy Borg, "Two Histories of the Far Eastern Policy of the United States: Tyler Dennett and A. Whitney Griswold," in Dorothy Borg and Shumpei Okamoto, eds., *Pearl Harbor as History: Japanese–American Relations, 1931–1941* [New York: Columbia University Press, 1973], 564).

78. Arthur A. Ekirch, "The Popular Desire for Peace as a Factor in Military Policy," in Harry L. Coles, ed., *Total War and Cold War: Problems in Civilian Control of the Military* (Columbus: Ohio State University Press, 1962), 163–164.

79. Ronald Spector, "The Military Effectiveness of the U.S. Armed Forces, 1919–39," in Allan R. Millett and Williamson Murray, eds., *Military Effectiveness, Vol. II: The Interwar Period* (Boston: Allen and Unwin, 1988), 70; Mark Skinner Watson, *United States Army in World War II, Chief of Staff: Prewar Plans and Preparations* (Washington, DC: Historical Division, Department of the Army, 1950); Louis Morton, "National Policy and Military Strategy," *The Virginia Quarterly Review* 36 (Winter 1960), 5; Russell F. Weigley, "The Role of the War Department and the Army."

80. Maurice Matloff, "The American Approach to War, 1919–1945," in Michael Howard, ed., *The Theory and Practice of War* (New York: Praeger, 1966), 228.

81. Russell F. Weigley, *History of the United States Army* (New York: Macmillan, 1967), 406–407.

82. The logic of the Color Plans has been invoked by Krepinevich, in *The QDR*, as relevant for the United States today, based on the premise "that it is risky to try and predict with any great degree of precision the character of future conflicts. It is riskier still to focus on one particular contingency (e.g., 'Desert Storm Equivalents') as a model for all plausible conflicts" (Krepinevich, *The Quadrennial Defense Review*, 53). He continues, "These plans helped the US military to hedge against an uncertain future by focusing its efforts on preparing to confront a range of plausible contingencies, as opposed to the most familiar or those believed to be the most likely" (56).

83. Steven T. Ross, ed., *Peacetime War Plans, 1919–1935. Volume I, Peacetime War Plans, 1919–1935 Series* (New York: Garland, 1992), x.

84. Ibid., xi.

85. Ibid., xxvii.

86. William R. Braisted, "On the American Red and Red-Orange Plans, 1919–1939," in Gerald Jordan, ed., *Naval Warfare in the Twentieth Century, 1900–1945: Essays in Honor of Arthur Marder* (New York: Crane Russak, 1977), 172.

87. Ross, *Peacetime War Plans*, xii.

88. Ibid., xxv.

89. Weigley, *History of the United States Army*, 405–406.

90. Matloff, "The American Approach to War," 220.

91. For Army contributions to fighting a Pacific War, see Brian McAllister Linn, *Guardians of Empire: The U.S. Army and the Pacific, 1920–1940* (Chapel Hill: University of North Carolina Press, 1997).

92. The Japanese Navy, unlike its Western counterparts, could make extensive use of long-range land-based bombers, which were subject to no arms control limits by operating them from the island chains mandated to Japan at the end of the war.

93. Moy, *Hitting the Beaches and Bombing the Cities*, 25

94. Quoted in Ibid., 29.

95. Amphibious assault, up to this point, had not superseded traditional peacetime functions *in practice* (Allan R. Millett, "Assault from the Sea: The Development of Amphibious Warfare between the Wars. The American, British, and Japanese Experiences," in Williamson Murray and Allan R. Millett, eds., *Military Innovation in the Interwar Period* [Cambridge UK: Cambridge University Press, 1996]; Allan R. Millett, *Semper Fidelis: The History of the United States Marine Corps* (New York: Free Press, 1991); Holland Smith and Percy Finch, *Coral and Brass* (New York: Scribner's, 1949); Moy, *Hitting the Beaches*, 44.

96. Jeter A. Isley and Philip A. Crowl, *The U.S. Marines and Amphibious War: Its Theory and Its Practice in the Pacific* (Princeton, NJ: Princeton University Press, 1951), 14–71; Millett, "Assault from the Sea," 337–341.

97. The Marine Corps historically assumed multiple responsibilities: guarding ships, shore installations, consulates, and embassies; serving as shore parties, boarding parties, and gun crews; acting as a hemispheric police force, as colonial light infantry, and as regular infantry during World War I (Millett, *Semper Fidelis*, 147–263, 318; Moy, *Hitting the Beaches*, 20). With America's acquisition of an insular empire after the Spanish-American War, the Marines also adopted the advanced base mission to defend the Navy's coaling stations and bases (Jack Shulimson, *The Marine Corps's Search for a Mission, 1880–1898* [Lawrence: University Press of Kansas, 1993], p. 207).

98. Ibid., 221.

99. C. M. Melhorn, *Two Block Fox: The Rise of the Aircraft Carrier 1911–1929* (Annapolis, MD: Naval Institute Press, 1974), 88.

100. Stephen Peter Rosen, *Winning the Next War: Innovation and the Modern Military* (Ithaca, NY: Cornell University Press, 1994), 69–71; Michael Vlahos, *The Blue Sword: The Naval War College and the American Mission, 1919–1941* (Newport, RI: Naval War College Press, 1980), remains the authority on the subject.

101. Rosen, *Winning the Next War*, 69–71.

102. The fleet problems were developed in the 1920s as a means of testing scenarios, and throughout the 1920s and 1930s they were a valuable testing ground for aviation concepts. In Fleet Problem IX in 1929, which included participation of the converted battle cruisers *Lexington* and *Saratoga*, Admiral Pratt's carrier task force achieved a devastating surprise attack on the Panama Canal (Archibald Turnbull and Clifford Lord, *History of United States Naval Aviation* [New Haven, CT: Yale University Press, 1949], 271–273; Thomas C. Hone and Mark D. Mandeles, "Interwar Innovation in Three Navies: USN, RN, IJN," *Naval War College Review* 40 [Spring 1987], 75–76).

103. Till, "Adopting the Aircraft Carrier," 197, 221.

104. George F. Hofmann, "The Demise of the U.S. Tanks Corps and Medium Tank Development Program," *Military Affairs* (February 1973), 21, 23.

105. Pershing's testimony was highly valued at the time. According to an *Army and Navy Journal* report, as quoted in Hofmann, "no one officer in the Army has wider knowledge or more complete grasp of the military lessons learned through the war" (Ibid., 23).

106. Ibid., 24; Timothy K. Nenninger, "The Development of American Armor 1917–1940, Part IV, A Revised Mechanization Policy," *Armor* 78 (September–October 1969), 45.

107. Robert K. Griffith Jr., *Men Wanted for the U.S. Army: America's Experience with an All-Volunteer Army between the World Wars* (Westport, CT: Greenwood Press, 1982), 53–58; Mark Skinner Watson, *United States Army in World War II*, 26.

108. Ibid., 23; Timothy K. Nenninger, "The Development of American Armor 1917–1940, Part I, The World War I Experience," *Armor* 78 (January–February 1969), 49.

109. Nenninger, "The Development of American Armor 1917–1940, Part I," 46–51.

110. The infantry and cavalry were also expected to develop greater mobility to support the army's defensive mission (Hofmann, "The Demise of the U.S. Tanks Corps," 23).

111. Timothy K. Nenninger, "The Development of American Armor 1917–1940, Part II, The Tank Corps Reorganized," *Armor* 78 (March–April 1969), 35.

112. Timothy K. Nenninger, "The Development of American Armor 1917–1940, Part III, The Experimental Mechanized Forces," *Armor* 78 (May–June 1969), 33–39.

113. Constance McLaughlin Green, Harry C. Thomson, and Peter C. Roots, *The Ordnance Department: Planning Munitions for War, U.S. Army in World War II: The Technical Services* 6, part 3 (Washington, DC: Office of the Chief of Military History, 1955), 195.

114. Williamson Murray, "Armored Warfare: The British, French, and German Experiences," in Williamson Murray and Allan R. Millett, eds., *Military Innovation in the Interwar Period* (Cambridge, UK: Cambridge University Press, 1996), 106.

115. Marvin A. Kreidberg and Merton G. Henry, *History of Military Mobilization in the United States Army, 1775–1945* (Washington, DC: Department of the Army, 1955), 413 (Department of the Army pamphlet ; no. 20-212).

116. Paul A. C. Koistinen, "The 'Industrial-Military Complex' in Historical Perspective: The Inter War Years," *The Journal of American History* (March 1970), 826.

117. Kreidberg and Henry, *History of Military Mobilization*, 498.

118. Ibid., 825.

119. Thomas Hone, "Fighting on Our Own Ground: The War of Production, 1920–1942," *Naval War College Review* (1992), 97–100, 106.

120. Harry B. Yoshpe, "Economic Mobilization Planning between the Two World Wars, Part II," *Military Affairs* 16 (Summer 1952), 72.

121. Koistinen, "The 'Industrial-Military Complex,'" 825. The IMP was revised in 1933, 1936, and 1939. Each revision benefited from increased Navy cooperation.

Planning for the creation and functioning of a key superagency to manage the wartime economy also progressed.

122. R. Elbertson Smith, *The Army and Economic Mobilization, U.S. Army in World War II: The War Department*, Vol. 4, part 5 (Washington, DC: Office of the Chief of Military History, 1959), 73–74.

123. Congress, for its part, was determined to avoid the procurement problems of the recent war and, by creating the OASW, provided a key political incentive for Army leaders to reevaluate how they executed their missions. Yet Congress failed to appropriate funds for staff, studies, and educational orders (Hone, "Fighting on Our Own Ground," 93–107). Only in 1937–1938 did Congress authorize educational orders, allocate modest resources for the stockpiling of essential strategic and raw materials, and slowly modify peacetime restraints on military contracting (Koistinen, "The 'Industrial-Military Complex,'" 838).

124. Ross, *Peacetime War Plans*, xi.

125. Robert A. Divine, *The Illusion of Neutrality* (Chicago: University of Chicago Press, 1962), viii.

126. Melvyn Leffler, "Political Isolationism, Economic Expansion or Diplomatic Realism? American Policy toward Western Europe, 1921–1933," *Perspectives in American History* 8 (1974), 413–461.

127. Ibid., 421.

128. Ibid., 423–432.

129. Ibid., 422.

130. Braeman, "Power and Diplomacy," 361–362.

131. Goldman, *Sunken Treaties*, 57.

132. Leffler, "Political Isolationism, Economic Expansion or Diplomatic Realism?" 414.

133. Revisionists maintain that the Philippines were really not important and that naval leaders called for their defense because it justified a large battle fleet and the Mahanian type engagement naval leaders hoped to engage in. This interpretation, however, slights the degree to which it was civilians who defined defense of the Philippines and the Open Door in China as in the national interest. The fact remained that Japan could not menace the continental United States nor the Western Hemisphere. It could, however, close the Open Door.

134. Vlahos, *The Blue Sword*, 17–19.

135. This also partly explains why the United States did not develop an independent air force at this time: instead, the U.S. Navy retained control over its air assets and made the administrative changes early on that paved the way for an air-centered vision of naval operations (Till, "Adopting the Aircraft Carrier," 203).

136. Ibid. See also Spector, "The Military Effectiveness of the U.S. Armed Forces, 1919–39," 73, 82, 89.

137. Braisted "On the American Red and Red-Orange Plans," 182.
138. Ibid.
139. Ibid.
140. Leffler, "Political Isolationism, Economic Expansion or Diplomatic Realism?" 426.
141. Ferris, *Men, Money, and Diplomacy*, 69.
142. Bond and Murray, "British Armed Forces," 120.
143. N. H. Gibbs, *Grand Strategy, Vol. 1, Rearmament Policy* (London: HMSO, 1976), 52; Bond, *British Military Policy*, 73.
144. Bond and Murray, "British Armed Forces," 115.
145. Ibid., 116–117.
146. In 1918, a unified Royal Air Force secured control over all air assets. The Fleet Air Arm was transferred back to the Navy in 1937, but the transfer took two years to complete, and centralization of aircraft procurement persisted. By 1938, the RAF was receiving the lion's share of service allocations, and it dramatically reduced funding for naval aircraft, championing seaplanes and long-range land-based aircraft as cheaper alternatives (Norman Friedman, *British Carrier Aviation* [Annapolis, MD: Naval Institute Press, 1989], 17).
147. Emily O. Goldman, "Receptivity to Revolution: Carrier Air Power in Peace and War," in Emily O. Goldman and Leslie C. Eliason, eds., *The Diffusion of Military Technology and Ideas* (Stanford, CA: Stanford University Press, 2003), 267–303.
148. Till, "Adopting the Aircraft Carrier," 203.
149. See, for example, Waldo H. Heinrichs Jr., "The Role of the United States Navy," in Dororthy Borg and Shumpei Okamoto, eds., *Pearl Harbor as History: Japanese-American Relations, 1931–1941* (New York: Columbia University Press, 1973), 201–202.
150. Thomas C. Hone, "Spending Patterns of the United States Navy, 1921–1941," *Armed Forces and Society* 8 (Spring 1982), 443–462.
151. Thomas C. Hone and Mark David Mandeles, "Managerial Style in the Interwar Navy: A Reappraisal," *Naval War College Review* 32 (September–October 1980), 97–98; Thomas C. Hone, "Navy Air Leadership: Rear Admiral William A. Moffett as Chief of the Bureau of Aeronautics," in *USAF Warrior Studies—Air Leadership: Proceedings of a Conference at Bolling Air Force Base April 13–14* (Washington, DC: GPO, 1984), 89–90.
152. Green et. al., *The Ordnance Department*, 195–196.
153. Weigley finds the experiential argument convincing. He writes, "Perhaps part of the explanation for the absence of an American Fuller, Liddell Hart, or Guderian after the World War is that, despite some worrying about the futility of warfare on the Western Front, the brief American participation in the war, with no Verdun or Passchendaele, did not provide so much inducement to American soldiers as to British or

German to look for ways to avoid repetition of the deadlock in the trenches" (Weigley, "The Role of the War Department and the Army," 219).

154. Bond and Murray, "British Armed Forces," 117, 120, 124.

155. Ibid., 99.

Chapter 5: United States, 1990–2010

1. Thomas Donnelly, *The Military We Need: The Defense Requirements of the Bush Doctrine* (Washington, DC: The AEI Press, 2005), 8.

2. Condoleezza Rice, "Campaign 2000: Promoting the National Interest," *Foreign Affairs* (January/February 2000).

3. Philip Bobbitt, *The Shield of Achilles: War, Peace, and the Course of History* (New York: Random House, 2002), xxi.

4. Harvey M. Sapolsky, Benjamin H. Friedman, and Brendan Rittenhouse Green, eds., *US Military Innovation since the Cold War: Creation without Destruction* (New York: Routledge, 2009).

5. Frederick Kagan, *Finding the Target: The Transformation of American Military Policy* (New York: Encounter Books, 2006).

6. Martin C. Libicki, "The Next Enemy," *Strategic Forum* 35 (July 1995); available at: www.dodccrp.org/libicki1.htm.

7. Colin S. Gray, "The 21st Century Security Environment and the Future of War," *Parameters* (Winter 2008–2009), 20, 23.

8. Stephen D. Biddle, Interview, "Military Victory in the Information Age," Conversations with History (Berkeley: University of California, 2006), available at http://globetrotter.berkeley.edu/people6/Biddle/biddle-con6.html.

9. Bruce Berkowitz, *Strategic Advantage: Challengers, Competitors, and Threats to America's Future* (Washington, DC: Georgetown University Press, 2008), 224.

10. Donald Kagan and Frederick W. Kagan, *While America Sleeps: Self-Delusion, Military Weakness, and the Threat to Peace Today* (New York: St. Martin's, 2000).

11. Barry Posen, "Command of the Commons: The Military Foundation of U.S. Hegemony," *International Security* 28 (Summer 2003), 5–46.

12. World Bank, "Gross Domestic Product," *World Development Indicators Database* (2008); available at: http://siteresources.worldbank.org/DATASTATISTICS/Resources/GDP.pdf

13. *The Knowledge Economy: Is the United States Losing Its Competitive Edge?* The Report of the Task Force on the Future of American Innovation (February 16, 2005); available at: www.futureofinnovation.org

14. Vladimir Putin, Annual Address to the Federal Assembly of the Russian Federation, the Kremlin, Moscow (April 25, 2005); available at: http://eng.kremlin.ru/speeches/2005/04/25/2031_type70029type82912_87086.shtml

15. Olga Oliker and Tanya Charlick-Paley, *Assessing Russia's Decline: Trends and Implications for the United States and the U.S. Air Force* (Santa Monica, CA: RAND, 2002).

16. Fareed Zakaria, "The Decline and Fall of Europe," *The Washington Post* (February 14, 2006), A15.

17. *Defense Strategy for the 1990s: The Regional Defense Strategy* (January 1993); available at: www.informationclearinghouse.info/pdf/naarpr_Defense.pdf

18. Robert Johnston, "U.S. Export Control Policy in the High Performance Computer Sector," *The Nonproliferation Review* (Winter 1998), 44–59; *Report of the Select Committee on U.S. National Security and Military/Commercial Concerns with the People's Republic of China* (1999); available at: www.house.gov/coxreport

19. Rice, "Campaign 2000."

20. *The 9/11 Commission Report* (2004); available at: http://govinfo.library.unt.edu/911/report/911Report.pdf

21. Ibid., 343.

22. Ryan Henry, "Defense Transformation and the 2005 Quadrennial Defense Review," *Parameters* (Winter 2005–2006), 12.

23. *National Defense Strategy of the United States of America* (Washington, DC: Department of Defense, 2005).

24. Henry, "Defense Transformation and the 2005 Quadrennial Defense Review," 7.

25. Ryan Henry, "Transforming the U.S. Global Defense Posture," *Naval War College Review* (Spring 2006), 13–28.

26. Mackubin Owens, "America's Long War(s)," Foreign Policy Research Institute E-Note (January 10, 2008).

27. A bus driver, Najibullah Zazi, was trained in Pakistan and now faces charges in federal court for planning to set off a series of bombs in the United States. An indictment that was unsealed in Chicago portrays an American citizen—David Headley—playing a pivotal role in last year's attack in Mumbai, which killed more than 170 people and dramatically raised tensions in South Asia. See also *Al Qaeda in Yemen and Somalia: A Ticking Time Bomb*, A Report to the Committee on Foreign Relations United States Senate One Hundred Eleventh Congress Second Session January 21, 2010 (Washington, DC: U.S. Government Printing Office, 2010).

28. U.N. General Assembly Security Council, "The Situation in Afghanistan and Its Implications for International Peace and Security," Report of the Secretary-General (December 28, 2009); available at: http://unama.unmissions.org/Portals/UNAMA/SG%20Reports/sgreportjan2010.pdf

29. David Anthony Denny, "U.S. Military Capability Much Better than in 2001, Rusmfeld Says," *The Washington File*, U.S. Department of State (May 17, 2006); available at: www.globalsecurity.org/military/library/news/2006/05/mil-060517-usia01.htm

30. Michael O'Hanlon, "U.S. Military Modernization: Implications for U.S. Policy in Asia," in Ashley J. Tellis and Michael Wills, eds., *Strategic Asia 2005–06: Military*

Modernization in an Era of Uncertainty (Seattle and Washington, DC: The National Bureau of Asian Research, 2005), 53.

31. Patrick E. Tyler, "U.S. Strategy Plan Calls for Insuring No Rivals Develop a One-Superpower World," *The New York Times* (March 8, 1992).

32. Patrick Tyler, "Pentagon Drops Goal of Blocking New Superpowers," *The New York Times* (May 24, 1992).

33. *Quadrennial Defense Review* (Washington, DC: 2001); *Nuclear Posture Review* (Washington, DC: 2001); *National Security Strategy* (Washington, DC: 2002); *National Military Strategy* (Washington, DC: 2004); *National Defense Strategy* (Washington, DC: 2005); *Quadrennial Defense Review* (Washington, DC: 2006). See Glen M. Segell, "Thoughts on Dissuasion," *Journal of Military and Strategic Studies* 10 (Summer 2008).

34. Quoted in Andrew F. Krepinevich, "Defense Transformation," Testimony before the U.S. Senate Committee on Armed Services (April 9, 2002).

35. Donald Rumsfeld, "21st Century Transformation," remarks delivered at National Defense University, Fort McNair, Washington, DC (January 31, 2002); available at: www.defense.gov/speeches/speech.aspx?speechid=183

36. Ibid.

37. U.S. Department of Defense. *Military Transformation: A Strategic Approach*. Washington, DC: Department of Defense, 2003.

38. Douglas J. Feith, "Transforming the U.S. Global Defense Posture," speech presented to the Center for Strategic and International Studies, Washington, DC (December 3, 2003); available at: www.defense.gov/Speeches/Speech.aspx?SpeechID=590

39. Winslow T. Wheeler and Lawrence J. Korb, *Military Reform: A Reference Handbook* (Westport, CT: Praeger, 2007).

40. Sapolsky et al., eds., *US Military Innovation since the Cold War*.

41. Terry Terriff, "Of Romans and Dragons: Preparing the US Marine Corps for Future Warfare," *Contemporary Security Policy* 28 (April 2007), 143–162.

42. O'Hanlon, "Limiting the Growth of the U.S. Defense Budget," 5.

43. Marcus Corbin, "Operation Enduring Freedom and Military Transformation," *The Defense Monitor* 31 (September 2002), 4–5.

44. Richard Andres, Craig Wills, and Thomas Griffith, "Winning with Allies: The Strategic Value of the Afghan Model," *International Security* 30 (Winter 2005–2006).

45. Thomas G. Mahnken, *Technology and the American Way of War since 1945* (New York: Columbia University Press, 2008), 195–204.

46. Stephen D. Biddle, "Allies, Airpower, and Modern Warfare: The Afghan Model in Afghanistan and Iraq," *International Security* 30 (Winter 2005–2006), 161–176; Stephen Biddle, "Afghanistan and the Future of Warfare," *Foreign Affairs* (March/April 2003).

47. Mahnken, *Technology and the American Way of War*, 211.

48. Biddle, "Allies, Airpower, and Modern Warfare."

49. Mark Mazzetti, "Iraq War Compels Pentagon to Rethink Big-Picture Strategy," *Los Angeles Times* (March 11, 2005).

50. Josh White, "Gates Sees Terrorism Remaining Enemy No. 1," *The Washington Post* (July 31, 2008), A1.

51. Andrew Bacevich, *The Limits of Power: The End of American Exceptionalism* (New York: Metropolitan Books, 2008).

52. Robert M. Gates, "Landon Lecture" (Manhattan: Kansas State University, 26 November 2007); available at: www.defense.gov/speeches/speech.aspx?speechid=1199

53. Mary Beth Sheridan and Greg Jaffe, "Gates Proposes $2 Billion in Funds to Aid Unstable Countries," *The Washington Post* (December 24, 2009), A02; Unclassified memo from Secretary Gates to Secretary Clinton (December 15, 2009), "Options for Remodeling Security Sector Assistance Authorities."

54. Thomas Donnelly and Gary Schmitt, "Obama and Gates Gut the Military," *Wall Street Journal Online* (April 7, 2009).

55. Ibid.

56. Kagan, *Finding the Target*, 364.

57. "White Paper of the Interagency Policy Group's Report on U.S. Policy toward Afghanistan and Pakistan"; available at: www.whitehouse.gov/assets/documents/afghanistan_pakistan_white_paper_final.pdf

58. COMISAF Initial Assessment (Unclassified) August 30, 2009; available at: www.washingtonpost.com/wp-dyn/content/article/2009/09/21/AR2009092100110.html?hpid=topnews

59. Rajiv Chandrasekaran, "Civilian, Military Planners Have Different Views on New Approach to Afghanistan," *Washington Post* (December 26, 2009), A01.

60. *A National Security Strategy of Engagement and Enlargement* (Washington, DC: 1994), 6.

61. Larry Berman and Emily O. Goldman, "Clinton's Foreign Policy at Midterm," in Colin Campbell and Bert A. Rockman, eds., *The Clinton Presidency: First Appraisals* (Chatham, NJ: Chatham House Publishers, 1996), 314.

62. Richard N. Haass, "Fatal Distraction: Bill Clinton's Foreign Policy," *Foreign Policy* (Fall 1997), 119.

63. Moisés Naím, "Clinton's Foreign Policy: A Victim of Globalization?" *Foreign Policy* (Winter 1997–1998), 34–69.

64. Berman and Goldman, "Clinton's Foreign Policy at Midterm," 298.

65. Robert G. Kaufman, *In Defense of the Bush Doctrine* (Lexington: University Press of Kentucky, 2007); Chris J. Dolan, *In War We Trust: The Bush Doctrine and the Pursuit of Just War* (Burlington, VT: Ashgate, 2005); Stephen M. Walt, *Taming American Power* (New York: W. W. Norton, 2006); Gary Rosen, *The Right War? The Conservative Debate on Iraq* (New York: Cambridge University Press, 2005); Andrew J.

Bacevich, *The New American Militarism: How Americans Are Seduced by War* (New York: Oxford University Press, 2006); Francis Fukuyama, *America at the Crossroads: Democracy, Power, and the Neoconservative Legacy* (New Haven, CT: Yale University Press, 2007).

66. Marc Trachtenberg, "Preventive War and U.S. Foreign Policy," *Security Studies* 16 (January 2007), 1–31; John Lewis Gaddis, *Surprise, Security and the American Experience* (Cambridge, MA: Harvard University Press, 2004).

67. Thomas E. Ricks, "For Pentagon, Asia Moving to Forefront," *The Washington Post* (May 26, 2000), A01.

68. "A Cold War China Policy," *The New York Times* (November 19, 2005).

69. Thomas Donnelly, "The Big Four Alliance: The New Bush Strategy," *AEI Online* (December 2, 2005).

70. Donnelly, *The Military We Need*, 25–26.

71. Thomas J. Christensen, "Shaping the Choices of a Rising China: Recent Lessons for the Obama Administration," *The Washington Quarterly* 32 (July 2009), 89–104.

72. "President Obama Delivers Remarks at U.S.–China Strategic and Economic Dialogue," *CQ Transcriptions* (July 27, 2009).

73. Robert Kagan and Dan Blumenthal, "Strategic Reassurance That Isn't," *The Washington Post* (November 10, 2009). See also Evan S. Medeiros, "Strategic Hedging and the Future of Asia-Pacific Stability," *The Washington Quarterly* 29 (Winter 2005/06), 145–167.

Chapter 6: Consequences of Strategic Choices

1. G. John Ikenberry, "Liberal Order Building," in Melvyn P. Leffler and Jeffrey W. Legro, eds., *To Lead the World: American Strategy after the Bush Doctrine* (New York: Oxford University Press, 2008), 91.

2. Kipp, "The Russian Navy and the Problem of Technological Transfer."

3. Robert F. Baumann, "The Russian Army, 1853–1881," in F. W. Kagan and R. Higham, eds., *The Military History of Tsarist Russia* (New York: Palgrave, 2002), 32–33; Fuller, *Strategy and Power in Russia*, 324.

4. Menning, *Bayonets before Bullets*.

5. Fuller, *Strategy and Power in Russia*, 339.

6. Ibid., 384.

7. Ibid., 375–379.

8. Ibid., 362–363.

9. Ibid., 325.

10. Goldman, "Cultural Foundations of Military Transformation," 69–91.

11. Emily O. Goldman, "Thinking about Strategy Absent the Enemy," *Security Studies* 4 (Autumn 1994), 40–85.

12. Ferris, *Men, Money, and Diplomacy*, 106.

13. Edgerton, *Warfare State*, 19, 43.

14. Michael Moissey Postan, *British War Production*, History of the Second World War Series, United Kingdom Civil Series (London: HMSO, 1952), 19, 40; Gordon, *British Seapower and Procurement between the Wars*, 133.

15. Peden, *Arms, Economics and British Strategy*, 139–140.

16. Ibid., 151.

17. Edgerton, *Warfare State*, 23, 43.

18. Some attribute problems in carrier aviation to the Navy's loss of control over the Fleet Air Arm (FAA) between 1918 and 1939. Others argue that even once the Admiralty regained control of the naval air arm, they did not change the method of supplying aircraft for the Fleet Air Arm (Vice Admiral Sir Arthur Hezlet, *Aircraft and Sea Power* [New York: Stein and Day, 1970], 127–128, 135).

19. Peden, *Arms, Economics and British Strategy*, 140.

20. Harris, "British Armour and Rearmament in the 1930s."

21. Correlli Barnett, *The Audit of War: The Illusion and Reality of Britain as a Great Nation* (London: Macmillan, 1986), 143–158, 161–164.

22. Harris, "British Armour and Rearmament," 223.

23. Bond points to the system of Treasury oversight, under which new items had to be explicitly justified and savings in one area could not be credited to expenditure in another and "which allowed virtually no flexibility, set too much emphasis on precedent, and did not provide for continuity in the kind of research, trials, and experiments essential to the development of mechanization" (Bond, *British Military Policy between the Two World Wars*, 135).

24. Harris, "British Armour and Rearmament," 228.

25. Bond and Murray, "The British Armed Forces, 1918–39," 103.

26. Ferris, *Men, Money, and Diplomacy*, 115.

27. Peden, *Arms, Economics and British Strategy*, 156.

28. Ibid., 144.

29. Howard, *The Continental Commitment*, 93.

30. Emily O. Goldman, "International Competition and Military Effectiveness: Naval Air Power, 1919–1945," in Risa A. Brooks and Elizabeth A. Stanley, eds., *Creating Military Power: The Sources of Military Effectiveness* (Stanford, CA: Stanford University Press, 2007).

31. The British "armored flight deck" carriers had armored hangars, which meant armoring part of the flight deck above the hangar and also the sides of the hangar. There was also a belt for side protection to resist cruiser shellfire.

32. The fundamental measure of offensive carrier effectiveness was the number of aircraft a carrier could launch for a given mission. See Barry Watts and Williamson Murray, "Military Innovation in Peacetime," in Williamson Murray and Allan R.

Millett, eds., *Military Innovation in the Interwar Period* (Cambridge, UK: Cambridge University Press, 1996), 399–400.

33. Till, "Adopting the Aircraft Carrier," 226.
34. Peden, *Arms, Economics and British Strategy*, 154–155.
35. Sumida, "British Naval Administration and Policy in the Age of Fisher," 4.
36. Ibid., 3.
37. Lambert, "Transformation and Technology in the Fisher Era," 290–291.
38. Kenneth L. Moll, "Politics, Power, and Panic: Britain's 1909 Dreadnought 'Gap.'" *Military Affairs* 29 (1965), 142.
39. Ibid.
40. Bryan Ranft, "The Protection of British Seaborne Trade and the Development of Systematic Planning for War, 1860–1906," in Bryan Ranft, ed., *Technical Change and British Naval Policy, 1860–1939* (London: Hodder and Stoughton, 1977).
41. Moll, "Politics, Power, and Panic," 144.
42. Peden, *Arms, Economics and British Strategy*, 48.
43. Trebilcock, "British Armaments and European Industrialization, 1890–1914," 258.
44. Ibid., 264.
45. Peden, *Arms, Economics and British Strategy*, 48.
46. Ibid., 45.
47. John Lewis Gaddis, "A Grand Strategy," *Foreign Policy* (November/December 2002), 55–57.
48. H. R. McMaster, "Learning from Contemporary Conflicts to Prepare for Future War," *Orbis* (Fall 2008), 565–566.
49. Ibid., 565.
50. Andrew Krepinevich, "Emerging Threats, Revolutionary Capabilities and Military Transformation," Testimony before the Senate Armed Services Subcommittee on Emerging Threats and Capabilities, March 5, 1999.
51. Clay Wilson, "Network Centric Operations: Background and Oversight Issues for Congress" (Washington, DC: Congressional Research Service, March 15, 2007).
52. Stephen D. Biddle. Interview, "Military Victory in the Information Age," Conversations with History (Berkeley, CA: University of California, 2006): available at: http://globetrotter.berkeley.edu/people6/Biddle/biddle-con6.html
53. Thomas Donnelly, *The Military We Need*, 16.
54. Biddle, "Military Victory in the Information Age."
55. Roxborough and Eyre, "Which Way to the Future?" 28–34.
56. *The 9/11 Commission Report*.
57. Charles Krauthammer, "Decline Is a Choice," *The Weekly Standard* (December 19, 2009).

BIBLIOGRAPHY

Al Qaeda in Yemen and Somalia: A Ticking Time Bomb. 2010. A Report to the Committee on Foreign Relations United States Senate One Hundred Eleventh Congress Second Session January 21, 2010. Washington, DC: U.S. Government Printing Office.

Alberts, David S., John J. Garstka, and Frederick P. Stein. 1999. *Network Centric Warfare: Developing and Leveraging Information Superiority,* 2nd ed., revised. Washington, DC: C4ISR Cooperative Research Program.

Allison, Graham T. 1971. *Essence of Decision.* Boston: Little, Brown and Company.

Altfeld, Michael F. 1984. "The Decision to Ally: A Theory and a Test." *Western Political Quarterly* 37: 523–544.

Andres, Richard, Craig Wills, and Thomas Griffith. 2005–2006. "Winning with Allies: The Strategic Value of the Afghan Model." *International Security* 30 (Winter).

"Annual Abstract of Statistics, 1935–1946" (1970; Reprinted). V. 84. Kraus Reprint (Central Statistical Office).

Arquilla, John, and David Ronfeldt. 1993. "Cyberwar Is Coming!" *Comparative Strategy* 12 (April–June): 141–165.

Art, Robert J. 2003. *A Grand Strategy for America.* Ithaca, NY, and London: Cornell University Press.

Aspin, Les. 1993. *Report of the Bottom-Up Review.* Washington, DC: Department of Defense (October).

Avant, Deborah D. 1994. *Political Institutions and Military Change: Lessons From Peripheral Wars.* Ithaca, NY: Cornell University Press.

Axelrod, Robert and Robert O. Keohane. 1985. "Achieving Cooperation under Anarchy: Strategies and Institutions." *World Politics* 38: 226–254.

Bacevich, Andrew J. 2006. *The New American Militarism: How Americans Are Seduced by War*. New York: Oxford University Press.

———. 2008. *The Limits of Power: The End of American Exceptionalism*. New York: Metropolitan Books.

Baldwin, David A. 1993. "Neoliberalism, Neoliberalism, and World Politics," in David A. Baldwin, ed., *Neorealism and Neoliberalism: The Contemporary Debate*. New York: Columbia University Press.

Barnett, Correlli. 1986. *The Audit of War: The Illusion and Reality of Britain as a Great Nation*. London: Macmillan.

Barnett, Jeffery R. 1996. *Future War: An Assessment of Aerospace Campaigns in 2010*. Maxwell AFB, AL: Air University Press.

Barnett, Michael N. 1992. *Confronting the Costs of War: Military Powers, State, and Society in Egypt and Israel*. Princeton, NJ: Princeton University Press.

Barnett, Michael N., and Jack S. Levy. 1991. "Domestic Sources of Alliances and Alignment: The Case of Egypt, 1962-73." *International Organization* 45: 369-395.

Barnett, Thomas P. M. 2004. *The Pentagon's New Map: War and Peace in the Twenty-First Century*. New York: Putnam.

Baumann, Robert F. 2002. "The Russian Army, 1853-1881," in F. W. Kagan and R. Higham, eds., *The Military History of Tsarist Russia*. New York: Palgrave.

Becker, Seymour. 1988. "Russia's Central Asia Empire, 1885-1917." In M. Rywkin, ed., *Russian Colonial Expansion to 1917*. London: Mansell Publishing.

Beeler, John. 1997. *British Naval Policy in the Gladstone-Disraeli Era, 1866-1880*. Stanford, CA: Stanford University Press.

Berkowitz, Bruce. 2003. *The New Face of War: How War Will Be Fought in the 21st Century*. New York: The Free Press.

———. 2008. *Strategic Advantage: Challengers, Competitors, and Threats to America's Future*. Washington, DC: Georgetown University Press.

Berman, Larry, and Emily O. Goldman. 1996. "Clinton's Foreign Policy at Midterm," in Colin Campbell and Bert A. Rockman, eds., *The Clinton Presidency: First Appraisals*. Chatham, NJ: Chatham House Publishers.

Beskrovnyi, Lyubomir G. 1973. *Russkaya Armiya I Flot v XIXv.: Voenno-Ekonomicheskii Potentsial Rossii* [Russia's Army and Navy in the 19th century: Military-Economic Potential of Russia]. Moscow: Nauka.

———. 1986. *Armiya I Flot Rossii v Nachale XXv.: Ocherki Voenno-Ekonomicheskogo Potentsiala (Russia's Army and Navy in the Beginning of the 20th century: Narratives on the Military-Economic Potential)*. Moscow: Nauka.

Betts, Richard. 1977. *Soldiers, Statesmen, and Cold War Crises*. Cambridge, MA: Harvard University Press.

———. 1992. "Systems for Peace or Causes of War? Collective Security, Arms Control, and the New Europe." *International Security* 17 (Summer): 5-43.

Biddle, Stephen. 2003. "Afghanistan and the Future of Warfare," *Foreign Affairs* (March/April).
———. 2004. *Military Power: Explaining Victory and Defeat in Modern Battle*. Princeton, NJ: Princeton University Press.
———. 2005–2006. "Allies, Airpower, and Modern Warfare: The Afghan Model in Afghanistan and Iraq," *International Security* 30 (Winter), 161–176.
———. 2006. Interview. "Military Victory in the Information Age." Conversations with History. Berkeley, CA: University of California, 2006. Available at: http://globetrotter.berkeley.edu/people6/Biddle/biddle-con6.html
Binnendijk, Hans, and Stuart Johnson, eds. 2003. *Transforming for Stabilization and Reconstruction Operations*. Washington, DC: Center for Technology and National Security Policy.
Black, Jeremy. 1999. "Enduring Rivalries: Britain and France." In W. R. Thompson, ed., *Great Power Rivalries*. Columbia: University of South Carolina Press.
———. 2001. *Western Warfare: 1775–1882*. Bloomington and Indianapolis: Indiana University Press.
Bobbitt, Philip. 2002. *The Shield of Achilles: War, Peace, and the Course of History*. New York: Random House.
Bond, Brian. 1980. *British Military Policy between the Two World Wars*. Oxford, UK: Oxford University Press.
Bond, Brian, and Williamson Murray. 1988. "The British Armed Forces, 1918–39," in Allan R. Millett and Williamson Murray, eds., *Military Effectiveness, Volume II: The Interwar Period*. Winchester, MA: Allen and Unwin.
Boot, Max. 2006. *War Made New: Technology, Warfare, and the Course of History 1500 to Today*. New York: Gotham Books.
Borg, Dorothy. 1973. "Two Histories of the Far Eastern Policy of the United States: Tyler Dennett and A. Whitney Griswold," in Dorothy Borg and Shumpei Okamoto, eds., *Pearl Harbor as History: Japanese–American Relations, 1931–1941*. New York: Columbia University Press.
Bower, J. L., and C. M. Christensen. 1995. "Disruptive Technologies: Catching the Wave." *Harvard Business Review*. (January-February): 43–53.
Bracken, Paul. 1993. "The Military after Next." *The Washington Quarterly*, 16: 157–174.
Bracken, P., L. Brandt, and S. E. Johnson. 2006. "The Changing Landscape of Defense Innovation." *Defense Horizons*, 47: 1–8.
Braeman, John. 1982. "Power and Diplomacy: The 1920s Reappraised," *Review of Politics*, 44.
Braisted, William R. 1977. "On the American Red and Red-Orange Plans, 1919–1939," in Gerald Jordan, ed., *Naval Warfare in the Twentieth Century, 1900–1945: Essays in Honor of Arthur Marder*, 167–185. New York: Crane Russak, 1977.
Brawley, Mark R. 1999. *Afterglow or Adjustment? Domestic Institutions and Responses to Overstretch*. New York: Columbia University Press.

Breemer, Jan S. 1999. "Technological Change and the New Calculus of War: The United States Builds a New Navy," in Peter Trubowitz, Emily O. Goldman, and Edward Rhodes, eds., *The Politics of Strategic Adjustment: Ideas, Institutions, and Interests*. New York: Columbia University Press.

Bridge, F. R., and Roger Bullen. 1980. *The Great Powers and the European State System: 1815–1914*. New York: Longman.

Broadberry, Stephen, and Mary O'Mahony. 2007. "Britain's Twentieth Century Productivity Performance in International Perspective." In Nicholas Crafts, Ian Gazeley, and Andrew Newell, eds., *Work and Pay in 20th Century Britain*. Oxford, UK: Oxford University Press.

Brodie, Bernard. 1976. "Technological Change, Strategic Doctrine, and Political Outcomes," in Klaus Knorr, ed., *Historical Dimensions of National Security Problems*. Lawrence: University of Kansas Press.

Brooks, Stephen G. 1997. "Dueling Realisms." *International Organization* 51 (Summer).

Brose, Eric D. 2001. *The Kaiser's Army: The Politics of Military Technology in Germany During the Machine Age, 1870–1918*. New York: Oxford University Press.

Budget of the United States Government: Historical Tables Fiscal Year 2008. Available at: www.gpoaccess.gov/USbudget/fy08/hist.html

Bush, George W. 1999. "A Period of Consequences." Speech at the Citadel, 23 September.

———. 2001. "Remarks by the President to the Troops and Personnel." Norfolk Naval Air Station, Norfolk, VA, 13 February.

Bushnell, John S. 1994. "Miliutin and the Balkan War: Military Reform vs. Military Performance," in Ben Eklof, John Bushnell, and Larissa Zakharova, eds., *Russia's Great Reforms, 1855–1881*. Bloomington: Indiana University Press.

Campbell, Donald T. 1988. "'Degrees of Freedom' and the Case Study," in E. Samuel Overman, ed., *Methodology and Epistemology for Social Science*. Chicago: University of Chicago Press.

Carlson, Lark J. 1998. *SOF Planning for Uncertainty: Creative Thinking in Dynamic Environments*. Naval Postgraduate School Thesis. December.

Casillas, Julio, Percy Crocker Jr., Frank Fehrenbach, Kevin Haug, and Ben Straley. 2000. "Disruptive Technologies: Strategic Advantage and Thriving in Uncertainty." In Mohanbir S. Sawhney and Ranjay Gulati (eds.), *Kellogg TechVenture 2000 Anthology*. Evanston, IL: Nminds Publications.

Cebrowski, Arthur K., and John J. Garstka. 1998. "Network-Centric Warfare: Its Origin and Future." U.S. Naval Institute *Proceedings* (January): 28–35.

Cha, Victor D. 2002. "Hawk Engagement and Preventive Defense on the Korean Peninsula." *International Security* 27: 40–78.

Chalmers, Malcolm. 1985. *Paying for Defence: Military Spending and British Decline*. London: Pluto Press.

Chandrasekaran, Rajiv. 2009. "Civilian, Military Planners Have Different Views on New Approach to Afghanistan." *Washington Post*. December 26: A01.

Chayes, Abram, Lara Olson, and George Raach. 1997. "The Development of U. S. Policy Toward the Former Soviet Union." In A. Arbatov, A. Chayes, A. H. Chayes, and L. Olson, eds. *Managing Conflict in the Former Soviet Union: Russian and American Perspectives*. Cambridge, MA: MIT Press.

Checkel, Jeffrey T. 1998. "The Constructivist Turn in International Relations Theory." *World Politics* 50: 324–348.

Christensen, C. M. 2002. "The Rules of Innovation." *Technology Review* 105: 33–38.

Christensen, C. M., M. W. Johnson, and D. K. Rigby. 2002. "Foundations for Growth: How to Identify and Build Disruptive New Businesses." *MIT Sloan Management Review* 43: 22–31.

Christensen, C. M., and M. Overdorf. 2000. "Meeting the Challenge of Disruptive Change." *Harvard Business Review* (March–April): 67–76.

Christensen, Clayton M. 2000. *The Innovator's Dilemma*. New York: HarperBusiness.

Christensen, Clayton M., Scott D. Anthony, and Erik A. Roth. 2004. *Seeing What's Next: Using the Theories of Innovation to Predict Industry Change*. Boston: Harvard Business School Press.

Christensen, Clayton M., and Michael E. Raynor. 2003. *The Innovator's Solution: Creating and Sustaining Successful Growth*. Boston: Harvard Business School Press.

Christensen, Thomas J. 1996. *Useful Adversaries: Grand Strategy, Domestic Mobilization, and Sino-American Conflict, 1947-1958*. Princeton University Press.

———. 2009. "Shaping the Choices of a Rising China: Recent Lessons for the Obama Administration." *The Washington Quarterly* 32 (July): 89–104.

Christensen, Thomas J., and Jack Snyder. 1990. "Chain Gangs and Passed Bucks: Predicting Alliance Patterns in Multipolarity." *International Organization* 44: 137–168.

Citino, Robert. 2005. "Beyond Fire and Movement: Command, Control and Information in German Blitzkrieg." In Emily O. Goldman, ed., *Information and Revolutions in Military Affairs*. London: Routledge.

Cohen, Eliot A. 1994. "The Mystique of U.S. Air Power." *Foreign Affairs* 73 (Jan/Feb): 109–124.

———. 1996. "A Revolution in Warfare." *Foreign Affairs* 75 (March/April 1996): 37–54.

Cohen, William S. 1997. *Report of the Quadrennial Defense Review*. Washington, DC: Department of Defense (May).

"A Cold War China Policy." 2005. *New York Times* (November 19).

COMISAF Initial Assessment (Unclassified). 2009. (August 30). Available at www.washingtonpost.com/wp-dyn/content/article/2009/09/21/AR2009092100110.html?hpid=topnews

Conetta, Carl. 2006. "We Can See Clearly Now: The Limits of Foresight in the Pre–World War II Revolution in Military Affairs (RMA)." Project of Defense Alternatives Research Monograph 12 (March).

Conybeare, John A. C. 1992. "A Portfolio Diversification Model of Alliances: The Triple Alliance and Triple Entente, 1879–1914." *Journal of Conflict Resolution* 36: 53–85.

———. 1994. "The Portfolio Benefits of Free Riding in Military Alliances." *International Studies Quarterly* 38: 405–419.

Cooley, Alexander. 2005. *Logics of Hierarchy: The Organization of Empires, States and Military Occupations*. Ithaca, NY: Cornell University Press.

Copeland, Dale C. 2000. *The Origins of Major War*. Ithaca, NY: Cornell University Press.

Corbin, Marcus, 2002. "Operation Enduring Freedom and Military Transformation." *The Defense Monitor*, 31 (September): 4–5.

Correll, John T. 2003. *Strategy, Requirements, and Forces: The Rising Imperative of Air and Space Power*. Air Force Association Special Report (February).

Courtney, Hugh G., Jane Kirkland, and S. Patrick Viguerie. 1997. "Strategy under Uncertainty." *Harvard Business Review* (November–December).

Coutau-Begarie, Herve. 1996. "French Naval Strategy: A Naval Power in a Continental Environment." In N. A. M. Rodger, ed., *Naval Power in the Twentieth Century*. Annapolis, MD: Naval Institute Press.

Cox, Michael, John G. Ikenberry, and Takashi Inoguchi. 2000. *American Democracy Promotion: Impulses, Strategies and Impact*. New York: Oxford University Press.

Crowe, Robert M., and Ronald C. Horn. 1967. "The Meaning of Risk." *Journal of Risk and Insurance*, 34: 459–474.

Das, T. K., and Bing-Sheng Teng. 2000. "Instabilities of Strategic Alliances: An Internal Tensions Perspective." *Organizational Science*, 11: 77–101.

Davis, Paul K., ed. 1994. *New Challenges for Defense Planning: Rethinking How Much Is Enough*. Santa Monica, CA: RAND.

Davis, Paul K., David Gompert, and Richard Kugler. 1996. *Adaptiveness in National Defense: The Basis of a New Framework*. Santa Monica, CA: RAND (August).

De Soysa, Indra, John R. Oneal, and Yong-Hee Park. 1997. "Testing Power Transition Theory Using Alternative Measures of National Capabilities." *Journal of Conflict Resolution*, 41: 509–528.

Defense Science Board. 2006. *Transformation: A Progress Assessment*. Vol. 1. Washington, DC: Office of the Under Secretary of Defense for Acquisition, Technology, and Logistics.

———. 2006. *Transformation: A Progress Assessment*. Vol. 2. *Supporting Reports*. Washington, DC: Office of the Under Secretary of Defense for Acquisition, Technology, and Logistics.

Defense Strategy for the 1990s: The Regional Defense Strategy. 1993 (January). Available at: www.informationclearinghouse.info/pdf/naarpr_Defense.pdf

Demchak, Chris C. 1991. *Complex Machines: Modernization in the U.S. Armed Services.* Ithaca, NY: Cornell University Press.

Denny, David Anthony. 2006. "U.S. Military Capability Much Better Than in 2001, Rusmfeld Says." *The Washington File.* U.S. Department of State (May 17). Available at: www.globalsecurity.org/military/library/news/2006/05/mil-060517-usia01.htm

Department of the Air Force. 1996. *Air Force Strategy: Global Engagement.* Available at: www.au.af.mil/au/awc/awcgate/global/nuvis.htm

——. 1992. *Global Reach—Global Power: The Evolving Air Force Contribution to National Security* (December). Arlington, VA: Aerospace Education Foundation.

Department of the Army. 1994. *Army Focus 94: Force XXI.* Washington, DC: U.S. Army Publication and Printing Command (September).

——. 1994. *Decisive Victory: America's Power Projection Army* (October).

Department of the Navy. 1986. "The Maritime Strategy." U.S. Naval Institute *Proceedings* Supplement (January).

——. 1992. *. . . From the Sea* (September). Washington, DC: Department of the Navy.

——. 1994. *Forward . . . from the Sea.* Washington, DC: Department of the Navy.

Dewar, James A. 2002. *Assumption-Based Planning: A Tool for Reducing Avoidable Surprises.* Santa Monica, CA: RAND.

Diehl, Paul F. 1994. "Substitutes or Complements? The Effects of Alliances on Military Spending in Major Power Rivalries." *International Interactions*, 19: 159–176.

DiMaggio, Paul J., and Walter W. Powell. 1983. "The Iron Cage Revisited: Institutional Isomorphism and Collective Rationality in Organizational Fields." *American Sociological Review*, 48 (April).

Divine, Robert A. 1962. *The Illusion of Neutrality.* Chicago: University of Chicago Press.

D'Lugo, David, and Ronald Rogowski. 1993. "The Anglo-German Naval Race and Comparative Constitutional 'Fitness,'" in Richard Rosecrance and Arthur A. Stein, eds., *The Domestic Bases of Grand Strategy.* Ithaca, NY: Cornell University Press.

Dolan, Chris J. 2005. *In War We Trust: The Bush Doctrine and the Pursuit of Just War.* Burlington, VT: Ashgate.

Dombrowski, Peter, and Eugene Gholz. 2006. *Buying Military Transformation: Technological Innovation and the Defense Industry.* New York: Columbia University Press.

Dombrowski, Peter J., Eugene Gholz, and Andrew L. Ross. 2003. *Military Transformation and the Defense Industry after Next: The Defense Industrial Implications of Network-Centric Warfare.* Newport Paper No. 18 Newport, RI: Naval War College Press.

Dombrowski, Peter J., and Andrew L. Ross. 2003. "Transforming the Navy: Punching a Featherbed?" *Naval War College Review*, 56: 107–131.

Donnelly, Thomas. 2005. "The Big Four Alliance: The New Bush Strategy." *AEI Online* (December 2).

———. 2005. *The Military We Need: The Defense Requirements of the Bush Doctrine.* Washington, DC: The AEI Press.

Donnelly, Thomas, and Gary Schmitt. 2009. "Obama and Gates Gut the Military." *Wall Street Journal Online* (April 7).

Dorff, Robert H. 2003. "The Current U. S. National Security Strategy and Policy: A Brief Appraisal," in M. G. Manwaring, E. G. Corr and R. H. Dorff, eds., *The Search for Security: A U. S. Grand Strategy for the Twenty-First Century.* Westport, CT: Praeger.

Doyle, Michael W. 1986. *Empires.* Ithaca, NY: Cornell University Press.

Doyle, Michael W. 1993. "Politics and Grand Strategy," in Richard Rosecrance and Arthur A. Stein, eds., *The Domestic Bases of Grand Strategy.* Ithaca, NY: Cornell University Press.

Doz, Yves L. 1996. "The Evolution of Cooperation in Strategic Alliances: Initial Conditions or Learning Processes?" *Strategic Management Journal,* 17: 55–83.

Dukes, Paul. 1990. *A History of Russia: Medieval, Modern, Contemporary,* 2nd edition. Houndmills, Basingstoke, Hampshire: Macmillan.

Edgerton, David. 2006. *Warfare State: Britain 1920–1970.* Cambridge, UK: Cambridge University Press.

Ekirch, Arthur A. "The Popular Desire for Peace as a Factor in Military Policy," in Harry L. Coles, ed., *Total War and Cold War: Problems in Civilian Control of the Military.* Columbus: Ohio State University Press, 1962.

Eklof, Ben, John Bushnell, and Larissa Zakharova, eds. 1994. *Russia's Great Reforms, 1855–1881.* Bloomington: Indiana University Press.

English, Richard, and Michael Kenny. 2000. "Conclusion: Decline or Declinism?" In Richard English and Michael Kenny, eds., *Rethinking British Decline.* Basingstoke, UK: Macmilllan.

English, Robert D. 2002. "Power, Ideas, and New Evidence on the Cold War's End." *International Security,* 26: 70–92.

Evangelista, Matthew. 1996. "Stalin's Revenge: Institutional Barriers to Internationalization in the Soviet Union," in Robert O. Keohane and Helen V. Milner, eds., *Internationalization and Domestic Politics.* Cambridge, UK: Cambridge University Press.

Evans, Gareth, and Mohamen Sahnoun. 2002. "The Responsibility to Protect." *Foreign Affairs,* 81.

Faulkenberry, Barbara J. 1990. *The Air Force and U.S. National Security: Global Reach—Global Power* (June). Maxwell AFB, AL: Air University Press.

Feinstein, C. H. 1972. *National Income, Expenditure and Output of the United Kingdom, 1855–1965.* Cambridge, UK: Cambridge University Press.

Feith, Douglas J. 2003. "Transforming the U.S. Global Defense Posture." Speech presented to the Center for Strategic and International Studies. Washington, DC (December 3). Available at: www.defense.gov/Speeches/Speech.aspx?SpeechID=590

Ferguson, Niall. 2004. *Empire: The Rise and Demise of the British World Order and the Lessons for Global Power.* New York: Basic Books.

Ferris, John Robert. 1989. *Men, Money, and Diplomacy.* Ithaca, NY: Cornell University Press.

Force XXI. 1995. Office of the Chief of Staff, Army (January 15).

Fordham, Benjamin. 1998. "The Politics of Threat Perception and the Use of Force: A Political Economy Model of U. S. Uses of Force, 1949–1994." *International Studies Quarterly*, 42: 567–590.

Frederick, Suzanne Y. 1999. "The Anglo-German Rivalry, 1890–1914," in W. R. Thompson, ed., *Great Power Rivalries.* Columbia: University of South Carolina Press.

Friedberg, Aaron. 1988. *The Weary Titan: Britain and the Experience of Relative Decline, 1895–1905.* Princeton, NJ: Princeton University Press.

Friedman, Norman. 1989. *British Carrier Aviation.* Annapolis, MD: Naval Institute Press.

Fukuyama, Francis. 2007. *America at the Crossroads: Democracy, Power, and the Neoconservative Legacy.* New Haven, CT: Yale University Press.

Fuller, William C. 1961. *The Conduct of War, 1789-1961.* New Brunswick, NJ: Rutgers University Press.

———. 1992. *Strategy and Power in Russia, 1600–1914.* New York City: Macmillan.

Gaddis, John L. 1992. *The United States and the End of the Cold War: Implications, Reconsiderations, Provocations.* New York: Oxford University Press.

———. 2002. "A Grand Strategy." *Foreign Policy* (November/December): 55-57.

———. 2004. *Surprise, Security and the American Experience.* Cambridge, MA: Harvard University Press.

Gamble, Andrew. 2000. "Theories and Explanations of British Decline," in Richard English and Michael Kenny, eds., *Rethinking British Decline.* Basingstoke, UK: Macmilllan.

Gates, Robert M. 2007. "Landon Lecture." Manhattan: Kansas State University. November 26. Available at www.defense.gov/speeches/speech.aspx?speechid=1199

Gellman, Barton. 1992. "Keeping the US First; Pentagon Would Preclude a Rival Superpower." *The Washington Post.* March 11.

Gemzell, Carl-Axel. 1973. *Organization, Conflict, and Innovation: A Study of German Naval Strategic Planning, 1888–1940.* Lund, Sweden: Esselte Studium.

George, James L. 1998. *History of Warships: From Ancient Times to the Twenty-First Century.* Annapolis, MD: Naval Institute Press.

Gerring, John. 2004. "What Is a Case Study and What Is It Good for?" *American Political Science Review,* 98:2 (May): 341–354.

Geyer, Dietrich. 1987. *Russian Imperialism: The Interaction of Domestic and Foreign Policy, 1860–1914.* Translated by B. Little. Oxford, UK: Berg.

Gibbs, N. H. 1976. *Grand Strategy, Vol. 1, Rearmament Policy.* London: HMSO.

Gintis, Herbert, Eric Alden Smith, and Samuel Bowles. 2001. "Cooperation and Costly Signaling." *Journal of Theoretical Biology,* 213: 103–119.

Glaser, Charles L. 1993. "Why NATO Is Still Best: Future Security Arrangements for Europe." *International Security,* 18: 5–50.

———. 1994/95. "Realists as Optimists: Cooperation as Self-Help." *International Security,* 19: 50–90.

———. 1997. "The Security Dilemma Revisited." *World Politics* 50: 171–201.

———. 2010. *Rational Theory of International Politics: The Logic of Competition and Cooperation.* Princeton, NJ: Princeton University Press.

Goldman, Emily O. 1994. *Sunken Treaties: Naval Arms Control between the Wars.* University Park: Pennsylvania State University Press.

———. 1994. "Thinking about Strategy Absent the Enemy," *Security Studies,* 4 (Autumn), 40–85.

———. 2003. "Receptivity to Revolution: Carrier Air Power in Peace and War," in Emily O. Goldman and Leslie C. Eliason, eds., *The Diffusion of Military Technology and Ideas.* Stanford, CA: Stanford University Press.

———. 2006. "Cultural Foundations of Military Transformation." *Review of International Studies,* 32 (January): 69–91.

———. 2007. "International Competition and Military Effectiveness: Naval Air Power, 1919–1945," in Risa A. Brooks and Elizabeth A. Stanley, eds., *Creating Military Power: The Sources of Military Effectiveness,* Stanford, CA: Stanford University Press, 2007.

Goldman, Emily O., and Larry Berman. 2000. "Engaging the World: First Impressions of the Clinton Foreign Policy Legacy." In Colin Campbell and Bert A. Rockman, eds., *The Clinton Legacy.* New York: Chatham House Publishers.

Goldman, Emily O., and Leo J. Blanken. 2005. "The Economic Foundations of Military Power," in Peter Dombrowski, ed., *Guns and Butter: The Political Economy of International Security.* Boulder, CO: Lynne Rienner.

Goldman, Emily O. and Leslie C. Eliason, eds. 2003. *The Diffusion of Military Technology and Ideas.* Stanford, CA: Stanford University Press.

Gordon, G. A. H. 1988. *British Seapower and Procurement between the Wars: A Reappraisal of Rearmament.* Annapolis, MD: Naval Institute Press.

Gray, Colin S. 2006. "Technology as a Dynamic of Defence Transformation." *Defence Studies,* 6: 26–51.

Gray, Colin S. 2008–2009. "The 21st Century Security Environment and the Future of War." *Parameters* (Winter): 14–26.

Green, Constance McLaughlin, Harry C. Thomson, and Peter C. Roots. 1955. *The Ordnance Department: Planning Munitions for War, U.S. Army in World War II:*

The Technical Services 6, part 3. Washington, DC: Office of the Chief of Military History.

Griffith, Robert K. Jr. 1982. *Men Wanted for the U.S. Army: America's Experience with an All-Volunteer Army between the World Wars*. Westport, CT: Greenwood Press.

Haass, Richard N. 1997. "Fatal Distraction: Bill Clinton's Foreign Policy." *Foreign Policy* (Fall).

———. 1997. *The Reluctant Sheriff: The United States After the Cold War*. Council on Foreign Relations.

Haggie, P. 1979. "The Royal Navy and War Planning in the Fisher Era," in Paul M. Kennedy, ed., *The War Plans of the Great Powers, 1880–1914*. London: George Allen & Unwin.

Harris, J. P. 1988. "British Armour and Rearmament in the 1930s." *The Journal of Strategic Studies*, 11.

Hattendorf, John B. 1991. "Alliance, Encirclement, and Attrition: British Grand Strategy in the War of the Spanish Succession, 1702–1713," in Paul Kennedy, ed., *Grand Strategies in War and Peace*. New Haven, CT: Yale University Press.

Heinrichs, Waldo H. Jr. "The Role of the United States Navy," in Dorothy Borg and Shumpei Okamoto, eds., *Pearl Harbor as History: Japanese–American Relations, 1931–1941*. New York: Columbia University Press.

Henderson, R. M., and K. B. Clark. 1990. "Architectural Innovation: The Reconfiguration of Existing Product Technologies and the Failure of Established Firms." *Administrative Science Quarterly*, 35: 9–30.

Henry, Ryan. 2005–2006. "Defense Transformation and the 2005 Quadrennial Defense Review." *Parameters* (Winter): 5–15.

———. 2006. "Transforming the U.S. Global Defense Posture." *Naval War College Review* (Spring): 13–28.

Herwig, Holger H. 1990. "Disjointed Allies: Coalition Warfare in Berlin and Vienna." *Journal of Military History*, 54: 265–280.

Heymann, Philip B. 2001/02. "Dealing with Terrorism: An Overview." *International Security*, 26: 24–38.

Hezlet, Vice Admiral Sir Arthur. 1970. *Aircraft and Sea Power*. New York: Stein and Day.

Hirsh, Michael. 2002. "Bush and the World." *Foreign Affairs*, 81: 18–43.

Hobsbawm, Eric. 1999. *Industry and Empire: The Birth of the Industrial Revolution*. New York: New Press.

Hoffman, Frank G. 2005. "Small Wars Revisited: The United States and Nontraditional Wars." *Journal of Strategic Studies*, 28 (December): 913–940.

Hofhansel, Claus. 1996. *Commercial Competition and National Security: Comparing U.S. and German Export Control Policies*. Westport, CT: Praeger.

Hofmann, George F. 1973. "The Demise of the U.S. Tanks Corps and Medium Tank Development Program." *Military Affairs* (February).

Hogan, Michael J. 1977. *Informal Entente: The Private Structure of Cooperation in Anglo-American Economic Diplomacy, 1918-1929.* Columbia: University of Missouri Press.

Hone, Thomas C. 1982. "Spending Patterns of the United States Navy, 1921-1941." *Armed Forces and Society* 8 (Spring): 443-462.

———. 1984. "Navy Air Leadership: Rear Admiral William A. Moffett as Chief of the Bureau of Aeronautics," in *USAF Warrior Studies—Air Leadership: Proceedings of a Conference at Bolling Air Force Base, April 13-14.* Washington, DC: GPO.

———. 1992. "Fighting on Our Own Ground: The War of Production, 1920-1942." *Naval War College Review.*

Hone, Thomas C., and Mark David Mandeles. 1980. "Managerial Style in the Interwar Navy: A Reappraisal." *Naval War College Review* 32 (September-October).

———. 1987. "Interwar Innovation in Three Navies: USN, RN, IJN." *Naval War College Review* 40 (Spring): 63-83.

Howard, Michael. 1972. *The Continental Commitment: The Dilemma of British Defence Policy in the Era of the Two World Wars.* London: Maurice Temple Smith.

———. 1983. "The Forgotten Dimension of Strategy," in Michael Howard, ed., *The Causes of War and Other Essays.* Cambridge, MA: Harvard University Press.

Huntington, Samuel P. 1997. "The Erosion of American National Interest." *Foreign Affairs,* 76.

Huth, Paul, Scott Bennett, and Christopher Gelpi. 1992. "System Uncertainty, Risk Propensity, and International Conflict among the Great Powers." *Journal of Conflict Resolution,* 36: 478-517.

Ikenberry, G. John. 2001. *After Victory: Institutions, Strategic Restraint, and the Rebuilding of Order after Major Wars.* Princeton, NJ: Princeton University Press.

———. 2002. "America's Imperial Ambition." *Foreign Affairs,* 81: 44-60.

———. 2002. "Introduction," in G. John Ikenberry, ed., *America Unrivaled: The Future of the Balance of Power.* Ithaca, NY: Cornell University Press.

———. 2008. "Liberal Order Building," in Melvyn P. Leffler and Jeffrey W. Legro, eds., *To Lead the World: American Strategy after the Bush Doctrine.* New York: Oxford University Press.

Imlay, Talbot C., and Monica Duffy Toft, eds. 2006. *The Fog of Peace and War Planning: Military and Strategic Planning under Uncertainty.* London and New York: Routledge.

Ingram, Edward. 1999. "Great Britain and Russia," in W. R. Thompson, ed., *Great Power Rivalries.* Columbia: University of South Carolina Press.

Isley, Jeter A., and Philip A. Crowl. 1951. *The U.S. Marines and Amphibious War: Its Theory and Its Practice in the Pacific.* Princeton, NJ: Princeton University Press.

Jaffe, Lorna S. 1993. *The Development of the Base Force, 1989-1992.* Washington, DC: U.S. Government Printing Office.

Jeffrey, K. 1984. *The British Army and the Crisis of Empire, 1918-1922.* Manchester, UK: Manchester University Press.

Jelavich, Barbara. 1964. *A Century of Russian Foreign Policy, 1814–1914*. Philadelphia: J. B. Lippincott.
———. 1974. *St. Petersburg and Moscow: Tsarist and Soviet Foreign Policy, 1814–1974*. Bloomington: Indiana University Press.
Jervis, Robert. 1976. *Perception and Misperception in International Politics*. Princeton, NJ: Princeton University Press.
———. 1978. "Cooperation Under the Security Dilemma." *World Politics*, 30: 167–214.
———. 1992. "Political Implications of Loss Aversion." *Political Psychology* 13: 187–204.
———. 2006. "The Remaking of a Unipolar World." *The Washington Quarterly* (Summer).
Joffe, Josef. 1995. "'Bismarck' or 'Britain'? Toward an American Grand Strategy after Bipolarity." *International Security* 19 (Spring): 94–117.
———. 2002. "Defying History and Theory: The United States as the 'Last Remaining Superpower,'" in G. John Ikenberry, ed., *America Unrivaled: The Future of the Balance of Power*. Ithaca, NY: Cornell University Press.
Johnston, Robert. 1998. "U.S. Export Control Policy in the High Performance Computer Sector," *The Nonproliferation Review* (Winter): 44–59.
Joint Chiefs of Staff. 1992. *National Military Strategy of the United States* (January). Washington, DC: Joint Chiefs of Staff.
Joint Chiefs of Staff. 1995. *National Military Strategy of the United States of America: A Strategy of Flexible and Selective Engagement*. Washington, DC: Joint Chiefs of Staff.
Joint Operations Concepts. 2003. Washington, DC: Joint Chiefs of Staff.
Joint Vision 2010. 1996. Washington, DC: Joint Chiefs of Staff.
Joint Vision 2020. 2000. Washington, DC: Joint Chiefs of Staff.
Jones, Archer and Andrew J. Keogh. 1985. "The Dreadnought Revolution: Another Look." *Military Affairs*, 49: 124–131.
Kagan, Donald, and Frederick W. Kagan. 2000. *While America Sleeps: Self-Delusion, Military Weakness, and the Threat to Peace Today*. New York: St. Martins.
Kagan, Frederick W. 2006. *Finding the Target: The Transformation of American Military Policy*. New York: Encounter Books.
Kagan, Robert. 2002. "Power and Weakness." *Policy Review*, 113 (June).
Kagan, Robert, and Dan Blumenthal. 2009. "Strategic Reassurance That Isn't." *The Washington Post* (November 10).
Kahler, Miles. 1984. *Decolonization in Britain and France: The Domestic Consequences of International Relations*. Princeton, NJ: Princeton University Press.
Katzenbach, Edward L. Jr. 1958. "The Horse Cavalry in the Twentieth Century: A Study in Policy Response." *Public Policy*, 7: 120–149.
Kaufman, Herbert. 1971. *The Limits of Organizational Change*. Tuscaloosa: University of Alabama Press.
Kaufman, Robert G. 2007. *In Defense of the Bush Doctrine*. Lexington: University Press of Kentucky.

Kennan, George F. 1986. *On Russian Diplomacy in the 19th Century and the Origins of World War I*. Washington, DC: Woodrow Wilson International Center for Scholars.

Kennedy, Paul M. 1979. "Imperial Cable Communications and Strategy, 1870–1917," in Paul M. Kennedy, ed., *The War Plans of the Great Powers, 1880–1914*. London: George Allen & Unwin.

———. 1983. "Mahan versus Mackinder: Two Interpretations of British Sea Power," in Paul Kennedy, ed., *Strategy and Diplomacy, 1870–1945: Eight Studies*. London: George Allen and Unwin.

———. 1983. *Strategy and Diplomacy, 1870–1945*. London: George Allen & Unwin.

———. 1987. *The Rise and Fall of the Great Powers: Economic Change and Military Conflict from 1500–2000*. New York: Random House.

———. 1991. "Grand Strategy in War and Peace: Toward a Broader Definition," in Paul M. Kennedy, ed., *Grand Strategies in War and Peace*. New Haven, CT: Yale University Press.

Keohane, Robert O. 1984. *After Hegemony: Cooperation and Discord in the World Political Economy*. Princeton, NJ: Princeton University Press.

Keynes, John Maynard. 1937. "The General Theory of Employment." *Quarterly Journal of Economics*, 51: 209–223.

Kim, W. 1989. "Power, Alliance, and Major Wars, 1816–1875." *Journal of Conflict Resolution*, 33: 255–273.

Kim, Woosang. 1991. "Alliance Transitions and Great Power War." *American Journal of Political Science*, 35: 833–850.

Kinsella, David. 1998. "Arms Transfer Dependence and Foreign Policy Conflict." *Journal of Peace Research*, 35: 7–23.

Kipp, Jacob W. 1994. "The Russian Navy and the Problem of Technological Transfer: Technological Backwardness and Military-Industrial Development, 1853–1876," in Ben Eklof, John Bushnell, and Larissa Zakharova, eds., *Russia's Great Reforms, 1855–1881*. Bloomington: Indiana University Press.

Kipp, Jacob W. 2002. "The Imperial Russian Navy, 1696–1900," in F. W. Kagan and R. Higham, eds., *The Military History of Tsarist Russia*. Basingstoke, UK: Palgrave.

———. 2004. "Strategic Railroads and the Dilemmas of Modernization," in David Schimmelpenninck Van Der Oye and Bruce W. Menning, eds., *Reforming the Tsar's Army: Military Innovation in Imperial Russia from Peter the Great to the Revolution*. Cambridge, UK: Cambridge University Press.

Knight, Frank H. 1971 (1921). *Risk, Uncertainty, and Profit*. Chicago: University of Chicago Press.

The Knowledge Economy: Is the United States Losing Its Competitive Edge? 2005. The Report of the Task Force on the Future of American Innovation (February 16). Available at: www.futureofinnovation.org.

Knox, MacGregor, and Williamson Murray, eds. 2001. *The Dynamics of Military Revolution 1300–2050*. Cambridge, UK: Cambridge University Press.

Koistinen, Paul A. C. 1970. "The 'Industrial-Military Complex' in Historical Perspective: The Inter War Years." *The Journal of American History* (March).

Krasner, Stephen D. 1976. "State Power and the Structure of International Trade." *World Politics*, 28: 317–47.

Krauthammer, Charles. 1990/91. "The Unipolar Moment." *Foreign Affairs*, 70: 23–33.

———. 2009. "Decline Is a Choice." *The Weekly Standard* (December 19).

Kreidberg, Marvin A., and Merton G. Henry. 1953. *History of Military Mobilization in the United States Army, 1775–1945*. Washington, DC: Department of the Army.

Krepinevich, Andrew F. 1994. "Cavalry to Computer: The Pattern of Military Revolutions." *The National Interest*, 37 (Fall): 10–42.

———. 2002. "Defense Transformation." Testimony before the U.S. Senate Committee on Armed Services (April 9).

———. 2005. *The Quadrennial Defense Review: Rethinking the US Military Posture*. Washington, DC: Center for Strategic and Budgetary Assessments.

Krepinevich, Andrew F. Jr. 1992 (2002). *The Military-Technical Revolution: A Preliminary Assessment*. Washington, DC: Center for Strategic and Budgetary Assessments.

———. 1999. "Emerging Threats, Revolutionary Capabilities and Military Transformation." Testimony before the Senate Armed Services Subcommittee on Emerging Threats and Capabilities. (March 5).

Kruger, G. K. 1994. "Russia's 'Disadvantaged Position' after the Crimean War: An Examination of the Root Causes and the Relevance of Military Material Technology." Draft (August).

Kupchan, Charles A. 1994. *The Vulnerability of Empire*. Ithaca, NY: Cornell University Press.

———. 2002. *The End of the American Era*. New York: Knopf.

———. 2002. "Hollow Hegemony or Stable Multipolarity?" in G. John Ikenberry, ed., *America Unrivaled: The Future of the Balance of Power*. Ithaca, NY: Cornell University Press.

Kupchan, Charles A. and Clifford A. Kupchan. 1995. "The Promise of Collective Security." *International Security*, 20: 52–61.

Kydd, Andrew. 1997. "Why Security Seekers Do Not Fight Each Other." *Security Studies*, 7 (Autumn): 114–154.

Lai, Brian, and Dan Reiter. 2000. "Democracy, Political Similarity, and International Alliances, 1816–1992." *Journal of Conflict Resolution*, 44: 203–227.

Lake, David A. 1988. *Power, Protection and Free Trade: International Sources of U.S. Commercial Strategy, 1887–1939*. Ithaca, NY: Cornell University Press.

Lamb, Christopher J. 2005. *Transforming Defense*. Washington, DC: National Defense University Press.

Lambert, Andrew D. 1995. "The Royal Navy, 1856–1914: Deterrence and the Strategy of World Power," in Keith Neilson and Elizabeth Jane Errington, eds., *Navies and Global Defense: Theories and Strategy*. Westport, CT: Praeger.

Lambert, Nicholas A. 1995. "Admiral Sir John Fisher and the Concept of Flotilla Defense." *Journal of Military History*, 59: 639–660.

———. 1995. "British Naval Policy, 1913–1914: Financial Limitation and Strategic Revolution." *Journal of Modern History*, 67: 595–626.

———. 1996. "Economy of Empire? The Fleet Unit Concept and the Quest for Collective Security in the Pacific, 1909–1914," in Keith Neilson and Greg Kennedy, eds., *Far Flung Lines: Studies in Imperial Defense in Honour of Donald Mackenzie Schurman*, 55–83. London: Frank Cass.

———. 1996. The Opportunities of Technology: British and French Naval Strategies in the Pacific, 1905–1909," in N. A. M. Roger, ed., *Naval Power in the Twentieth Century*. Annapolis, MD: Naval Institute Press.

———. 1999. *Sir John Fisher's Naval Revolution*. Columbia: University of South Carolina Press.

———. "Dreadnought—The Revolution that Never Was." Draft manuscript, n.d.

———. 2004. "Transformation and Technology in the Fisher Era: The Impact of the Communications Revolution." *The Journal of Strategic Studies*, 27 (June): 272–297.

Lamborn, Alan C. 1991. *The Price of Power: Risk and Foreign Policy in Britain, France and Germany*. Boston: Unwin Hyman.

Larson, Eric V., David T. Orletsky, and Kristen Leuschner. 2001. *Defense Planning in a Decade of Change: Lessons from the Base Force, Bottom-Up Review, and Quadrennial Defense Review*. Santa Monica, CA: RAND.

Layne, Christopher. 1993. "The Unipolar Illusion: Why New Great Powers Will Rise." *International Security*, 17: 5–51.

———. 1997. "From Preponderance to Offshore Balancing: America's Future Grand Strategy." *International Security*, 22: 86–124.

Leeds, Brett A. 2000. "Credible Commitments and International Cooperation: Guaranteeing Contracts without External Enforcement." *Conflict Management and Peace Science*, 18: 49–71.

Leffler, Melvyn. 1974. "Political Isolationism, Economic Expansion or Diplomatic Realism? American Policy Toward Western Europe, 1921–1933." *Perspectives in American History*, 8: 413–461.

Leonard, Major Steven M. 2001. *Inevitable Evolutions: Punctuated Equilibrium and the Revolution in Military Affairs*. Fort Leavenworth, KS: School of Advanced Military Studies, U.S. Army Command and General Staff College.

Levy, Jack S. 1983. "Misperception and the Causes of War: Theoretical Linkages and Analytical Problems." *World Politics*.

———. 1992. "Introduction to Prospect Theory." *Political Psychology*, 13: 171–186.

———. 1992. "Prospect Theory and International Relations: Theoretical Applications and Analytical Problems." *Political Psychology*, 13: 283–310.
Libicki, Martin C. 1995. "The Next Enemy." *Strategic Forum* 35 (July). Available at: www.dodccrp.org/libicki1.htm
Linn, Brian McAllister. 1997. *Guardians of Empire: The U.S. Army and the Pacific, 1920–1940*. Chapel Hill: University of North Carolina Press.
Lobell, Steven E. 1999. "Second Image Reversed Politics: Britain's Choice of Freer Trade or Imperial Preferences, 1903-1906, 1917-1923, 1930-1932." *International Studies Quarterly* 43: 671–694.
———. 2002/3. "War Is Politics: Offensive Realism, Domestic Politics, and Security Strategies." *Security Studies* 12 (Winter): 165–195.
———. 2003. *The Challenge of Hegemony: Grand Strategy, Trade and Domestic Politics*. Ann Arbor: University of Michigan Press.
Long, Andrew G. 2003. "Defense Pacts and International Trade." *Journal of Peace Research*, 40: 537–552.
Lowe, C. J. 1967. *The Reluctant Imperialists: British Foreign Policy 1878–1902*. London: Routledge and Keegan Paul.
Macgregor, Douglas A. 2003. *Transformation under Fire: Revolutionizing How America Fights*. Westport, CT: Praeger.
Macleod, Roy M., and Kay Andrews. 1971. "Scientific Advice in the War at Sea, 1915–1917: The Board of Invention and Research." *Journal of Contemporary History*, 6: 3–40.
Mahnken, Thomas. 2008. *Technology and the American Way of War since 1945*. New York: Columbia University Press.
Mahoney, James, and Gary Goertz. 2004. "The Possibility Principle: Choosing Negative Cases in Comparative Research." *American Political Science Review*, 98 (November): 653–669.
Maoz, Zeev. 1996. *Domestic Sources of Global Change*. Ann Arbor: University of Michigan Press.
Marder, Arthur J. 1952. *Fear God and Dread Nought: The Correspondence of Admiral of the Fleet Lord Fisher of Kilverstone, Vol 1*. London: Jonathan Cape.
———. 1956. *Fear God and Dread Nought: The Correspondence of Admiral of the Fleet Lord Fisher of Kilverstone, Vol. II*. London: Jonathon Cape.
———. 1959. *Fear God and Dread Nought: The Correspondence of Admiral of the Fleet Lord Fisher of Kilverstone, Vol III*. London: Jonathan Cape.
———. 1976. *The Anatomy of British Sea Power: A History of British Naval Policy in the Pre-Dreadnought Era, 1880–1905*. New York: Octagon Books.
Marshall, Andrew. W. 1993. "Some Thoughts on Military Revolutions." Memorandum for the Record (27 July). Washington, DC: Office of Net Assessment, Department of Defense.

Martin, Lisa L. 1992. *Coercive Cooperation: Explaining Multilateral Economic Sanctions*. Princeton, NJ: Princeton University Press.

———. 1992. "Interests, Power, and Multilateralism." *International Organization*, 46: 765–792.

Matloff, Maurice. 1966. "The American Approach to War, 1919–1945," in Michael Howard, ed., *The Theory and Practice of War*. New York: Praeger.

May, Ernest, ed. 1984. *Knowing One's Enemies: Intelligence Assessment before the Two World Wars*. Princeton, NJ: Princeton University Press.

Mazzetti, Mark. 2005. "Iraq War Compels Pentagon to Rethink Big-Picture Strategy." *Los Angeles Times* (March 11).

McCalla, Robert B. 1996. "NATO's Persistence after the Cold War." *International Organization*, 50: 445–475.

McDermott, J. 1979. "The Revolution in British Military Thinking from the Boer War to the Moroccan Crisis," in Paul M. Kennedy, ed., *The War Plans of the Great Powers, 1880–1914*. London: George Allen & Unwin.

McDougall, Dan. 2005. "India is the New American Dream." *Scotland on Sunday* (July 24).

McMaster, H. R. 2008. "Learning from Contemporary Conflicts to Prepare for Future War," *Orbis* (Fall), 565–566.

Mearsheimer, John J. 1990. "Back to the Future: Instability in Europe after the Cold War." *International Security*, 15: 5–56.

———. 1994/95. "The False Promise of International Institutions." *International Security*, 19: 5–49.

———. 2001. *The Tragedy of Great Power Politics*. New York: Norton.

Medeiros, Evan S. 2005/06. "Strategic Hedging and the Future of Asia-Pacific Stability." *The Washington Quarterly*, 29 (Winter): 145–167.

Melhorn, C. M. 1974. *Two Block Fox: The Rise of the Aircraft Carrier 1911–1929*. Annapolis, MD: Naval Institute Press.

Menke, S. M. 2004. "Pentagon Weighs Satellite Needs." *The Washington Post* (November 22): E4.

Menning, Bruce W. 1992. *Bayonets before Bullets: The Imperial Russian Army, 1861–1914*. Bloomington: Indiana University Press.

———. 2002. "Mukden to Tannenberg: Defeat to Defeat, 1905–1914." In F. W. Kagan and R. Higham, eds. *The Military History of Tsarist Russia*. London: Palgrave.

Mercer, Jonathan. 1995. "Anarchy and Identity." *International Organization*, 49: 229–252.

Metz, S. 2006. "America's Defense Transformation: A Conceptual and Political History." *Defence Studies*, 6: 1–25.

Metz, Stephen, 1997. "Which Army after Next? The Strategic implications of Alternative Futures." *Parameters*, XXVII (Autumn): 15–26.

Midlarsky, Manus. 1983. "Absence of Memory in the Nineteenth Century Alliance System: Perspectives from Queuing Theory and Bivariate Probability Distributions." *American Journal of Political Science*, 27: 762–784.

Millett, Allan R. 1991. *Semper Fidelis: The History of the United States Marine Corps.* New York: Free Press.

———. 1996. "Assault from the Sea: The Development of Amphibious Warfare between the Wars. The American, British, and Japanese Experiences," in Williamson Murray and Allan R. Millett, eds., *Military Innovation in the Interwar Period.* Cambridge, UK: Cambridge University Press.

———. 2003. "Vague Threats and Concrete Dangers: The Global Security Environment at the Start of the Twenty-First Century," in M. G. Manwaring, E. G. Corr, and R. H. Dorff, eds., *The Search for Security: A U. S. Grand Strategy for the Twenty-First Century.* Westport, CT: Praeger.

Milner, Helen V. 1997. *Interests, Institutions, and Information: Domestic Politics and International Relations.* Princeton, NJ: Princeton University Press.

Milner, Helen V., and Robert O. Keohane. 1996. "Internationalization and Domestic Politics: An Introduction," in Robert O. Keohane and Helen V. Milner, eds., *Internationalization and Domestic Politics.* Cambridge, UK: Cambridge University Press.

Mitchell, B. R. 1988. *British Historical Statistics.* Cambridge, UK: Cambridge University Press.

Mitchell, Donald W. 1974. *A History of Russian and Soviet Sea Power.* New York: Macmillan.

Mitchell, Paul T. 2006. *Network Centric Warfare: Coalition Operations in the Age of US Military Primacy.* Adelphi Paper 385. London and New York: Routledge.

Mitzen, Jennifer . 2006. "Ontological Security in World Politics: State Identity and the Security Dilemma." *European Journal of International Relations,* 12: 341–370.

Moll, Kenneth L. 1965. "Politics, Power, and Panic: Britain's 1909 Dreadnought 'Gap.'" *Military Affairs,* 29: 133–144.

Moran, Theodore H. 1990. "The Globalization of America's Defense Industries: Managing the Threat of Foreign Dependence." *International Security,* 15: 57–99.

———. 1996. "Grand Strategy: The Pursuit of Power and the Pursuit of Plenty." *International Organization,* 50: 175–205.

Moreman, T. R. 1996. "'Small Wars' and 'Imperial Policing': The British Army and the Theory and Practice of Colonial Warfare in the British Empire, 1919–1939." *The Journal of Strategic Studies,* 19: 105–131.

Morgan, Clifton T., and Glenn Palmer. 2003. "To Protect and to Serve: Alliances and Foreign Policy Portfolios." *Journal of Conflict Resolution,* 47 (2): 180–203.

Morrow, James D. 1991. "Alliances and Asymmetry: An Alternative to the Capability Aggregation Model of Alliances." *American Journal of Political Science,* 35: 904–933.

———. 1993. "Arms Versus Allies: Trade-Offs in the Search for Security." *International Organization,* 47: 207–233.

Morton, Louis. 1959. "War Plan ORANGE: Evolution of a Strategy." *World Politics* (January): 221–250.

———. 1960. "National Policy and Military Strategy." *The Virginia Quarterly Review,* 36 (Winter).

Moss, Walter G. 2002. *A History of Russia. Vol. I: To 1917.* London: Anthem Press.
Moy, Timothy David. 1987. *Hitting the Beaches and Bombing the Cities: Doctrine and Technology for Two New Militaries, 1920–1940.* PhD Dissertation, University of California Berkeley.
Mueller, John. 1993. "The Impact of Ideas on Grand Strategy," in Richard Rosecrance and Arthur A. Stein, eds., *The Domestic Bases of Grand Strategy.* Ithaca, NY: Cornell University Press.
Muller, Richard R. 1996. "Close Air Support: The German, British, and American Experiences, 1918–1941," in Williamson Murray and Allan R. Millett, eds., *Military Innovation in the Interwar Period.* Cambridge, UK: Cambridge University Press.
Murray, Robert K. 1969. *The Harding Era: Warren G. Harding and His Administration.* Minneapolis: University of Minnesota Press.
Murray, Williamson. 1996. "Armored Warfare: The British, French, and German Experiences," in Williamson Murray and Allan R. Millett, eds., *Military Innovation in the Interwar Period.* Cambridge, UK: Cambridge University Press.
———. 1996. "Innovation: Past and Future," in Williamson Murray and Allan R. Millett, eds., *Military Innovation in the Interwar Period.* Cambridge, UK: Cambridge University Press.
———. 1996. "Strategic Bombing: The British, American, and German Experiences," in Williamson Murray and Allan R. Millett, eds., *Military Innovation in the Interwar Period.* Cambridge, UK: Cambridge University Press.
Murray, Williamson, and Allan R. Millett, eds. 1996. *Military Innovation in the Interwar Period.* Cambridge, UK: Cambridge University Press.
Naím, Moisés. 1997–1998. "Clinton's Foreign Policy: A Victim of Globalization?" *Foreign Policy* (Winter): 34–69.
Narizny, Kevin. 2003. "Both Guns and Butter, or Neither: Class Interests in the Political Economy of Rearmament." *American Political Science Review,* 97 (May): 203–220.
National Defense Panel. 1997. *Transforming Defense: National Security in the 21st Century.* Arlington, VA: National Defense Panel.
National Defense Strategy. 2008. Available at: www.strategicstudiesinstitute.army.mil/pdffiles/nds2008.pdf
National Defense Strategy of the United States of America (2005). Washington, DC: Department of Defense.
A National Security Strategy for A New Century. 1998. (October) Available at: www.fas.org/man/docs/nssr-98.pdf
Nelson, Richard R., ed. 1993. *National Innovation Systems: A Comparative Analysis.* New York and Oxford: Oxford University Press.
Nenninger, Timothy K. 1969. "The Development of American Armor 1917–1940, Part I, The World War I Experience." *Armor,* 78 (January–February).
———. 1969. "The Development of American Armor 1917–1940, Part II, The Tank Corps Reorganized." *Armor,* 78 (March–April).

———. 1969. "The Development of American Armor 1917–1940, Part III, The Experimental Mechanized Forces." *Armor*, 78 (May–June).

———. 1969. "The Development of American Armor 1917–1940, Part IV, A Revised Mechanization Policy." *Armor*, 78 (September–October).

Nincic, Miroslav, Roger Rose, and Gerard Gorski. 1999. "The Social Foundations of Strategic Adjustment," in Peter Trubowitz, Emily O. Goldman, and Edward Rhodes, eds. *The Politics of Strategic Adjustment: Ideas, Institutions, and Interests*. New York: Columbia University Press.

The 9/11 Commission Report. 2004. Available at http://govinfo.library.unt.edu/911/report/911Report.pdf.

Nish, Ian. 1972. *Alliance in Decline*. London: Athlone Press.

Nye, Joseph S. 2002. *The Paradox of American Power: Why the World's Only Superpower Can't Go It Alone*. New York: Oxford University Press.

———. 2003. "U. S. Power and Strategy After Iraq." *Foreign Affairs*, 82: 60–73.

Office of Force Transformation. 2003. *Military Transformation: A Strategic Approach*. Washington, DC: Department of Defense.

Office of Force Transformation. 2004. *Elements of Defense Transformation*. Washington, DC: Department of Defense.

Office of Force Transformation. 2005. *The Implementation of Network-Centric Warfare*. Washington, DC: Department of Defense.

Office of Force Transformation. 2005. *Supporting Force Transformation: An Office of Force Transformation "Progress Report."* Washington, DC: Department of Defense.

Office of the Deputy Under Secretary of Defense (Industrial Policy). 2003. *Transforming the Defense Industrial Base: A Roadmap*. Washington, DC: Department of Defense. (February).

Office of the Secretary of Defense. 2005. *Unmanned Aircraft Systems Roadmap, 2005–2030*. Washington, DC: Department of Defense.

O'Hanlon, Michael E. 2002. "Limiting the Growth of the U.S. Defense Budget." *Policy Brief*. Washington, DC: The Brookings Institution (March).

———. "U.S. Military Modernization: Implications for U.S. Policy in Asia," in Ashley J. Tellis and Michael Wills, eds., *Strategic Asia 2005–06: Military Modernization in an Era of Uncertainty*. Seattle and Washington, DC: The National Bureau of Asian Research.

Oliker, Olga and Tanya Charlick-Paley. 2002. *Assessing Russia's Decline: Trends and Implications for the United States and the U.S. Air Force*. Santa Monica, CA: RAND.

Owens, Mackubin. 2008. "America's Long War(s)." Foreign Policy Research Institute E-Note (January 10).

Owens, W. A. 1995. "The Emerging System of Systems." U.S. Naval Institute *Proceedings* (May): 36–39.

———. 2002. "The Once and Future Revolution in Military Affairs." *Joint Forces Quarterly*, 31: 55–61.

Owens, William A., with Ed Offley. 2001. *Lifting the Fog of War*. Baltimore, MD: The Johns Hopkins University Press.

P. 1141, Series Y 904-916. *Military Personnel on Active Duty: 1789 to 1970* (table adapted).

Palmer, Glenn. 1990. "Alliance Politics and Issue Areas: Determinents of Defense Spending." *American Journal of Political Science*, 34: 190–211.

———. 1990. "Corralling the Free Rider: Deterrence and the Western Alliance." *International Studies Quarterly*, 34: 147–164.

Paret, Peter. 1988. "Foreword," in Harold R. Winton. *To Change an Army*. Lawrence: University Press of Kansas.

Peden, G. C. 2007. *Arms, Economics and British Strategy: From Dreadnoughts to Hydrogen Bombs*. Cambridge, UK: Cambridge University Press.

Petter, Wolfgang. 1985. "'Enemies' and 'Reich Enemies': An Analysis of Threat Perceptions and Political Strategy in Imperial Germany, 1871–1914," in W. Deist, ed., *The German Military in the Age of Total War*. Oxford, UK: Berg.

Pierce, Terry C. 2004. *Warfighting and Disruptive Technologies: Disguising Innovation*. London and New York: Frank Cass.

Pintner, Walter M. 1984. "The Burden of Defense in Imperial Russia, 1725–1914." *The Russian Review*, 43: 231–259.

Pollard, Sidney. 1989. *Britain's Prime and Britain's Decline: The British Economy 1870–1914*. London: Edward Arnold.

Posen, Barry R. 1984. *The Sources of Military Doctrine: France, Britain, and Germany between the World Wars*. Ithaca, NY: Cornell University Press.

———. 2001. "The Struggle Against Terrorism: Grand Strategy, Strategy, and Tactics." *International Security*, 26: 39–55.

———. 2003. "Command of the Commons: The Military Foundation of U. S. Hegemony." *International Security*, 28: 5–46.

Posen, Barry R., and Andrew L. Ross. 1996/97. "Competing Visions of U. S. Grand Strategy." *International Security*, 21: 5–53.

Postan, Michael Moissey. 1952. *British War Production*, History of the Second World War Series, United Kingdom Civil Series (London: HMSO).

"President Obama Delivers Remarks at U.S.–China Strategic and Economic Dialogue." 2009. *CQ Transcriptions*. (July 27).

Putin, Vladimir. 2005. Annual Address to the Federal Assembly of the Russian Federation. The Kremlin, Moscow (April 25). Available at: http://eng.kremlin.ru/speeches/2005/04/25/2031_type70029type82912_87086.shtml.

Putnam, Robert. 1988. "Diplomacy and Domestic Politics: The Logic of Two-Level Games." *International Organization*, 42: 427–460.

Ranft, Bryan. 1977. "The Protection of British Seaborne Trade and the Development of Systematic Planning for War, 1860–1906," in Bryan Ranft, ed., *Technical Change and British Naval Policy, 1860–1939*. London: Hodder and Stoughton.

Rapoport, Anatol. 1969. *Strategy and Conscience*. New York: Schocken Books.
Rasor, Eugene L. 1980. "The Manning Question in the Royal Navy in the Early Ironclad Era," in Robert William Love Jr., ed., *Changing Interpretations and New Sources in Naval History*. New York: Garland Publishing.
Reid, D. J., G. Goodman, W. Johnson, and R. E. Giffin. 2005. "All That Glistens: Is Network-Centric Warfare Really Scientific?" *Defense & Security Analysis*, 21: 335–367.
Reiter, Dan. 1996. *Crucible of Beliefs: Learning, Alliances, and World Wars*. Ithaca, NY: Cornell University Press.
Report of the Defense Science Board Task Force on Strategic Communication. 2004. Washington, DC: Office of the Under Secretary of Defense for Acquisition, Technology, and Logistics (September).
Report of the Select Committee on U.S. National Security and Military/Commercial Concerns with the People's Republic of China. 1999. Available at: www.house.gov/coxreport
Resende-Santos, Joao. 1996. "Anarchy and Emulation of Military Systems: Military Organizations and Technology in South America, 1870–1930." *Security Studies*, 5 (Spring).
Rice, Condoleezza. 2000. "Campaign 2000: Promoting the National Interest." *Foreign Affairs*, 79 (January/February): 45–62.
———. 2006. "Transformational Diplomacy." Washington, DC (January 18); available at: www.actfl.org/i4a/pages/index.cfm?pageid=4260
Ricks, Thomas E. 2000. "For Pentagon, Asia Moving to Forefront." *The Washington Post* (May 26).
Ring, Peter Smith. 1989. "The Environment and Strategic Management," in Jack Rabin et al., eds., *Handbook of Strategic Management*. New York: Marcel Dekker.
Robertson, Paul L. 1974. "Technical Education in the British Shipbuilding and Marine Engineering Industries, 1863–1914." *Economic History Review*, 27: 222–235.
Roeder, Philip G. 1985. "The Ties That Bind: Aid, Trade, and Political Compliance in Soviet-Third World Relations." *International Studies Quarterly*, 29: 191–216.
Rogers, Clifford J., ed. 1995. *The Military Revolution Debate: Readings on the Military Transformation of Early Modern Europe*. Boulder, CO: Westview.
Rosecrance, Richard, and Arthur A. Stein. 1993. "Beyond Realism: The Study of Grand Strategy," in Richard Rosecrance and Arthur A. Stein, eds., *The Domestic Bases of Grand Strategy*. Ithaca, NY: Cornell University Press.
Rosecrance, Richard, and Zara Stein. 1993. "British Grand Strategy and the Origins of World War II," in Richard Rosecrance and Arthur A. Stein, eds., *The Domestic Bases of Grand Strategy*. Ithaca, NY: Cornell University Press.
Rosen, Gary. 2005. *The Right War? The Conservative Debate on Iraq*. New York: Cambridge University Press.
Rosen, Stephen Peter. 1991. *Winning the Next War: Innovation and the Modern Military*. Ithaca, NY: Cornell University Press.

Rosenberger, Leif. 2003. "The Major Economic Challenge in the Global Security Environment: Competing in an Interdependent World," in M. G. Manwaring, E. G. Corr, and R. H. Dorff, eds., *The Search for Security: A U. S. Grand Strategy for the Twenty-First Century*. Westport, CT: Praeger.

Roskill, Stephen. 1968. *Naval Policy between the Wars*. London: Collins.

Ross, Steven T., ed. 1992. *Peacetime War Plans, 1919–1935. Volume I, Peacetime War Plans, 1919–1935 Series*. New York: Garland.

Roxborough, Ian, and Dana Eyre. 1999. "Which Way to the Future?" *Joint Forces Quarterly* (Summer): 28–34.

Rumsfeld, Donald H. 2002. "Transforming the Military." *Foreign Affairs*, 81: 20–32.

———. 2002. "21st Century Transformation." Remarks delivered at National Defense University. Fort McNair, Washington DC (January 31). Available at: www.defense.gov/speeches/speech.aspx?speechid=183.

Sandler, Todd. 1999. "Alliance Formation, Alliance Expansion, and the Core." *Journal of Conflict Resolution*, 43: 727–747.

Sapolsky, Harvey M., Benjamin H. Friedman, and Brendan Rittenhouse Green, eds. 2009. *US Military Innovation since the Cold War: Creation without Destruction*. New York: Routledge.

Schimmelpenninck Van Der Oye, David. 2004. "Reforming Military Intelligence," in David Schimmelpenninck Van Der Oye and Bruce W. Menning, eds., *Reforming the Tsar's Army: Military Innovation in Imperial Russia from Peter the Great to the Revolution*. Cambridge, UK: Cambridge University Press.

Schroeder, Paul W. 1994. "Historical Reality vs. Neo-realist Theory." *International Security*, 19: 108_148.

Schweller, Randall L. 1992. "Domestic Structure and Preventive War: Are Democracies More Pacific?" *World Politics*, 44: 235–269.

———. 1994. "Bandwagoning for Profit: Bringing the Revisionist State Back In." *International Security*, 19: 72–107.

———. 1996. "Neorealism's Status-Quo Bias: What Security Dilemma?" *Security Studies*, 5 (Spring): 90–121.

———. 2006. *Unanswered Threats: Political Constraints on the Balance of Power*. Princeton, NJ: Princeton University Press.

Schultz, Kenneth A. 2001. *Democracy and Coercive Diplomacy*. Cambridge, UK: Cambridge University Press.

Segell, Glen M. 2008. "Thoughts on Dissuasion." *Journal of Military and Strategic Studies*, 10 (Summer).

Sheridan, Mary Beth, and Greg Jaffe. 2009. "Gates Proposes $2 Billion in Funds to Aid Unstable Countries." *The Washington Post* (December 24), A02.

Sherman, Richard, and M. Scott Solomon. 2001. "IR Theory's Evolving Economic Metaphor." Paper presented at the International Studies Association Hong Kong Conference (July).

Showalter, Dennis E. 1975. *Railroads and Rifles: Soldiers, Technology, and the Unification of Germany*. Hamden, CT: Archon Books.

———. 1991. "Total War for Limited Objectives: An Interpretation of German Grand Strategy," in Paul M. Kennedy, ed., *Grand Strategy in War and Peace*. New Haven, CT: Yale University Press.

Shulimson, Jack. 1993. *The Marine Corps's Search for a Mission, 1880-1898*. Lawrence: University Press of Kansas.

Simes, Dimitri K. 2003. "America's Imperial Dilemma." *Foreign Affairs*, 82: 91-102.

Singer, J. D., S. Bremer, and J. Stucket. 1972. "Capability Distribution, Uncertainty, and Major Power War, 1820-1965," in Bruce Russett, ed., *Peace, War, and Numbers*. Beverly Hills, CA: Sage Publications.

Singer, P. W. 2003. *Corporate Warriors: The Rise of the Privatized Military Industry*. Ithaca, NY: Cornell University Press.

Siverson, Randolph M., and Harvey Starr. 1994. "Regime Change and the Restructuring of Alliances." *American Journal of Political Science*, 38: 145-161.

Skalnes, Lars S. 2000. *Politics, Markets, and Grand Strategy*. Ann Arbor: University of Michigan Press.

Sked, Alan. 1987. *Britain's Decline. Problems and Perspectives*. Oxford, UK: Basil Blackwell.

Smith, Holland, and Percy Finch. 1949. *Coral and Brass*. New York: Scribner's.

Smith, R. Elbertson. 1959. *The Army and Economic Mobilization. U.S. Army in World War II: The War Department. Vol. 4. Part 5*. Washington, DC: Office of the Chief of Military History.

Snyder, Glenn H. 1984. "The Security Dilemma in Alliance Politics." *World Politics*, 36: 461-495.

Snyder, Jack. 1984. *The Ideology of the Offensive*. Ithaca, NY: Cornell University Press.

———. 1990. "Averting Anarchy in the New Europe." *International Security*, 14: 5-40.

———. 1991. *Myths of Empire: Domestic Politics and International Ambition*. Ithaca, NY: Cornell University Press.

Solingen, Etel. 1998. *Regional Orders at Century's Dawn: Global and Domestic Influences on Grand Strategy*. Princeton, NJ: Princeton University Press.

Solingen, Etel. 2001. "Mapping Internationalization: Domestic and Regional Impacts." *International Studies Quarterly*, 45: 517-555.

Spector, Ronald. 1988. "The Military Effectiveness of the U.S. Armed Forces, 1919-39," in Allan R. Millett and Williamson Murray, eds., *Military Effectiveness, Vol. II: The Interwar Period*. Boston: Allen and Unwin.

Spiers, Edward M. 1980. *The Army and Society, 1815-1914*. London and New York: Longman.

Spiezio, Edward K. 1990. "British Hegemony and Major Power War, 1815-1939: An Empirical Test of Gilpin's Model of Hegemonic Governance." *International Studies Quarterly*, 34: 165-181.

Statistical Abstract for the United Kingdom. 1927. For each of the fifteen years from 1911 to 1925.

Statistical Abstract for the United Kingdom. Reprinted in 1966 by Kraus Reprint LTD. No 82: 1913 and 1924–1937.

Statistical Abstract Relating to British India From 1903–04 to 1912–13. 1915. London: His Majesty's Stationary Office.

Statistical Abstract Relating to British India From 1910–11 to 1919–1920. 1922. London: His Majesty's Stationary Office.

"Statistical Abstract for the United Kingdom for Each of the Fifteen years 1913 and 1918 to 1931" (published in 1933; No. 76: 1913 and 1918–1931) [See *pp. 126–127, Table No. 103.—Number of Officers, Men and Boys Borne on the Books of His Majesty's Ships, at the Royal Marine Divisions*; tables adapted; numbers as of March of each year].

"Statistical Abstract for the United Kingdom for Each of the Fifteen Years from 1911 to 1925" (1927). V.70. London

"Statistical Abstract for the United Kingdom for Each of the Fifteen Years from 1913 and 1918 to 1931" (1930). V.76. London

"Statistical Abstract for the United Kingdom for Each of the Fifteen Years from 1913 and 1924 to 1937" (1966; Reprinted). V.82. London

Statistical History of the United States from Colonial Times to the Present. 1976. New York: Basic Books.

Stein, Arthur A. 1990. *Why Nations Cooperate: Circumstance and Choice in International Relations.* Ithaca, NY: Cornell University Press.

———. 1993. "Domestic Constraints, Extended Deterrence, and the Incoherence of Grand Strategy: The United States, 1938–1950," in Richard Rosecrance and Arthur A. Stein, eds., *The Domestic Bases of Grand Strategy.* Ithaca, NY: Cornell University Press.

Stokesbury, James L. 1983. *Navy and Empire.* New York: William Morrow and Company.

Sturgis, James. 1984. "Britain and the New Imperialism," in C. C. Eldridge, ed., *British Imperialism in the Nineteenth Century.* London: Macmillan.

Sumida, Jon Tetsuro. 1979. "British Capital Ship Design and Fire Control in the Dreadnought Era: Sir John Fisher, Arthur Hungerford Pollen, and the Battle Cruiser." *Journal of Modern History,* 51: 205–230.

———. 1989. *In Defense of Naval Supremacy: Finance, Technology and British Naval Policy, 1889–1914.* Boston: Unwin Hyman.

———. 1990. "British Naval Administration and Policy in the Age of Fisher." *Journal of Military History,* 54: 1–26.

———. 1995. "Sir John Fisher and the Dreadnought: The Sources of Naval Mythology." *Journal of Military History,* 59: 619–637.

———. 2001. "The Admiralty and British Imperial Grand Strategy, 1889–1918." Draft paper. (June 28).

———. 2001. "Geography, Technology, and British Naval Strategy before the First World War: Mahanian Theory versus Fisherian Practice in the Dreadnought Era." Draft paper. (March 7).

Taliaferro, Jeffrey W. 2000/01. "Security Seeking under Anarchy: Defensive Realism Revisited." *International Security*, 25 (Winter).

Taylor, A. J. P. 1954. *The Struggle for Mastery in Europe: 1848–1918*. Oxford, UK: Clarendon Press.

Taylor, Shelley. 1982. "The Availability Bias in Social Perception and Interaction," in Daniel Kahneman, Paul Slovic, and Amos Tversky, eds., *Judgment under Uncertainty: Heuristics and Biases*. Cambridge, UK: Cambridge University Press.

Terriff, Terry. 2007. "Of Romans and Dragons: Preparing the US Marine Corps for Future Warfare." *Contemporary Security Policy*, 28 (April): 143–162.

Thompson, William R., and David P. Rapkin. 1981. "Collaboration, Consensus, and Detente: The External Threat-Bloc Cohesion Hypothesis." *Journal of Conflict Resolution*, 25: 615–637.

Till, Geoffrey. 1996. "Adopting the Aircraft Carrier: The British, American, and Japanese Case Studies," in Williamson Murray and Allan R. Millett, eds., *Military Innovation in the Interwar Period*. Cambridge, UK: Cambridge University Press.

———. 1996. "Luxury Fleet? The Sea Power of (Soviet) Russia," in N. A. M. Rodger, ed., *Naval Power in the Twentieth Century*. Annapolis, MD: Naval Institute Press.

Tin-bor Hui, Victoria. 2004. "Toward a Dynamic Theory of International Politics: Insights from Comparing Ancient China and Early Modern Europe." *International Organization*, 58 (Winter).

Toffler, Alvin, and Heidi Toffler. 1993. *War and Anti-War*. New York: Warner.

Trachtenberg, Marc. 2007. "Preventive War and U.S. Foreign Policy," *Security Studies*, 16 (January), 1–31.

Trebilcock, Clive. 1973. "British Armaments and European Industrialization, 1890–1914." *Economic History Review*, 26: 254–272.

Trubowitz, Peter. "Geography and Strategy: The Politics of American Naval Expansion," in Peter Trubowitz, Emily O. Goldman, and Edward Rhodes, eds., *The Politics of Strategic Adjustment: Ideas, Institutions, and Interests*. New York: Columbia University Press.

———. 1998. *Defining the National Interest*. Chicago: University of Chicago Press.

Turnbull, Archibald, and Clifford Lord. 1949. *History of United States Naval Aviation*. New Haven, CT: Yale University Press.

Tversky, Amos, and Daniel Kahneman. 1973. "Availability: A Heuristic for Judging Frequency and Probability." *Cognitive Psychology*, 5: 207–232.

———. 1974. "Judgment under Uncertainty." *Science* 185: 1124–1131.

Tyler, Patrick. 1992. "Pentagon Drops Goal of Blocking New Superpowers." *The New York Times* (May 24).

———. 1992. "U.S. Strategy Plan Calls for Insuring No Rivals Develop a One-Superpower World." *The New York Times* (March 8).

Unclassified memo from Secretary Gates to Secretary Clinton. 2009. "Options for Remodeling Security Sector Assistance Authorities." (December 15).

U.N. General Assembly Security Council. 2009. "The Situation in Afghanistan and Its Implications for International Peace and Security." Report of the Secretary-General (December 28). Available at: http://unama.unmissions.org/Portals/UNAMA/SG%20Reports/sgreportjan2010.pdf.

U.S. Air Force. 2002, 2003, 2004. *Air Force Transformation Flight Plan*. Washington, DC: Headquarters U.S. Air Force, Future Concepts and Transformation Division.

———. 2005. *Air Force Transformation: The Edge*. Washington, DC: Headquarters U.S. Air Force, Future Concepts and Transformation Division.

U.S. Army. 2002, 2003, 2004. *Army Transformation Roadmap*, Washington, DC: Department of the Army.

U.S. Department of Defense. 2001. *Quadrennial Defense Review Report*. Washington, DC: Department of Defense (September).

———. 2003. *Military Transformation: A Strategic Approach*. Washington, DC: U.S. Department of Defense.

———. 2003. *Transformation Planning Guidance*. Washington, DC: Department of Defense (April).

———. 2004. *Logistics Transformation Strategy: Achieving Knowledge-Enabled Logistics*. Washington, DC: Department of Defense (December).

———. 2006. *Quadrennial Defense Review Report*. Washington, DC: Department of Defense (February).

———. 2010. Active Duty Military Personnel Strengths. Available at: www.defense.gov/faq/pis/mil_strength.html

U.S. Joint Forces Command. 2004. *Joint Transformation Roadmap*, Washington, DC: Department of Defense.

U.S. Marine Corps. 2000. *Marine Corps Strategy 21*. Washington, DC: Headquarters United States Marine Corps.

U.S. Navy. 2002, 2003. *Naval Transformation Roadmap*. Washington, DC: Department of the Navy.

Van der Vat, Dan. 2000. *Standard of Power: The Royal Navy in the Twentieth Century*. London: Hutchinson.

Van Evera, Stephen. 1998. "Offense, Defense, and the Causes of War." *International Security* 22 (Spring): 5–43.

———. 1999. *Causes of War: Power and the Roots of Conflict*. Ithaca, NY: Cornell University Press.

Vayrynen, Raimo. 1983. "Economic Cycles, Power Transitions, Political Management and Wars between Major Powers." *International Studies Quarterly*, 27: 389–418.
Virmani, Arvind. 2005. "Global Power from the 18th to 21st Century: Power Potential, Strategic Assets and Actual Power." Working Paper No. 175. New Delhi: Indian Council for Research on International Economic Relations (November).
Vlahos, Michael. 1980. *The Blue Sword: The Naval War College and the American Mission, 1919–1941*. Newport, RI: Naval War College Press.
Voenno-Morskaya Ideya Rossii: Duhovnoe Nasledie Imperatorskogo Flota. 1999. (Military-Naval Thought of Russia: Heritage of the Imperial Fleet.). Vol. Moscow: Russkii Put.
Wagner, R. Harrison. 1993. "What Was Bipolarity?" *International Organization*, 47: 77–106.
Walt, Stephen M. 1985. "Alliance Formation and the Balance of World Power." *International Security*, 9: 3–43.
———. 1987. *The Origins of Alliances*. Ithaca, NY: Cornell University Press.
———. 2001. "Beyond bin Laden: Reshaping U. S. Foreign Policy." *International Security*, 26: 56–78.
———. 2002. "Keeping the World 'Off-Balance': Self-Restraint and U. S. Foreign Policy," in G. John Ikenberry, ed., *America Unrivaled: The Future of the Balance of Power*. Ithaca, NY: Cornell University Press.
———. 2005. *Taming American Power*. New York: W. W. Norton.
Waltz, Kenneth. 1979. *Theory of International Politics*. Reading, MA: Addison-Wesley.
———. 1996. "International Politics is Not Foreign Policy." *Security Studies*, 6: 54–57.
Waltz, Kenneth N. 1954. *Man, the State, and War: A Theoretical Analysis*. New York: Columbia University Press.
Watson, Mark Skinner. 1950. *United States Army in World War II, Chief of Staff: Prewar Plans and Preparations*. Washington, DC: Historical Division, Department of the Army.
Watts, Anthony J. 1990. *The Imperial Russian Navy*. London: Arms and Armour Press.
Watts, Barry, and Williamson Murray. 1996. "Military Innovation in Peacetime," in Williamson Murray and Allan R. Millett, eds., *Military Innovation in the Interwar Period*. Cambridge, UK: Cambridge University Press, 1996.
Weigley, Russell F. 1967. *History of the United States Army*. New York: Macmillan.
———. 1973. "The Role of the War Department and the Army," in Dorothy Borg and Shumpei Okamoto, eds., *Pearl Harbor as History: Japanese–American Relations, 1931–1941*. New York: Columbia University Press.
Weinstein, Franklin B. 1969. "The Concept of a Commitment in International Relations." *Journal of Conflict Resolution*, 13: 39–56.
Weir, Gary E. 1992. *Building the Kaiser's Navy: The Imperial Navy Office and German Industry in the von Tirpitz Era, 1890–1919*. Annapolis, MD: Naval Institute Press.

Weitsman, Patricia A. 1997. "Intimate Enemies: The Politics of Peacetime Alliances." *Security Studies*, 7 (August): 156–192.

———. 2004. *Dangerous Alliances: Proponents of Peace, Weapons of War*. Stanford, CA: Stanford University Press.

Wendt, Alexander. 1992. "Anarchy Is What States Make of It." *International Organization*.

———. 1995. "Constructing International Politics." *International Security*, 20: 71–81.

Wheeler, Winslow T., and Lawrence J. Korb. *Military Reform: A Reference Handbook* (Westport, CT: Praeger, 2007).

White, Josh. 2008. "Gates Sees Terrorism Remaining Enemy No. 1." *The Washington Post* (July 31): A1.

White House. 1995. *A National Security Strategy of Engagement and Enlargement* (February).

———. 2002. *The National Security Strategy of the United States* (September).

———. 2006. *The National Security Strategy of the United States* (March).

Williamson, Samuel R. 1969. *The Politics of Grand Strategy: Britain and France Prepare for War, 1904–1914*. Cambridge, MA: Harvard University Press.

Wilson, Clay. 2007. "Network Centric Operations: Background and Oversight Issues for Congress." Washington, DC: Congressional Research Service (March 15).

Wilson, Herbert Wrigley. 1969. *Battleships in Action*. Boston: Little, Brown and Company.

Wilson, Keith M., ed. 1986. *British Foreign Secretaries and Foreign Policy: From Crimean War to First World War*. London: Croon Helm.

Winham, Gilbert R. 1977. "Negotiations as a Management Process." *World Politics*, 30: 87–114.

Wohlforth, William C. 1987. "The Perception of Power: Russia in the Pre-1914 Balance." *World Politics*, 39 (April): 353–381.

———. 1994/95. "Realism and the End of the Cold War." *International Security*, 19 (Winter): 91–129.

———. 1999. "The Stability of a Unipolar World." *International Security*, 24: 5–41.

———. 2002. "U. S. Strategy in a Unipolar World," in G. John Ikenberry, ed., *America Unrivaled: The Future of the Balance of Power*. Ithaca, NY: Cornell University Press.

Wolfers, Arnold. 1962. *Discord and Collaboration: Essays on International Politics*. Baltimore, MD: The Johns Hopkins University Press.

World Bank. 2008. "Gross Domestic Product." *World Development Indicators Database*. Available at: http://siteresources.worldbank.org/DATASTATISTICS/Resources/GDP.pdf

Yoshpe, Harry B. 1952. "Economic Mobilization Planning between the Two World Wars, Part II." *Military Affairs*, 16 (Summer).

Zahavi, Amotz. 1975. "Mate Selection: A Selection for Handicap." *Journal of Theoretical Biology*, 53: 205–214.

Zakaria, Fareed. 2006. "The Decline and Fall of Europe." *The Washington Post* (February 14): A15.

Zanini, Michele, and Sean J. A. Edwards. 2001. "The Networking of Terror in the Information Age," in John Arquilla and David Ronfeldt, eds., *Networks and Netwars: The Future of Terror, Crime, and Militancy*. Santa Monica, CA: RAND.

INDEX

ABM treaty, 156
Acheson, Dean, 145
adapting strategy, 5, 19, 20–21, 27, 183n30; of declining powers, 7, 9, 22–23, 25, 80, 165–69, 176, 187n75; and defense spending, 26, 33, 34, 81, 137, 139–41; of defensively advantaged states, 26, 80–81, 129–30; diplomatic indicators of, 31, 32, 33, 34, 97, 165–166; economic indicators of, 31, 32, 33, 34; and global interests/number and diversity of threats, 26, 37, 38, 81, 129–30, 155, 161, 165–66, 168–69; of Great Britain, 9, 60–62, 81, 82, 84–101, 108, 118, 119, 120–21, 123–24, 129, 155, 165–69, 168; military indicators of, 31–32, 33, 34, 60–62, 81, 100, 137; and near-term readiness, 26, 33, 34, 37, 60–62, 93–94, 100–101, 108, 118, 119, 123–24, 130, 139, 141, 155, 159; of preeminent powers, 22, 25, 38, 129, 155, 161, 175; as reactive strategy, 6, 21; relationship to cognitive limitations, 29, 123–24; risks of, 6, 22; and technological change, 25, 26, 31–32, 33, 34, 60–62, 96, 97, 100–101, 119; of United States, 9, 129–30, 137, 139–41, 142, 150, 154–56, 159, 161, 175
Afghanistan: US war in, 1, 10, 128, 130, 134–35, 143, 147, 148, 150–51, 152, 153–54, 160, 172–73
Allison, Graham T.: *Essence of Decision*, 185n57

Al-Qaeda, 132–33, 134–35, 151, 153, 174, 175
Al Qaeda in Yemen and Somalia, 202n27
Amery, Leopold, 193n21
Andres, Richard, 203n44
Anglo-Boer War, 60, 70, 72
Annual Report on the Military Power of the People's Republic of China (1999), 157
"Anytime, Anywhere: A Navy for the 21st Century," 149
Army Vision 2010, 146
Arnoldson, Derek, 65
Arquilla, John, 182n15
asymmetric strategies, 22, 63, 134, 147, 151, 175
Australia, 67
Austria-Hungary: as declining power, 36; vs. Great Britain, 70; relations with Great Britain, 58; relations with Prussia, 71; relations with Russia, 39, 40–41, 51–52, 74; vs. Russia, 42, 50

Bacevich, Andrew: *The Limits of Power*, 204n51; *The New American Militarism*, 204n65
Balkans, 138; Bosnia, 132, 141, 148, 155, 173, 184n43; Kosovo, 132, 146, 173; Serbia, 144, 150
Barnett, Correlli: *The Audit of War*, 206n23
Barnett, Thomas P. M.: *The Pentagon's New Map*, 179n1
Baumann, Robert F., 205n3
Beeler, John, 59

241

Belgium, 98, 99, 166
Berkowitz, Bruce: Strategic Advantage, 201n9
Berman, Larry, 182n23, 204nn61,64
Betts, Richard K., 182n21; Soldiers, Statesmen, and Cold War, 185n57
Biddle, Stephen, 127, 174, 203n46, 204n48
Biden, Joseph, 154
Bin Laden, Osama, 132–33
bipolar vs. multipolar systems, 13, 15, 25
Blanken, Leo J., 184nn38,41
Blumenthal, Dan, 158
Bobbitt, Philip, 126
Bond, Brian, 121, 193n22, 194nn32,34,41, 43–45, 195n56, 200nn140–43, 201nn152,153, 206nn23,25
Borg, Dorothy, 195n77
Bosnia, 132, 141, 148, 155, 173, 184n43
Bottom Up Review (BUR) (1993), 131–32, 141
Bower, J. L., 182n20
Bowles, Samuel, 181n10
Braeman, John, 115–16, 195nn73, 74
Braisted, William R., 196n84, 200nn137–39
Brawley, Mark R., 193n6, 194n26
Breemer, Jan: on rapid technological change, 27
Bridge, F. R., 187n1
Broadberry, Stephen, 193nn9,10
Brooks, Stephen G., 186n64
Bullen, Roger, 187n1
Bush, George W., 145; Citadel speech of 1999, 142; religious convictions of, 180n13; second inaugural speech, 156
Bushnell, John, 45, 188nn13,27–29

Campbell, Donald T., 187n71
case selection and coding, 12, 28–35; diplomatic indicators, 31, 32, 33–34, 34, 37–38, 41, 51–52, 53, 55, 77, 97, 119, 159, 165, 172, 173–74; economic indicators, 31, 32, 33, 34, 40–42, 45, 48, 52–53, 65, 77, 103, 163, 175; military indicators, 31–32, 33, 34, 37, 38, 39, 40, 41, 43–45, 46–47, 48–51, 52–53, 60–62, 77, 81, 137, 138, 163–64, 165
Casillas, Julio, 180n15
causality: and intentions, 35; vs. correlation, 35
Cebrowski, Arthur, 142
Chalmers, Malcolm: Paying for Defence, 193n14

Chamberlain, Joseph, 72, 186n66
Chanak crisis, 83
Chandrasekaran, Rajiv, 204n59
Charlick-Paley, Tanya: Assessing Russia's Decline, 202n15
Cheney, Dick, 133; Defense Strategy for the 1990s, 131
China: defense spending, 129; military policies, 134; reforming and reconstituting strategy of, 187n73; relations with Great Britain, 167; relations with Japan, 102, 116, 121; relations with United States, 1, 20, 102, 109, 116, 121, 125, 127, 129, 132, 153, 157–58, 174, 175, 195n77, 199n133; as rising power, 3, 4, 31, 129, 157–58, 174, 175; unification of, 102; and WTO, 158
Christensen, Clayton M., 182n20; The Innovator's Dilemma, 180n14
Christensen, Thomas J., 205n71
Churchill, Winston, 67, 76–77
Citino, Robert, 184n36
Clinton, Bill, 132, 154–56
Cohen, Eliot A., 182n15
Cold War: bipolarity during, 15; vs. current situation, 1, 15, 130–31; nostalgia regarding, 16; United States during, 9, 24
collective security, 17, 32
complexity of security environment: diversity of treats, 1, 4, 14–15, 19, 24–25, 26, 29, 30, 37, 38, 81, 82, 118, 119, 120, 124, 125–27, 129, 130, 133–34, 135, 143, 155, 165–66, 168, 169; interdependence, 1, 7–8, 14, 15, 26, 30, 124, 133, 179n1; number of threats, 1, 4, 14, 16, 19, 24, 26, 29, 30, 37, 38, 81, 82, 124, 129, 133, 155, 158–59; proximity of threats, 7, 16, 24, 26, 68, 80–82, 119–20, 121, 124, 129–30, 184nn42,43, 186n64; relationship to strategic choices, 2, 5, 7–8, 12, 24–25, 26, 34–35, 37, 58–59, 77, 79–81, 124, 128, 129–30, 131–34, 159, 161
Conetta, Carl, 192n2; on RMAs, 26
Cooley, Alexander: Logics of Hierarchy, 179n9
Copeland, Dale C.: The Origins of Major War, 184n38
Corbin, Marcus, 203n43
costly signals, 13, 181n10
Counterinsurgency Field Manual, FM 3-24, 147–48

INDEX 243

Courtney, Hugh G., 181n4, 183n28
Crocker, Percy, Jr., 180n15
Crowl, Philip A.: The U.S. Marines and Amphibious War, 197n96
Cuba, 169–170
Curzon, George, 193n21

defense spending, 25, 27, 29, 74; in adapting strategy, 26, 33, 34, 81, 137, 139–41; by Great Britain, 54, 58–68, 70, 71, 81, 84–94, 97, 100, 102, 103, 120, 123, 166–67, 168–69, 194n27, 200n144, 206n23; for long-term transformation, 18, 22, 26, 33, 34, 42, 48, 60–62, 81, 93–94, 108, 118, 130, 138–40; for near-term readiness, 18, 22, 26, 33, 34, 42, 48, 62–62, 81, 84, 96, 138–40; in reforming and reconstituting strategy, 22, 29, 33, 34, 37, 41, 42, 48, 53, 163–64, 168–69; by Russia, 39, 41, 42, 43–44, 48, 50, 52, 53, 163–64; in shaping strategy, 26, 33, 34, 58–59, 137; by United States, 102, 103–8, 113, 118, 119, 120, 121–22, 135–40, 145, 150, 152–53, 158, 160, 161
Demchak, Chris C., 180n10; Complex Machines, 182n12
Dening, B. C., 95
Denny, David Anthony, 202n29
DiMaggio, Paul J., 28
diplomatic policies: in adapting strategy, 31, 32, 33, 34, 97, 165; flexibility in, 32, 33–34, 51–52, 72–74, 97–99, 100, 114, 120, 156, 157, 159, 172; of Great Britain, 54–55, 72–74, 94, 96, 97–99, 165, 170–71, 172; of Japan, 102, 109; multilateralism, 154–55, 156, 157, 159, 163; in reforming and reconstituting strategy, 31, 32, 33, 34, 37–38, 41, 51–52, 53, 55, 77; of Russia, 40, 41, 51–52, 53, 75, 77, 129; in shaping strategy, 31, 32, 33–34, 159, 170, 172, 173–74; of United States, 102, 103, 114–16, 120, 154–58, 169–70, 173–74, 195n 77
Divine, Robert A.: The Illusion of Neutrality, 199n125
Dolan, Chris J.: In War We Trust, 204n65
domestic politics: economic nationalists, 27, 29, 185n51; free traders/internationalists, 27, 29, 185n51; relationship to strategic choices, 8, 12, 25–27, 29, 32, 80, 124, 160, 162
Dominican Republic, 169

Donnelly, Thomas, 153, 201n1, 204nn54,55, 205nn69,70, 208n62
Dukes, Paul, 192n133

economic policies: in adapting strategy, 31, 32, 33, 34; balance between nondefense spending and, 16, 18, 32, 34, 58, 60, 84, 85, 91, 103; engagement, 20, 21, 32, 132, 158, 187nn68,69; of Great Britain, 54, 64–65, 70, 76, 79, 80, 88, 91, 92, 100, 103, 166, 168, 186n66; in reforming and reconstituting strategy, 31, 32, 33, 34, 37, 40–42, 45, 48, 52–53, 77, 163, 175; of Russia, 40–42, 45, 48, 52–53, 77, 163–65; in shaping strategy, 31, 32, 33, 65, 103; trade policies, 16, 17, 21, 27, 32, 33, 34, 37, 41, 65, 70, 158, 172, 186n66; of United States, 20, 103, 113–14, 115–16, 117–18, 122, 131, 132, 153, 158, 160, 175, 198n121
Edgerton, David, 93, 194n50, 195n53; Warfare State, 206nn15,19
Edwards, Sean J. A., 180n16
Ekirch, Arthur A., 196n78
Eliason, Leslie: The Diffusion of Military Technology and Ideas, 182n17
English, Richard, 193n8; Rethinking British Decline, 192n3
Europe: as declining, 31; during post-Cold War period, 3, 31, 129
Eyre, Dana, 183n33, 208n55

Fashoda incident of 1898, 72
Fehrenbach, Frank, 180n15
Feith, Douglas, 145
Ferris, John Robert: on British defense spending, 88, 91; Men, Money, and Diplomacy, 192n5, 193nn17–19, 194nn25,36,40,49, 195nn54,57,58,60,61,66–67, 200n141, 205n12, 206n26
Finch, Percy: Coral and Brass, 197n95
firms: and advertising, 6; and industry standards, 20; responses to uncertainty in marketplace, 4, 5–6, 7, 12, 19, 21; vs. states, 5–6, 7, 12, 19, 20, 21, 27, 127, 179n9
Fisher, Sir John, 60–68, 74, 76, 149, 171–72
Forward . . . From the Sea, 148, 149
Four Power Treaty, 99, 116
France: colonial policies, 78; vs. Germany, 36; vs. Great Britain, 54, 70, 97;

France *(Continued)*
  during inter-world war period, 30;
  mass-conscription armies of, 22, 37, 70;
  military policies, 97, 112–13; navy, 57,
  59–60, 62–63, 64–65, 72, 73; relations
  with Belgium, 166; relations with
  Germany, 40, 51, 98, 102, 115–16, 117–18;
  relations with Great Britain, 38, 55, 56,
  58, 59–60, 62, 64–65, 67, 72, 73, 74, 82,
  94, 96, 97–99, 100, 116, 172; relations
  with Japan, 99, 116; relations with
  Prussia, 49, 51, 71; relations with Russia,
  39, 40, 49, 51, 52, 55, 56, 72, 76–77;
  relations with United States, 99, 115–16,
  117–18, 156; during Revolution, 22;
  vs. Russia, 36, 45
Franco-Prussian War, 49, 51, 71
Frederick, Suzanne Y., 189nn55,56,59
Friedberg, Aaron: The Weary Titan, 183n35,
  184n37, 192nn3,4, 193n7
Friedman, Benjamin H.: US Military
  Innovation since the Cold War, 201n4,
  203n40
Friedman, Norman: British Carrier Aviation,
  200n144
... From the Sea, 148
Fukuyama, Francis: America at the
  Crossroads, 205n65
Fuller, William C.: on Russian intelligence
  capabilities, 51; on Russian railway
  construction, 164; on Russian threat
  assessment, 50, 51, 75, 164; Strategy and
  Power in Russia, 188nn9,12,14,18,24,
  189n39–43,45,47–52, 192nn132,134,139

Gaddis, John L., 207n56; *Surprise, Security
  and the American Experience*, 205n66
Gallipoli, 111
Gates, Robert, 151, 152–53
Germany: air power, 121; economic policies,
  54; vs. France, 36; vs. Great Britain, 36,
  38, 54, 55, 60, 66, 80, 97, 167, 184n42;
  during inter-world war period, 22, 31;
  military policies, 22, 55–56, 72, 102,
  184n36; navy, 55–56, 59, 60, 66, 67, 166,
  171; during post-Crimean War period,
  31, 36; relations with France, 40, 51, 98,
  102, 115–16, 117–18; relations with Great
  Britain, 54, 55–56, 58, 59, 60, 66, 67–68,
  71, 72–73, 74, 80, 82, 97–98, 99, 127,
  166, 171, 172; relations with Russia, 40,
  49–50, 51–52, 72–73, 74, 77, 164; relations
  with United States, 20, 115–16, 117–18,
  142, 156; as rising power, 22, 31, 38; vs.
  Russia, 42, 50, 165; unification of, 36, 37,
  40, 51; and Versailles Treaty, 78, 98, 110;
  as weak state, 31. See also Prussia
Gerring, John, 179n7, 187n74; on formal vs.
  informal units, 186n62; on intentions
  and causality, 35
Geyer, Dietrich, 192n140
Gibbs, N. H.: Grand Strategy, 200n141
Gintis, Herbert, 181n10
Glaser, Charles L., 181n9; Rational Theory of
  International Politics, 183n27
Global Engagement: A Vision for the 21st
  Century Air Force, 150
global interests, 24–25, 74, 162, 176; and
  adapting strategy, 26, 37, 38, 81, 129–30,
  155, 161, 165–66, 168–69; of Great
  Britain, 38, 80, 81, 82, 83–84, 94–96,
  100–101, 119, 120–21, 155, 165–66,
  168–69; and shaping strategy, 25, 26,
  119–20; of United States, 126, 129–30,
  144, 149, 155, 159, 161
globalization, 1, 126, 129–30, 135, 144, 174
Global Reach—Global Power, 150
Global Vigilance, Reach, and Power, 150
Goertz, Gary, 186n61
Good Neighbor Policy, 170
Gorchakov, A. M., 39, 41
Gordon, G. A. H.: British Seapower and
  Procurement between the Wars, 194n33
Gorski, Gerard, 25
Gray, Colin S., 127
Great Britain: adapting strategy of, 9,
  60–62, 81, 82, 84–101, 108, 118, 119,
  120–21, 123–24, 129, 155, 165–69; 168;
  air power, 83–84, 88, 91, 92, 93, 96–97,
  98–99, 100, 101, 117, 120, 121, 165–66,
  168, 200n144, 206nn20,33; army, 68–71,
  79, 80, 83, 87, 88, 89, 90, 92–93, 94–96,
  98–99, 100–101, 120–21, 165–67, 168;
  vs. Austria, 70; Boer War, 60, 70, 72;
  Cardwell system, 95–96; colonial
  policies, 53, 56, 60, 69–70, 70, 72, 73–74,
  78, 94–96, 98–99, 100, 102, 120–21, 123;
  Conservative Party, 70–71; as declining
  power, 9, 79–82, 97, 119, 120, 127,
  165–69, 174, 183n35; defense spending,
  54, 58–68, 70, 71, 81, 84–94, 97, 100,
  102, 103, 120, 123, 166–67, 168–69,

194n27, 200n146, 206n25; as defensively advantaged, 68, 80–81, 121, 184n42; diplomatic policies, 54–55, 72–74, 94, 96, 97–99, 165, 170–71, 172; economic policies, 54, 64–65, 70, 76, 79, 80, 88, 91, 92, 100, 103, 166, 168, 186n66; English Civil War, 68–69; Fisher, 60–68, 74, 76, 149, 171–72; fleet unit concept, 66–67, 149; vs. France, 54, 70, 97; general staff, 68, 69; vs. Germany, 36, 38, 54, 55, 60, 66, 80, 97, 167, 184n42; imperial policing by, 94–96, 98–99, 100, 102, 120–21, 123, 167, 168, 193n16; intelligence capabilities, 9, 63–64, 79; during inter-world war period, 9, 29, 31, 38, 79–101, 102, 119, 120–21, 122–24, 129, 155, 165–69, 170–72, 173, 174–76; Irish rebellion, 83; vs. Japan, 96, 168; Liberal Party, 70; and Locarno Pact, 98–99; military policies, 54, 55–71, 75–76, 77, 81, 83–97, 98–99, 100–101, 112–13, 119, 120–21, 123, 165–69, 193n24; navy, 9, 38, 53, 54–58, 59–68, 71, 72, 73, 74–75, 76, 77, 79, 84, 87, 88, 92, 93, 94, 96, 99, 100–101, 102, 108, 121, 165–66, 168, 170, 171–72, 193n16, 200n146, 206nn20,33; plunging policies, 64–65, 76; during post-Crimean War period, 9, 31, 38, 53–76, 99, 170–74, 175; as preeminent power, 9, 38, 58–59, 60–62, 68, 72, 77, 170–74; vs. Prussia, 68–69, 70; relations with Australia, 67; relations with Austria-Hungary, 58; relations with Belgium, 98, 99; relations with China, 167; relations with Dominions, 66–67, 83, 97; relations with France, 38, 55, 56, 58, 59–60, 62, 64–65, 67, 72, 73, 74, 82, 94, 96, 97–99, 116, 165–66, 172; relations with Germany, 54, 55–56, 58, 59, 60, 66, 67–68, 71, 72–73, 74, 80, 82, 97–98, 99, 100, 127, 166, 171, 172; relations with Italy, 67, 92, 166; relations with Japan, 66, 67, 72, 73, 80, 82, 94, 96, 97, 99, 100, 101, 102, 110, 116, 127, 170–71; relations with Prussia, 71; relations with Russia, 38, 39, 45, 48, 49, 51, 52, 53, 54–55, 56, 58, 59–60, 62, 65, 67, 72–74, 76–77, 82, 83, 99, 171, 172; relations with Turkey, 82, 83, 111; relations with United States, 56, 67, 72, 82, 94, 96, 97, 98, 99, 102, 109–10, 116, 117, 127, 170; vs. Russia, 36, 54, 70, 75–77; security environment during inter-world period, 82–84, 124; security environment during post-Crimean War period, 53–58; shaping strategy of, 9, 38, 58–75, 77, 170–72, 173, 175; and Suez Canal, 54–55; and technological change, 57–58, 60–68, 74–75, 76, 94, 119, 165–67, 170, 171–72; Ten Year Rule adopted by, 80, 94–95, 165; two-power standard adopted by, 59–60, 62, 77, 170; vs. United States, 31, 36, 38, 79–82, 96, 97, 101, 108, 111, 117, 118, 119–24, 129, 149, 155, 166, 168, 169, 170–76; during World War I, 111; during World War II, 92–93, 121, 123, 166, 167

Great Depression, 103, 115, 118
Greece: relations with Turkey, 83
Green, Brendan Rittenhouse: *US Military Innovation since the Cold War*, 201n4, 203n40
Green, Constance McLaughlin, 198n113, 200n152
Griffith, Robert K., Jr.: *Men Wanted for the U.S. Army*, 198n107
Griffith, Thomas, 203n44
Gulf War of 1991, 131, 139, 141, 148, 160–61

Haass, Richard N., 155
Haiti, 132, 138, 148, 155, 169
Harris, J. P., 194n48, 206nn22,24,26
Haug, Kevin, 180n15
Hay-Pauncefote Treaty, 72
Headley, David, 202n27
hedging strategies, 21, 22, 162
Heinrichs, Waldo H., Jr., 200n149
Henry, Merton G.: *History of Military Mobilization in the United States Army, 1775–1945*, 198nn115,117,118
Hezbollah, 134
Hezlet, Sir Arthur, 206n18
Hoffman, Frank G., 182n13
Hofhansel, Claus: *Commercial Competition and National Security*, 186n67
Hofmann, George F., 197n104, 198nn105,106,110
Hogan, Michael J.: *Informal Entente*, 195n75
Hone, Thomas C., 122, 197n100, 198n119, 199n123, 200nn150,151
Hoover, Herbert, 169
Howard, Michael, 190n80, 195n59; on Britain's imperial policing, 167; on societal support, 18

Ikenberry, G. John: on risks, 162–63
Imlay, Talbot C.: The Fog of Peace and War Planning, 179n5
India: British army in, 69–70, 73–74, 83, 88, 89, 95–96, 120, 167; Mumbai attack, 202n27; relations with United States, 142, 157, 158; as rising power, 3, 4, 31; Sepoy/White Mutinies, 69–70
Industrial Revolution, 31, 36–37, 80
Ingram, Edward, 192nn125,129
innovation, 6, 67, 182n16, 186n63; amphibious warfare, 78, 103, 110, 111, 117, 119, 169, 197n95; carrier aviation, 78, 96–97, 110, 111, 112, 117, 121–22, 165–66, 168, 169, 197n102, 206nn20,33,34; as disruptive, 4, 10–11, 17, 61–62, 65–66, 180n14; dreadnoughts, 65–66, 171–72; and economic growth, 193n9; by Great Britain, 60–68, 74, 76, 149, 171–72; incentives to innovate, 22, 24, 25, 26, 38, 74, 118, 171; leadership in, 31, 38, 93, 118, 119–20, 171; mechanized/armored warfare, 22, 78, 95, 96, 100, 112–13, 120, 122–23, 166–67, 184n36; network-centric warfare, 149, 173; research and development (R&D), 18, 32, 33, 64–65, 91, 117, 128, 139, 150, 169, 170; revolutions in military affairs (RMAs), 15, 16, 19, 22, 26, 60, 138, 142, 144, 145–46, 161, 175; satellites, 10–11; in shaping strategy, 20, 21, 26, 31, 33, 34, 38, 64–66, 108, 119–20, 169, 170, 171–73; strategic bombing, 113, 120; by United States, 128, 143, 145–47, 148, 149, 150–51, 161, 169, 173–74; unmanned aerial vehicles (UAVs), 140, 150. See also technological change
intelligence capabilities, 126, 143; of Great Britain, 9, 63–64, 79; of Russia, 51, 53
interdependence, 1, 7–8, 14, 15, 26, 30, 124, 133, 179n1
interface standards, 17
international relations theory, 20–21; and management literature, 12, 179n9; and uncertainty, 13. See also realism
Internet, 10, 134, 135
Iran: invasion of Kuwait, 131, 160–61; nuclear program of, 1; relations with United States, 1, 127, 132, 140, 161
Iraq: and Al-Quaeda, 135; Gulf War of 1991, 131, 139, 141, 148, 160–61; US war in, 1, 10, 21, 128, 130, 147, 148, 150–51, 152, 153, 154, 156, 160, 172–73
Isley, Jeter A.: The U.S. Marines and Amphibious War, 197n94
Israel-Hezbollah war, 134
Italy: air power, 121; colonial policies, 78; navy, 100; relations with Great Britain, 67, 92, 166; relations with Russia, 39

Jaffe, Greg, 204n53
Japan: air power, 121; diplomatic policies of, 102, 109; vs. Great Britain, 96, 168; Meiji Restoration, 31, 36, 78; military policies, 66, 102, 196n90; navy, 56, 60, 67, 102, 168, 196n90; relations with China, 102, 116, 121; relations with France, 99, 116; relations with Great Britain, 66, 67, 72, 73, 80, 82, 94, 96, 97, 99, 100, 101, 102, 110, 116, 127, 170–71; relations with United States, 82, 99, 102, 109–12, 113, 116, 117, 121, 142, 157, 158, 169, 170, 199n131; as rising power, 31, 36, 78; Russo-Japanese War, 36, 40, 53, 55, 56, 60, 67, 72, 74, 75, 77, 78, 164; in Tokugawa period, 31
Jeffrey, K., 193n18
Jervis, Robert, 25, 180nn10–13, 182n23
Joffe, Josef, 184n42
Johnston, Robert, 202n18
Joint Vision 2010, 146
Joint Vision 2020, 144, 157–58

Kagan, Donald: *While America Sleeps*, 201n10
Kagan, Frederick W., 126, 153; *While America Sleeps*, 201n10
Kagan, Robert, 158, 179n6
Kahneman, Daniel, 186n58
Katzenbach, Edward L., Jr., 185n57
Kaufman, Herbert: *The Limits of Organizational Change*, 185n57
Kaufman, Robert G.: *In Defense of the Bush Doctrine*, 204n65
Kellogg-Briand Pact, 114–15
Kennedy, Paul M., 24, 80, 189n61, 195n55
Kenny, Michael, 193n8; *Rethinking British Decline*, 192n3
Keynes, John Maynard, 181n3
Kipp, Jacob W., 188nn8,15,19–22,25,26,30–33, 189nn34–38, 205n2
Kirkland, Jane, 181n4, 183n28

INDEX

Knight, Frank H.: Risk, Uncertainty, and Profit, 181n2
Knowledge Economy, The, 201n13
Koistinen, Paul A. C., 198nn116,121, 199n123
Konstantin Nikolaevich, Grand Duke, 49
Korb, Lawrence J.: Military Reform, 203n39
Kosovo, 132, 146, 173
Krauthammer, Charles, 208n57
Kreidberg, Marvin A.: History of Military Mobilization in the United States Army, 1775–45, 198nn115,117,118
Krepinevich, Andrew F., 182n15, 187n2, 192n1, 207n59; on color plans, 196n82; The Quadrennial Defense Review, 180n17, 196n82
Kruger, G. K., 188n23
Krulak, Charles C., 149
Kupchan, Charles A.: The Vulnerability of Empire, 183n34
Kydd, Andrew, 181n10

Lamb, Christopher J., 183n25
Lambart, Frederick, 94–95
Lambert, Andrew D., 189n53
Lambert, Nicholas A., 193n16, 194n52, 195n64; on decline of British naval dominance, 54; on Fisher, 60, 61–62, 63–65, 66–67, 76, 171; on late nineteenth century, 38
League of Nations, 114, 115
Leffler, Melvyn, 115, 199n132, 200n140
Leonard, Steven M.: Inevitable Evolutions, 182n16
Levy, Jack S., 182n23
Libicki, Martin C., 201n6
Linn, Brian McAllister: Guardians of Empire, 196n89
Lobell, Steven E., 185n51; The Challenge of Hegemony, 186n67, 187n69
Locarno Pact, 98–99, 118
London Naval Treaty, 102, 109
long-term transformation: defense spending for, 18, 22, 26, 33, 34, 42, 48, 60–62, 81, 93–94, 108, 118, 130, 138–40; vs. near-term readiness, 8, 18, 22, 26, 33, 34, 42, 48, 60–62, 81, 82, 84, 93–94, 108, 118, 130, 138–40, 141, 164, 176; and shaping strategy, 8, 22, 33, 108, 120, 130, 155, 169, 172–73
Lord, Clifford: History of United States Naval Aviation, 197n102

Mahnken, Thomas: *Technology and the American Way of War since 1945*, 203nn45,47
Mahoney, James, 186n61
Mandeles, Mark David, 197n102, 200n151
Marder, Arthur, 67, 190nn67,73,76, 191n102,113
Matloff, Maurice, 196nn80,90
May, Ernest: Knowing One's Enemies, 181n5
Mazzetti, Mark, 204n49
McChrystal, Stanley, 154
McDermott, J., 71, 190n64, 192nn122,126,127
McMaster, H. R., 207nn48,49
Mearsheimer, John J.: The Tragedy of Great Power Politics, 181n8
Medeiros, Evan S., 205n73
Melhorn, C. M.: Two Block Fox, 197n99
Menning, Bruce W., 75–76, 180n1, 187n3, 189n44, 192nn135,136,141, 205n4
Mesopotamia, 83
military policies: in adapting strategy, 31–32, 33, 34, 60–62, 81, 100, 137; of France, 97, 112–13; of Germany, 22, 55–56, 72, 102, 184n36; of Great Britain, 54, 55–71, 75–76, 77, 81, 83–97, 98–99, 100–101, 112–13, 119, 120–21, 123, 165–69, 193n24; of Japan, 66, 102, 196n92; in reforming and reconstituting strategy, 31–32, 33, 34, 37, 39, 40, 41, 43–45, 46–47, 48–51, 52–53, 77, 163–64; of Russia, 39, 40, 41, 42, 43–45, 46–47, 48–51, 52–53, 59–60, 65, 75–76, 77, 163–64; in shaping strategy, 31–32, 33, 38, 137, 138; of United States, 102–14, 116–17, 118–20, 121–23, 125–27, 130, 135–54, 169–70, 172–76, 197n97, 199n133, 200n153, 203n37
Millett, Allan R., 197nn95-97
Milner, Alfred, 193n21
Milutin, Dmitri, 41, 45, 49, 52
Mitzen, Jennifer: on physical vs. ontological security, 16–17
Moffett, William, 122
Moll, Kenneth L., 207nn38,39,41
Moreman, T. R., 193n24, 194nn39,47, 195n68, 195n69
Morocco crisis of 1905, 56, 73
Morton, Louis, 195n76, 196n79
Moy, Timothy David: Hitting the Beaches and Bombing the Cities, 185n57, 196n93, 197nn95,97
multilateralism, 154–55, 156, 157, 159, 163
Murray, Robert K.: The Harding Era, 195n75

Murray, Williamson, 121, 179n2, 194nn32,45, 198n114, 200n142, 201n154,155, 206nn25,32

Naím, Moisés, 204n63
Napoleonic Wars, 36, 37
Narizny, Kevin, 185n52
National Defense Strategy of the United States of America (2005), 133, 203n33
National Military Strategy (2004), 203n33
National Security Strategy (1991), 131
National Security Strategy (1997), 132
National Security Strategy (2002), 142–43, 203n33
National Security Strategy of Engagement and Enlargement (1994), 131, 154–55
National Strategy to Combat Weapons of Mass Destruction Proliferation (2002), 156
NATO expansion, 155, 156, 187n72
near-term readiness: and adapting strategy, 26, 33, 34, 37, 60–62, 93–94, 100–101, 108, 118, 119, 123–24, 130, 139, 141, 155, 159; defense spending for, 18, 22, 24, 26, 33, 34, 42, 48, 62–62, 81, 84, 96, 138–40; vs. long-term transformation, 8, 18, 22, 26, 33, 34, 42, 48, 60–62, 81, 82, 84, 93–94, 108, 118, 130, 138–40, 141, 164, 176
Nenninger, Timothy K., 198nn104,106,107,109,110
neoliberalism, 180n9
Nicaragua, 169
niche strategies, 162
Nincic, Miroslav, 25
9/11 Commission Report, 132–33, 175
Nine Power Treaty, 116
Nish, Ian: Alliance in Decline, 195n65
North Korea, 156; relations with United States, 1, 127, 132, 140, 141, 144, 161

Obama, Barack: on China, 158; West Point speech (Dec. 8, 2009), 153–54
Obruchev, N. N., 49
O'Hanlon, Michael E., 202n30, 203n42
Oliker, Olga: Assessing Russia's Decline, 202n15
O'Mahony, Mary, 193nn9,10
Operational Maneuver from the Sea (OMFTS), 149
Ottoman Empire. See Turkey

Overdorf, M., 182n20
Owens, Mackubin, 134

Pakistan, 134–35
Palestine, 83
Panama, 132
Paret, Peter, 180n1
Peden, G. C.: Arms, Economics and British Strategy, 187n4, 190n68, 191nn107,108, 192nn119,123, 207nn36,51,54,55; on Britain during inter-world war period, 100, 101, 167; on British diplomatic flexibility, 172
Pershing, John, 112, 122, 123, 198n105
Persia, 49, 83
Pierce, Terry C.: Warfighting and Disruptive Technologies, 180n14
Pinter, Walter M., 41
Platt Amendment, 170
Pollard, Sidney: Britain's Prime and Britain's Decline, 192n3
Posen, Barry R., 201n11; The Sources of Military Doctrine, 180n9, 183n31, 185nn55,57, 186n63
Postan, Michael Moissey: British War Production, 206n16
Powell, Colin, 140
Powell, Walter W., 28
preemptive war, 10, 156
preventive war, 20, 21, 130, 156, 158, 172, 173
prospect theory, 182n23
Prussia: general staff, 30–31; vs. Great Britain, 68–69, 70; relationship with France, 49, 51, 71; relations with Austria, 71; relations with Great Britain, 71; relations with Russia, 39, 40; as rising power, 36
Putin, Vladimir, 129

Quadrennial Defense Review, 133–34, 141–42, 144, 159, 203n33

Ranft, Bryan, 207n49
Rasor, Eugene L., 190n71
realism, 5, 7; and balance of power, 2, 3–4; defensive realists, 24, 186nn64,68; neorealism of Waltz, 180n9; offensive realists, 17, 163, 186nn64,68; and uncertainty, 17–18
Reeves, Joseph, 122
reforming and reconstituting strategy, 5, 19, 27, 80, 176, 183n30; of declining powers,

22–23, 25, 42, 80, 168, 187n75, 193n15; and defense spending, 22, 29, 33, 34, 37, 41, 48, 53, 163–64, 168–69; diplomatic indicators of, 31, 32, 33, 34, 37–38, 41, 51–52, 53, 55, 77; economic indicators of, 31, 32, 33, 34, 37, 40–42, 45, 48, 52–53, 77, 163, 175; and long-term transformation, 29, 33, 34, 37, 42, 48, 80, 163–64; military indicators of, 31–32, 33, 34, 37, 39, 40, 41, 43–45, 46–47, 48–51, 52–53, 77, 163–64; risks of, 6, 22, 163–64; of Russia, 9, 37–38, 40–53, 55, 77, 163–65, 187n73; of Soviet Union, 7, 23; as strategy of necessity, 165; and technological change, 31–32, 33, 37, 39, 45, 48, 49, 50–51, 53, 77, 164–65; of weak states, 6–7, 21, 23, 25, 37–38, 77, 163
regime change policies, 7, 10, 20, 130, 172
relative international standing: declining powers, 7, 9, 22–23, 25, 31, 32, 34, 79–82, 119, 158, 168–69, 175, 176, 183n35, 187n70, 193n15; perceptions of, 23, 183n35; preeminent powers/hegemons, 2, 3, 3–4, 7, 9–10, 22, 24–25, 31, 32, 34, 38, 58–59, 60–62, 68, 118, 127–30, 158, 161, 165, 169, 170, 175, 184n35, 187n70; relationship to economic power, 23–24; relationship to strategic choices, 5, 6–7, 8, 12, 22–24, 25, 34–35, 37–38, 58–59, 77, 79–82, 124, 128, 129, 163; relationship to transfer of technology, 32, 33, 34, 37, 65, 172; rising powers, 3, 4, 7, 9, 20, 22, 25, 31, 32, 36, 102–3, 116, 157–58, 169, 184n35; weakest powers/states in trough of power curve, 6–7, 10, 21, 23, 25, 31, 32, 34, 37, 77, 184n35
Resende-Santos, Joao, 184n46, 186n60
Reutern, Count, 41
Rice, Condoleezza, 180n12, 201n2, 202n19
Ricks, Thomas E., 205n67
Ring, Peter Smith, 183n24, 184n45
risks: of adapting strategy, 6, 22; Ikenberry on, 162–63; of reforming and reconstituting strategy, 6, 22, 163–64; risk vs. uncertainty, 13, 181n4; of shaping strategy, 6, 19, 21–22, 29, 153, 169, 170, 171, 173–74
Robertson, Paul L., 191n105
Rogers, Clifford J.: The Military Revolution Debate, 182nn15,16
Ronfeldt, David, 182n15

Roots, Peter C., 198n113, 200n152
Rose, Roger, 25
Rosen, Gary: The Right War?, 204n65
Rosen, Stephen Peter: Winning the Next War, 197nn100,101
Roskill, Stephen, 193n20
Ross, Steven T.: Peacetime War Plans, 1919–1935, 114, 196nn83,85,87,88, 199n122
Roxborough, Ian, 183n33, 208n55
Rumsfeld, Donald, 133, 140, 145, 148, 160; on mission and coalition, 32, 156; strategy for Iraq, 21, 126; on transformation goals, 143–44
Russia: Alexander II, 41; Alexander III, 165; vs. Austria, 42, 50; defense spending, 39, 41, 42, 43–44, 48, 50, 52, 53, 163–64; diplomatic policies, 40, 41, 51–52, 53, 75, 77, 129; Duma created in, 75; economic policies, 40–42, 45, 48, 52–53, 77, 163–65; vs. France, 36, 45; vs. Germany, 42, 50, 165; Gorchakov, 39, 41; vs. Great Britain, 36, 54, 70, 75–77; intelligence capabilities, 51, 53; Grand Duke Konstantin, 49; military policies, 39, 40, 41, 42, 43–45, 46–47, 48–51, 52–53, 59–60, 65, 75–76, 77, 163–64; Milutin, 41, 45, 49, 52; as multinational state, 40; during post-Cold War period, 31, 127, 129; during post-Crimean War period, 9, 16, 29, 31, 37–38, 39–53, 58, 59–60, 65, 67, 72–74, 75–77, 99, 163–65, 187n73; Putin, 129; railroad construction in, 41–42, 50, 164; reforming and reconstituting strategy of, 9, 37–38, 40–53, 55, 77, 163–65, 187n73; relations with Austria, 39, 40–41, 51–52, 74; relations with France, 39, 40, 49, 51, 52, 55, 56, 72, 76–77; relations with Germany, 40, 49–50, 51–52, 72–73, 74, 77, 164; relations with Great Britain, 38, 39, 45, 48, 49, 51, 52, 53, 54–55, 56, 58, 59–60, 62, 65, 67, 72–74, 76–77, 82, 83, 99, 171, 172; relations with Italy, 39; relations with Prussia, 39, 40; relations with Turkey, 39, 40, 45, 49, 50, 51, 53, 65, 73, 77, 164; relations with United States, 1, 127, 129, 132, 141; Reutern, 41; revolution/civil war in, 78, 83, 194n27; Russo-Japanese War, 36, 40, 53, 55, 56, 60, 67, 72, 73, 74, 75, 77, 78, 164; Russo-Turkish War, 40, 45, 50, 51,

Russia: Russo-Turkish War *(Continued)*
53, 65, 77, 164; and technological change, 36–37, 39, 45, 48, 49, 50–51, 65, 77, 164–65; as weak state, 4, 9, 31, 37, 77

Sahel, the, 135
Sapolsky, Harvey M.: US Military Innovation since the Cold War, 201n4, 203n40
Schimmelpenninck Van Der Oye, David, 187n3
Schleswig-Holstein Affair of 1864, 71
Schmitt, Gary, 204nn54,55
Schultz, Kenneth A.: Democracy and Coercive Diplomacy, 181n10
Schweller, Randall L.: Unanswered Threats, 179n3, 181n9, 184n37
security environment: high threat periods, 2, 3, 5, 12, 15; lack of strategic rival, 1–3, 7, 16–17, 27–28, 29, 114, 130–31, 161; low threat periods, 1–3, 5, 18; regionalization of, 158–59, 160–61; rising threat periods, 5. See also complexity of security environment; uncertainty
Segell, Glen M., 203n33
Serbia, 144, 150
Seven Weeks War, 71
shaping strategy, 5, 23, 25, 183nn29,30; and border pressure, 26; criticism of, 172–73; and defense spending, 26, 33, 34, 58–59, 137; diplomatic indicators of, 31, 32, 33–34, 159, 169–70, 172, 173–74; and domestic politics, 27; economic indicators of, 31, 32, 33, 65, 103; and global interests/number and diversity of threats, 25, 26, 119–20; of Great Britain, 9, 38, 58–75, 77, 170–72, 173, 175; innovation in, 20, 21, 26, 31, 33, 34, 38, 64–66, 108, 118, 119–20, 170, 171–73; and long-term transformation, 8, 22, 33, 108, 118, 120, 130, 155, 172–73; military indicators of, 31–32, 33, 38, 137, 138; of preeminent powers, 7–8, 22, 25, 38, 129–30, 169, 170, 175–76; preventive war, 20, 21, 130, 156, 158, 172, 173; as proactive strategy, 4, 6, 19–20; regime change, 7, 10, 20, 130, 172; of revolutionary regimes, 22, 29; of rising powers, 7, 22, 25, 102–3, 169; risks of, 6, 19, 21–22, 29, 118, 153, 170, 171, 173–74; and technological change, 25, 26, 31, 33, 34, 38, 57–58, 64–66, 74–75, 118, 119–20, 161, 170, 171, 172–73, 174–75; of United States, 7, 8, 9–10, 21–22, 82, 102–3, 108, 118–20, 127–28, 129, 130, 137, 140, 141–51, 153, 154, 156–58, 159–60, 161, 169–70, 172–74, 175, 180n13
Sheridan, Mary Beth, 204n53
Sherman, Richard, 180n9
Shinseki, Eric, 146
Shulimson, Jack: The Marine Corps's Search for a Mission, 197nn97,98
Sims, William, 122
Singer, P. W.: Corporate Warriors, 182n14
Sked, Alan: Britain's Decline, 192n3
Smith, Eric Alden, 181n10
Smith, Holland: Coral and Brass, 197n95
Smith, R. Elbertson, 199n122
Smuts, Jan, 193n21
Snyder, Jack: The Ideology of the Offensive, 185n56; Myths of Empire, 183n34
Solingen, Etel, 185n51
Solomon, M. Scott, 180n9
Somalia, 132, 135, 138, 141, 148, 152, 155
South African War, 60, 70, 72
Soviet Union: breakup of, 10, 129, 131, 141, 149; as declining state, 7, 23; under perestroika, 7, 23; relations with United States, 3, 16. See also Russia
Spanish-American War, 197n97
Spector, Ronald, 196n79
Stark, Harold R., 117, 170
states: as democratic, 26–27, 74; as dictatorships, 26–27, 29; vs. firms, 5–6, 7, 10, 12, 19, 20, 21, 27, 175; as revisionist, 13, 16, 26–27, 29, 99, 187n68; as security seeking, 13; as status quo, 13, 16, 22, 26–27, 29
Straley, Ben, 180n15
strategic choices: relationship to cognitive limitations, 8, 12, 27, 28, 29, 76–77, 119–20, 122–24, 160–61; relationship to complexity of strategic environment, 2, 5, 7–8, 12, 24–25, 26, 34–35, 37, 58–59, 77, 79–81, 124, 128, 129–30, 131–34, 159, 161; relationship to domestic politics, 8, 12, 25–27, 29, 32, 80, 124, 160, 162; relationship to organizational/institutional tendencies, 8, 12, 27–28, 29, 75–76, 120–22, 123, 124, 161; relationship to proximity of potential adversaries, 7, 16, 24, 26, 68, 80–82, 112, 113, 118, 119–20, 121, 124, 129–30, 184nn42,43, 186n64; relationship to rapid technological change, 4, 18, 25, 27, 29, 60, 77, 79,

101, 160; relationship to relative power, 5, 6–7, 8, 12, 22–24, 25, 34–35, 37–38, 58–59, 77, 79–82, 124, 128, 129, 163; and state-firm analogy, 5–6, 7, 12, 19, 20, 21, 27, 127, 179n9. See also adapting; reforming and reconstituting; shaping
Sturgis, James, 187n5
Sumida, Jon Tetsuro, 74, 187n7, 189nn54,58, 190nn66,72,74,77–79,81–83, 191nn91,99,104,116, 192nn129,130, 207nn35,36
Sweden, 39, 49
Sykes, Sir Mark, 193n21

Taliaferro, Jeffrey W., 25, 186n64
Taylor, Shelley, 186n58
technological change: and adapting strategy, 25, 26, 31–32, 33, 34, 60–62, 96, 97, 100–101, 119; in artillery, 70; cyberwar, 174–75; and diversity of threats, 135; fast-follower strategy/adaptation regarding, 31–32, 42, 45, 48, 53, 61–62, 77, 81, 108, 119, 165; as gradual and incremental, 182n16; Industrial Revolution, 31, 36–37, 80; in information technology, 1–2, 9, 19, 36, 62, 63–64, 67, 127, 132, 134, 135, 138, 143, 144, 146, 148, 150–51, 173, 174–75, 180n16, 184n43; missiles, 10–11, 127, 140, 153, 156, 174; in naval technology, 57–58, 60, 61–66, 74–75, 76, 78–79, 96, 97, 110, 111, 112, 117, 118, 121–22, 165–66, 169, 170, 171–72; precision guided munitions, 145, 146, 148, 150, 161, 174; as rapid, 1–2, 4, 18, 25, 27, 29, 30, 60, 77, 79, 82, 101, 160, 182n16; and reforming and reconstituting strategy, 31–32, 33, 37, 39, 45, 48, 49, 50–51, 53, 77, 164–65; revolutions in military affairs (RMAs), 15, 16, 19, 22, 26, 60, 138, 142, 144, 145–46, 161, 175, 182nn15,16; in rifles, 70; and shaping strategy, 25, 26, 31, 33, 34, 38, 57–58, 64–66, 74–75, 118, 119–20, 161, 170, 171, 172–73, 174–75; transfer of technology, 16, 17, 21, 32, 33, 34, 37, 65, 172; unmanned aerial vehicles (UAVs), 140, 150; weapons of mass destruction (WMD), 1, 10–11, 131, 132, 156–57, 184n43
Terriff, Terry, 203n41
terrorism, 1, 11, 126, 127, 144, 151–52, 202n27; Al-Qaeda, 132–33, 134–35, 151, 153, 174, 175; embassy bombings of 1998, 132; September 11th attacks, 1, 9–10, 30, 130, 132–33, 143, 157, 159, 160
Thomson, Harry C., 198n113, 200n152
threats: diversity of, 1, 4, 14–15, 19, 24–25, 26, 29, 30, 37, 38, 81, 82, 118, 119, 120, 124, 125–27, 129, 130, 133–34, 135, 143, 155, 165–66, 168, 169; number of, 1, 4, 14, 16, 19, 24, 26, 29, 30, 37, 38, 81, 82, 124, 129, 133, 155, 158–59; taxonomy of, 133–34; uncertainty regarding, 1–3, 4, 5–6, 7–9, 10–11, 12, 13–19, 29–30, 60, 124, 131–34, 144, 162–63, 168, 169–70, 173–76
Three Emperors' League, 40, 51–52
Till, Geoffrey, 194n51, 197n101, 200n146, 207nn35, 38–40
Tin-bor Hui, Victoria, 21
Tirpitz, Alfred von, 55, 72
Toffler, Alvin and Heidi, 182n15
Toft, Monica Duffy: The Fog of Peace and War Planning, 179n5
Trachtenberg, Marc, 205n66
Treaty of Berlin, 54–55
Treaty of Paris, 77
Treaty of San Stefano, 54
Treaty of Versailles, 78, 98, 110, 114, 115
Trebilcock, Clive, 65, 207nn52,53
Trenchard, Hugh, 120
Trubowitz, Peter, 185n49; Defining the National Interest, 185n51
Turkey: adapting strategy of, 187n75; collapse of Ottoman Empire, 78, 84; as declining power, 31, 36, 187n75; reforming and reconstituting strategy of, 165; relations with Great Britain, 82, 83, 111; relations with Greece, 83; relations with Russia, 39, 40, 45, 49, 50, 51, 53, 65, 73, 77, 164
Turnbull, Archibald: History of United States Naval Aviation, 197n100
Tversky, Amos, 186n58
Tyler, Patrick, 203nn31,32

uncertainty: regarding allies, 15, 16, 17, 97; regarding capabilities of adversaries, 13, 15, 16, 17, 18, 27, 29, 59, 77, 160, 162; regarding defense spending, 16, 18; defined, 12, 13; and institutionalism, 28, 29; regarding intentions of adversaries, 13, 15, 16, 18, 27, 29, 77, 160, 183n27; in marketplace, 4, 5–6, 7, 12, 19, 21; regarding national capabilities and commitment, 15, 16, 17–18; and organization theory, 27–28, 29;

uncertainty *(Continued)*
   as property of agents, 14; as property of international system, 13–14; relationship to cognitive limitations, 14, 27, 28, 29; relationship to lack of great power rivalry, 16–17, 29, 125–26; vs. risk, 13, 181n4; of threat, 1–3, 4, 5–6, 7–9, 10–11, 12, 13–19, 29–30, 60, 124, 125–26, 131–34, 144, 162–63, 168, 169–70, 173–76. *See also* complexity of security environment
unilateralism, 17, 32
United Nations, 155, 156, 157
United States: adapting strategy of, 9, 129–30, 137, 139–41, 142, 150, 154–56, 159, 161, 175; aircraft industry in, 97, 113; air power, 113, 117, 121, 122, 150, 153, 168, 199n135, 207n38; army, 103, 105, 106, 107, 108, 109, 113–14, 117, 118, 122–23, 146–47, 169, 196n91, 199n123; Army Industrial College (AIC), 113–14; Base Force review, 140–41, 161; George H. W. Bush administration, 131, 140–41, 142; George W. Bush administration, 10, 130, 132–34, 137, 140, 141–45, 142, 150, 154, 156–57, 159–60, 161, 180n13; Civil War, 37; Clinton administration, 131–32, 137, 140, 141, 154–56, 158, 159, 160; during Cold War, 9, 24; Color Plans, 108–10, 111, 117, 170, 196n82; counterinsurgency warfare (COIN), 126–27, 130, 144, 147–48, 151, 154, 173, 174, 175–76; counterterrorism policies, 126, 127, 130, 134, 143, 144, 151–52, 153–54, 156, 159, 173, 174, 175–76, 202n27; defense spending, 102, 103–8, 113, 118, 119, 120, 121–22, 135–40, 145, 150, 152–53, 158, 160, 161; as defensively advantaged, 81–82, 112, 113, 118, 119–20, 129–30; democracy promoted by, 7, 119, 128, 156; diplomatic policies, 102, 103, 114–16, 120, 154–58, 169–170, 173–74, 195n77; doctrine of military preponderance, 142–43; economic conditions in, 79, 103, 113–14, 115, 118, 128–29, 153, 174; economic policies, 20, 103, 113–14, 115–16, 117–18, 122, 131, 132, 153, 158, 160, 175, 198n121; embassy bombings of 1998, 132; engagement policies of, 20, 132, 158; Experimental Force (EXFOR), 146; Force XXI, 146; Future Combat System (FCS), 147; Gates, 151, 152–53;
Good Neighbor Policy, 119; vs. Great Britain, 31, 36, 38, 79–82, 96, 97, 101, 108, 111, 117, 118, 119–24, 129, 149, 155, 166, 168, 169, 170–76; and Great Depression, 103, 115, 118; Harding administration, 110; Industrial Mobilization Plan (IMP) of 1930, 114, 198n121; information superiority policies, 19; during interworld war period, 9, 16, 29, 31, 79–82, 101–20, 121–23, 124, 161; isolationism in, 80, 114; Latin American policies, 169–170; Major Regional Contingency (MRC) planning guidelines, 160; marines, 103, 106, 107, 108, 111, 117, 147, 148, 149–50, 169–170, 197n97; Marshall Plan, 20; military policies of, 102–14, 116–17, 118–20, 121–23, 125–27, 130, 135–54, 169–70, 172–76, 197n97, 199n133, 200n153, 203n37, 207n38; Monroe Doctrine, 102, 109; Naval War College, 112, 149; navy, 66, 96, 102, 103, 105, 106, 107, 108, 109, 110–11, 112, 116–17, 118, 120, 121–22, 148–49, 153, 166, 168, 169, 197n102, 198n121, 199nn133,135, 207n38; nonproliferation policies, 131, 142, 156; Obama administration, 153–54, 157–58; Objective Force/Future Force, 146–47; Office of Net Assessment (ONA)/Dept. of Defense, 161; peacekeeping operations, 132, 140, 141, 148, 155, 159, 165; and Philippines, 102, 109, 110–11, 112, 121, 199n131; during post-cold war period, 16, 28–29, 31, 38, 125–61, 169–70, 172–76, 183n23; as preeminent power, 2, 3–4, 7, 9–10, 22, 118, 127–30, 155; preemption policies, 10, 156; preventive war policies, 130, 158, 172, 173; Proliferation Security Initiative (PSI), 156–57; Rainbow Plans, 108, 117, 170; Reagan administration, 135, 140; regime change policies, 7, 10, 20, 130, 172; regional security policies, 131, 133; relations with China, 1, 20, 102, 109, 116, 121, 125, 127, 129, 132, 153, 157–58, 174, 175, 195n77, 199n133; relations with failed states, 127, 132, 141, 174; relations with France, 99, 115–16, 117–18, 156; relations with Germany, 20, 115–16, 117–18, 142, 156; relations with Great Britain, 56, 67, 72, 82, 94, 96, 97, 98, 99, 102, 109–10, 116, 117, 127, 170; relations with India, 142, 157, 158; relations with Indonesia, 157;

relations with Iran, 1, 127, 132, 140, 161; relations with Japan, 82, 99, 102, 109–12, 113, 116, 117, 121, 142, 157, 158, 169, 170, 199n133; relations with North Korea, 1, 127, 132, 140, 141, 144, 161; relations with Russia, 1, 127, 129, 132, 141; relations with Serbia, 144, 150; relations with Singapore, 158; relations with Soviet Union, 3, 16; relations with Vietnam, 157, 158; as rising power, 9, 81–82, 102–3, 119–20, 166, 169; Rumsfeld, 21, 32, 126, 133, 140, 143–44, 145, 148, 156, 160; security environment during inter-world war period, 16, 82, 101–2, 124; security environment during post-Cold War period, 125–26, 130–35; September 11th attacks, 1, 9–10, 30, 130, 132–33, 143, 157, 159, 160; shaping strategy of, 7, 8, 9–10, 21–22, 82, 102–3, 108, 118–20, 127–28, 129, 130, 137, 140, 141–51, 153, 154, 156–58, 159–60, 161, 169–70, 172–74, 175, 180n13; Special Forces, 126, 127, 140, 150–51, 160; technological innovation by, 128, 143, 145–47, 148, 149, 150–51, 161, 169, 173–74; war in Afghanistan, 1, 10, 128, 130, 134–35, 143, 147, 148, 150–51, 152, 153–54, 160, 172–73; war in Iraq, 1, 10, 21, 128, 130, 147, 148, 150–51, 152, 153, 154, 156, 160, 172–73; Wilson administration, 170; during World War I, 122–23, 200n151; during World War II, 110, 112, 113, 170

Van der Vat, Dan, 55–56, 189nn60,62,63
Van Evera, Stephen: on uncertainty and military capabilities, 13
Viguerie, S. Patrick, 181n4, 183n28
Virmani, Arvind, 184n39
Vlahos, Michael: The Blue Sword, 197n100, 199n134

Walt, Stephen: balance of threat theory, 14, 181n11; *The Origins of Alliances*, 181n11, 182n18; *Taming American Power*, 204n65
Waltz, Kenneth: on international system, 13; neorealism of, 180n9; *Theory of International Politics*, 180n9, 181n6
Warfighting Publication 3-33.5, 147–48
Washington Naval Conference of 1921–22, 110, 114–15, 116
Washington Naval Treaty, 102, 109, 110–11
Watson, Mark Skinner, 196n79
Watts, Barry, 206n32
weapons of mass destruction, 10–11, 132, 156–57; biological and chemical weapons, 1; nuclear weapons, 1, 131, 142, 156, 184n43
Weigley, Russell F., 195n76, 196nn81,89, 200n153
Weitsman, Patricia A., 186n65
Wheeler, Winslow T.: Military Reform, 203n39
White, Josh, 204n50
Williamson, Samuel R., 191n117, 192nn120,121,124,128
Wills, Craig, 203n44
Wilson, Clay, 207n51
Wilson, Herbert Wrigley, 190n69
Wilson, Sir Henry, 80
Wilson, Woodrow, 169
Wohlforth, William C., 184n35, 187n70
Wolfers, Arnold, 179n4
Wolfowitz, Paul, 133, 142–43

Yemen, 135, 152, 156
Yoshpe, Harry B., 198n120

Zahavi, Amotz, 181n10
Zakaria, Fareed, 202n16
Zanini, Michele, 180n16
Zazi, Najibullah, 202n27

The authorized representative in the EU for product safety and compliance is:
Mare Nostrum Group
B.V Doelen 72
4831 GR Breda
The Netherlands